209
233

Meetings, Conventions, and Expositions

An Introduction to the Industry

Meetings, Conventions, and Expositions

An Introduction to the Industry

Rhonda J. Montgomery, Ph.D.
and
Sandra K. Strick, Ph.D.

VNR VAN NOSTRAND REINHOLD
An International Thomson Publishing Company

New York • London • Bonn • Boston • Detroit • Madrid • Melbourne • Mexico City
Paris • Singapore • Tokyo • Toronto • Albany NY • Belmont CA • Cincinnati OH

Copyright © 1995 by Van Nostrand Reinhold

Library of Congress Catalog Card Number 93-40899
ISBN 0-442-00838-4

I(T)P   Van Nostrand Reinhold, an International Thomson Publishing Company.
        ITP logo is a trademark under license.

Printed in the United States of America.

Van Nostrand Reinhold   International Thomson Publishing GmbH
115 Fifth Avenue   Königswinterer Strasse 418
New York, New York 10003   53227 Bonn
                                     Germany

International Thomson Publishing
Berkshire House   International Thomson Publishing Asia
168-173 High Holborn   221 Henderson Road
London WC1V 7AA   #05 10 Henderson Building
England   Singapore 0315

Thomas Nelson Australia   International Thomson Publishing Japan
102 Dodds Street   Hirakawacho Kyowa Building, 3F
South Melbourne, Victoria 3205   2-2-1 Hirakawa-cho Chiyoda-ku,
Australia   Tokyo 102
                                     Japan

Nelson Canada
1120 Birchmount Road
Scarborough, Ontario
M1K 5G4, Canada

ARCFF 16   15   14   13   12   11   10   9   8   7   6   5   4

Library of Congress Cataloging-in-Publication Data

Montgomery, Rhonda J.
    Meetings, conventions, and expositions : an introduction to the
industry / by Rhonda J. Montgomery and Sandra K. Strick.
        p.   cm.
    Includes index.
    ISBN 0-442-00838-4
    1. Hospitality industry.   2. Congresses and conventions—Planning.
3. Meetings—Planning.   I. Strick, Sandra K.   II. Title.
TX911.2.M66   1994
647.94—dc20   93-40899
                                                        CIP

To Mick and Jackie.
To Harry, Matt, Anna, and Michelle.
For all their support, love, and encouragement.

Contents

Chapter 3   Players in the Industry   41

Chapter 4   The Sponsor   65

Preface

With the growth in revenue generated from conventions, meetings, and expositions exceeding $44.5 billion in 1989 as compared with $38.1 billion in 1988, changes in the educational structure must be made to meet the growing needs of this vast industry. Students in hospitality programs must be introduced to the specifics of the convention, meeting, and exposition industry. Ten years ago students graduating from hospitality management programs basically received no specific education in the field of conventions, meetings, and expositions. Today's hospitality program graduates will be directly influenced by this segment of the hospitality industry and therefore must have a working knowledge of how conventions, meetings, and expositions operate.

Students in our classrooms today must be prepared to deal with an industry that is becoming much more sophisticated. Modern consumers have a wide variety of choices; therefore, students must have a comprehensive understanding of the industry to compete in this market.

Today's convention attendees are educated consumers and have high expectations regarding services provided. Advances in meeting technology as well as changes in convention facilities warrant a detailed review of current trends. In order to effectively manage today's conventions and meetings, students must further have a thorough understanding of the roles of various players in providing the necessary services.

This textbook is designed to introduce students to the meeting and convention industry. Its intent is to:

1. Provide a broad overview of the industry;
2. Provide an awareness of the growth and coinciding changes that this industry has experienced;
3. Provide the basic framework for planning a meeting, convention, or exposition; and
4. Provide students with the skills necessary for interacting with the various players involved in this industry.

This book is by no means intended to be a detailed "how-to" guide to the meetings, conventions, and expositions industry. Its purpose is to introduce students to a very exciting and growing segment of hospitality and perhaps pique an interest to further explore the possibilities.

Acknowledgments

With sincere gratitude we acknowledge all those who collaborated with us in putting this book together. We recognize that this is an industry that has many dedicated professionals who are willing and eager to share their expertise.

Melvin Barrington
Charlotte Gant
Tony Sylvester
Jane Lorimar
Patti Shock
Richard Newman
Melissa Berry
Ed Polivka
Harry E. Varney
Craig Smith
Ellen Beckert
William Hogan
Dale Finley
Charlotte St. Martin
Lauren Kennedy
Denney Rutherford

1

History of Meetings, Conventions, and Expositions

Learning Objectives

1. To provide a historical perspective of tourism and meetings, conventions, and expositions.
2. To briefly describe the tourism industry and how meetings, conventions, and expositions fit into the grand scheme of tourism.
3. To define conferences, conventions, expositions, and meetings.
4. To identify the growth factors influencing meetings, conventions, and expositions.
5. To explain the economic impact of meetings, conventions, and expositions on the host city.

Introduction to the Tourism Industry

The meetings and conventions industry is an exciting and lucrative segment of the hospitality industry that is often overlooked by individuals entering the field. This text is designed to introduce individuals to meetings, conventions, and expositions. However, before this segment of the hospitality industry is explored, it is important to understand how this segment fits into the overall picture of the hospitality industry.

The hospitality industry, often referred to as the tourism industry, is the sum total of tourist expenditures. Within a nation this figure is computed and classified along with other national industries. The hospitality industry encompasses the global industry of travel, attractions, lodging, and transportation, as well as related components, such as food and entertainment, that meet the needs and wants of tourists.

A tourist is defined by the United Nations as one who spends more than one night but less than a year away from home for pleasure or business, except diplomats, military personnel, and enrolled students.

History of Tourism

A brief history of tourism is essential to provide the framework from which we can begin our exploration into the world of meetings, conventions, and expositions. Even though tourism for the masses is a relatively new phenomenon, historical documents provide accounts of travel and tourism throughout history. Fossil evidence indicates the nomadic lifestyle of the earliest humans. Until recently, most travel was done for specific reasons. Usually, travels were precipitated by the changing seasons that resulted in a depletion of food sources or the need to escape danger. Travel was hard work. It was no coincidence that travel and travail (heavy labor) have the same root word. Our ancestors did not think that the word "travel" was synonymous with the word "pleasure," as so many of us do today. Travel was difficult and dangerous and only undertaken for reasons of necessity.

Travel for the purpose of trade and pleasure can for all intents and purposes be traced to the Sumerians of Babylonia. About 4000 B.C. the Sumerians were credited with inventing money, cuneiform writing, and the wheel. All of these inventions played an important role in tourism. With these inventions people were able to pay for transportation and accommodations through bartering or monetary exchange.

As travel evolved, it took on many forms, such as peace-making voyages like the one described on the walls of the Temple of Deit El Bahari at Luxor, where Queen Hatshepust traveled to the lands of Punt (now referred to as Somalia) in 1490 B.C. for the purposes of establishing peace as well as touring the foreign land. Travel was also undertaken for trade and religious purposes like those described in the Old Testament. In 776 B.C. with the first Olympic games, came one of the earliest forms of planned attractions where people traveled to a far-off land to see an event and paid to stay in accommodations. To this day the Olympics remain one of the largest attractions in the world and generate millions of dollars for the host city.

The Roman empire was also an important player in the development of tourism. Because of their affluent lifestyle and their technological advances, the Romans were able to establish a network of road systems previously unheard of. These roads enabled travelers to journey in more comfort and with greater speed to their destinations. The Romans also provided safety for travelers by their roaming militias, which were designed to keep the roadways safe. Further, their intense interest in foreign cultures and willingness to spend money to travel to far-off places to view attractions (such as the pyramids and monuments of Egypt) helped set the foundation for modern tourism.

As road systems developed and travel was made easier and safer, the wealthy began to travel more often for pleasure. Because of this increase in travelers, cities and provinces developed local carnivals, sporting competitions, and trade markets to entice people to visit their cities. It is noted that during the reign of Alexander the Great over 600,000 tourists traveled to Ephesus (now referred to as Turkey) to attend exhibitions put on by acrobats, animal trainers, jugglers, and magicians. While there, tourists also visited the trade markets that made Ephesus famous.

With the fall of the Roman Empire came the beginning of the Dark Ages (450 A.D. to 1450 A.D.). Travel became a thing of the past. Roads and passageways were no longer safe, as travelers were robbed or killed by bands of road or sea pirates. The only notable travel was done for religious purposes associated with the Crusades. Travel for anything but necessity did not resume until the

Industrial Revolution (about 1745 A.D.). At this time the invention of steamboats, stagecoaches, and railroads made travel much easier. The Industrial Revolution gave birth to a new generation of people—the middle class. These individuals not only had the time and the money for travel, but also they were hungry to explore new areas of the world.

The invention of the automobile in the twentieth century and the eventual development of motor coaches helped evolve travel further. The automobile became accessible to the middle class traveler, who then demanded that better road systems be developed and maintained. As in the time of the Roman empire, a well-constructed, maintained, and patrolled road system led to increased travel and tourism.

Tourism as we know it today began in the late 1950s. It was around this time that travel was no longer the domain of the wealthy, but became accessible to the masses. There are a number of factors that influenced this change in travel:

1. A relatively peaceful political environment.
2. Postwar posterity.
3. Jet travel.
4. Economical rates for air travel.
5. Increased car ownership.
6. Expanded and improved road systems.
7. Increased desire on the part of people to explore new territory.

History of Meetings, Conventions, and Expositions

For as long as there have been people, there have been meetings. Archaeologists, in their investigations of ancient cultures, have found primitive ruins that functioned as common areas where people would gather to discuss communal interests, such as hunting plans, war-time activities, negotiations for peace, or the organization of tribal celebrations. This occurred as nomadic lifestyle gave way to civilizations based in one geographic area. Each village, hamlet, or city had its common gathering place. As certain geographic areas grew and became centers of commerce, dynamic cities emerged as gathering places for people wanting to trade goods or discuss public problems.

Cities have always had a plethora of financial, technical, and intellectual resources that have made them an important factor in the history of mankind (Gartrell 1988). As cities became the hub of activity for geographic regions and as transportation from location to location improved, the ability to gather for the discussion of common interest became more prevalent. Trade associations as well as professional, fraternal, and religious organizations assembled to address issues relevant to their membership. Discussions of trade regulations and the selling or trading of goods were also important reasons for congregating.

"Though there were many trade, professional, fraternal and religious associations with historical roots throughout Europe, it wasn't until the mid 1800's that such activity took place along the

Figure 1-1   1910 Automobile Trade Show in Chicago. (Courtesy: Kitzing Inc.)

eastern seaboard of North America (Gartrell 1988, p. 4)." As America grew, so did its trade, professional, fraternal, and religious associations. Figures 1-1 and 1-2 reflect the mood of trade shows in the early 1900s.

Increased association activity led to the need for more meetings among association members. In 1896, a group of Detroit businessmen decided that these groups and the meetings they held provided significant revenue to whatever host city they met in. They acknowledged that these organizations and the meetings, conventions, and expositions they held were something desirable to have in one's community. These businessmen had the forethought to develop what is now recognized as the first convention bureau. The purpose of this bureau was to attract these organizations to

Figure 1-2   1932 Radio Show at the Chicago Coliseum. (Courtesy: Kitzing Inc.)

the city of Detroit. It was not too much later that other cities followed suit.

Shortly after the turn of the century (1910), the hospitality industry founded its first professional organizations in the form of The American Hotel Protective Association, presently called the American Hotel and Motel Association. The convention bureaus that were forming all over the country organized themselves in 1914 to form the International Association of Convention Bureaus. This association later became known as the International Association of Convention and Visitor Bureaus (IACVB). In 1927, the Hotel Sales Management Association was formed, this association evolved into the Hotel Sales and Marketing Association International. These associations were the forerunners of numerous associations designed to improve and professionalize individuals and corporations associated with the hospitality industry. In 1949, the meetings, conventions, and expositions industry was growing at a tremendous rate, as were the associations affiliated with this segment of the hospitality industry. Therefore, it was deemed necessary to develop the Convention Liaison Council to provide a centralized clearinghouse of information related to the meetings, conventions, and expositions industry.

Although this segment of the industry was experiencing growing pains within its ranks, it was also experiencing other more serious problems. Hotels were not designed to host groups and basically had no desire to play an active role in this very dynamic segment of the industry. It was not until hotel chains, such as Holiday Inn, Sheraton, Hilton, Marriott, and Hyatt, began recognizing the importance of meetings, conventions, and expositions to their economic well being that hotels solicited group business. These chains took the purely functional meeting facilities of the 1950s and built upon the concept and worked with the meeting planners and association executives to design state of the art meeting facilities fashioned to promote meetings, conventions, and expositions.

In conjunction with the changes being made in the physical facilities, hotels realized the need for individuals whose primary responsibilities were to service meetings, conventions, and expositions. The concept of the convention service manager is often attributed to Jim Collins, a young salesperson at the Chicago Conrad Hilton hotel. Collins recognized the need for someone to act on behalf of the groups meeting at their properties as well as someone to work in conjunction with the group's meeting planner and the association executives (Lofft 1992). In 1989 the Convention Service Managers united to form their own professional association, the Association for Convention Operation Management (ACOM). It was also in this year that the U.S. Department of Labor added the job title of meeting and convention planner to its National Occupational Code Directory.

Tourism Today

Tourism is quickly becoming one of the largest industries in the world. For many countries tourism is the number one commodity in the international trade market. The economic importance of tourism can be seen from the following figures (Mill 1990, p. 29):

- Global travel volume is over 4 billion arrivals; domestic tourism is about 90 percent of total travel worldwide; about 90 percent of domestic tourism occurs in Europe and the Americas.
- There are over 340 million international arrivals annually; excluding transportation, international tourism receipts were over $120 billion. Europe receives about two-thirds of all international arrivals, although East Asia, the Pacific, the Middle East, and Africa are recording the highest proportional gains. International tourism receipts are over $120 billion annually.
- U.S. citizens make close to 30 million international trips a year, spending about $25 billion in the process. Over 22 million international tourists visit the United States and spend over $15 billion (including payments to U.S. flag carriers). Receipts from domestic tourism in the United States exceed $240 billion.

Within the United States, tourism (McIntosh & Goeldner 1990, p. 20):

- Is the third largest retail industry, following food stores and automotive deals;
- Is the second largest private employer in the nation;
- Is one of the top three employers in 39 states;
- Accounts for $323 billion in domestic and foreign visitor spending, exceeding 6.4 percent of the gross national product;

- Directly employs 5.5 million Americans at every level of skill;
- Generates more than $70 billion a year in wages and salaries and more than $36 billion a year in federal, state, and local tax revenues; and
- Is a highly diversified industry with more than 1 million component companies, ranging from small travel agencies, restaurants, and souvenir shops to large airlines and hotel chains, with 99 percent of these companies classified as small businesses.

The Four Components of Tourism

The tourism industry is comprised of thousands of companies whose primary purpose is to provide services and products for tourists. The companies involved are as varied as they are numerous and include everything from "mom and pop" diners to multinational corporations.

There are four basic components of the tourism industry. The four components are attractions, transportation, lodging, and food and beverage. The combined efforts of these four components make it possible, even desirable, for people to travel.

Attractions

People travel for many different reasons. Some travel because of business obligations, while others travel for pleasure. Those traveling for pleasure usually travel to visit relatives or to experience new and different attractions around the world. Attractions are what draw individuals to specific destinations. "They may be based on natural resources, culture, ethnicity or entertainment" (Mill 1990, p. 22). Tourists have always traveled to natural areas of beauty to seek solace from their everyday lives. Today this type of tourism is called ecotourism. Ecotourism is a type of environmentally oriented tourism in which tourists from around the globe seek out natural wonders (Fridgen 1991). The U.S. National Park System attracted 9 million foreign visitors, accounting for more than 20 percent of the total foreign visitors to the country (Ridenour 1990). There are over 1,100 national parks and 3,200 nature preservations across the world. In countries such as Africa, national parks are their primary attractions. Many undeveloped areas are studying ways to capitalize on their natural resources without changing or destroying the natural beauty.

Other man-made attractions range from the Pyramids in Egypt and the Incan ruins in Peru to Disney World in Florida. There are attractions designed to meet the needs of everyone. If one has the desire to study about ancient cultures, there are attractions that have preserved the artifacts from these cultures and that provide tours to enhance the sightseer's visit. If one's desires lean toward the more fanciful, there are hundreds of theme parks from which to choose. With the overwhelming success of both Disneyland and Disney World, there has been a flourish of imitators developed to provide tourists with the excitement they are seeking at theme parks.

Gaming has also become a major player in the tourism industry. Las Vegas, Nevada, (figure 1-3) has experienced overwhelming success in this industry. Currently, gaming has made tourism the number one industry in the state. Gone is the misconception that Las Vegas is a "den of iniquity"; Las Vegas is now promoting itself as a family vacation destination. Theme hotels and theme parks are helping the city to entice families there. Gaming is quickly becoming popular in other parts of the United States as well. It is also popular in other parts of the world as well as on cruise ships.

Transportation

As was made evident in the discussion of the history of tourism, transportation has been a vital component to the success of the tourism industry. The earliest travelers journeyed on foot or horseback in caravans or groups to provide safety and comfort to one another. As vehicles of travel were invented and fine tuned, travel became more prominent.

Worldwide, domestic tourists generally travel by automobile. In 1990, according to the Federal Highway Administration, Americans traveled more than 2 trillion intercity passenger-miles. Of those 2 trillion miles, 81 percent were by car, while air travel accounted for 17 percent. Rail passenger transportation and motor coach transportation also play an important but smaller role in domestic travel, providing the most support in intracity travel. International tourism relies predominantly on the airline industry. In 1988, the number of paying passengers was 335.8 billion (Fridgen 1991). Air travel has revolutionized the tourism industry. Today air travel is not only reasonably priced, but easy to do. It takes only one

Figure 1-3   Every year over 22 million visitors and convention attendees enjoy the lights and sounds of Las Vegas and the glittering strip. Las Vegas currently has the ten largest resort hotels in the world. (Courtesy: Las Vegas News Bureau.)

phone call to book passage on any of a number of major carriers to almost anywhere in the world. The primary advantage to air travel is the speed in which the traveler can reach his or her destination. In a relatively short period of time (5–6 hours), an individual can fly from coast to coast. The airlines now make it possible for people to travel to faraway destinations in short periods of time—this supports the new trend of more frequent but shorter vacations. The airlines have also provided easy access for business travelers to their many business meetings and conferences.

Lodging

As soon as people began to travel, they needed places to sleep and take nourishment. Historical accounts of roadside inns and lodging facilities have been found in documents dating back to ancient

Persia. These lodging facilities were located along trade and caravan routes. Early lodging facilities provided lodging for both the traveler and their animals. Many of the earliest travelers were religious individuals, and inns were developed because people wanted to open their homes to the clergymen.

People traveling for pleasure or for business needed a place to sleep. The lodging industry is an extremely important component of the tourism industry. Lodging encompasses a broad spectrum of supplier businesses. Accommodation categories can include hotels, motels, conference centers, inns, bed and breakfasts, resort condominiums, youth hostels, and health spas. In 1992 total industry revenues for the U.S. lodging industry reached $66 billion.

Food and Beverage

Tourists need to eat and drink while away from home. In fact, with the current emphasis placed on dining out, eating is not only necessary, but it is in many cases a source of entertainment for tourists. In 1992 the food and beverage industry saw sales exceeding $248 billion. Regarding lodging and transportation foodservice sales, the National Restaurant Association concluded that 1991 restaurant sales at lodging establishments (which include hotel restaurants, motor restaurants, and motor hotel restaurants) reached $15.7 billion in 1991. Transportation foodservice sales (on airlines, passenger/cargo lines, and railroads) exceeded $2.9 billion in that same year.

Meetings, Conventions, and Expositions

A major source of revenue for the tourism industry comes from the meetings, conventions, and expositions segment of the industry. As stated earlier, a tourist is someone who spends more than one night but less than one year away from home for business or pleasure. This definition applies to a large percentage of individuals attending meetings, conventions, or expositions. In the 1991 Successful Meetings' Industry Study, the average number of meetings per year that required hotel accommodations was 9.3 for both association and corporate planners (McNabb/DeSoto & Company

1991). Conventions/expositions were the largest type of meeting booked, with an average of 804 attendees generating an average of 396 hotel rooms used for the convention/exposition.

Meetings, conventions, and expositions generate a tremendous amount of revenue within the hospitality industry. A *meeting* is a conference, workshop, seminar, or other event designed to bring people together for the purpose of exchanging information. Meetings do not include exhibits. An *exposition* is "an event designed to bring together purveyors of products, equipment, and services in an environment in which they can demonstrate their products and services to a group of attendees at a convention or trade show (Rutherford 1990, p. 44)." When meetings are combined with expositions, the event is called a *convention*.

Historically, the meetings, conventions, and expositions industry has mirrored the changes in the overall hospitality industry. As the hospitality industry saw great increases in expenditures, meetings, conventions, and expositions experienced great growth as well. In 1989, when the lodging industry encountered its best year yet with revenues well above $55 billion dollars, the meetings, conventions, and expositions industry also saw a tremendous growth in expenditures. With the many changes the hospitality industry has undergone in the past 20 years, the importance of meetings, conventions, and expositions has become more recognized. The need to communicate with one another face to face has been the driving force behind the growth of this industry. In 1991 the meetings industry spent approximately $38.7 billion on conventions, meetings, and expositions; this number is predicted to swell to over $50 billion in 1995. This figure accounts for over half of the total lodging industry revenue. Figure 1-4 hints at the growth that the meeting and convention industry has experienced in recent years.

There are four major components of the conventions industry: planners and the groups they represent, host facilities, services, and exhibitors. Planners are individuals or groups that plan meetings, conventions, and expositions. Planners fall into a number of categories. There are corporate meeting planners who work exclusively for a corporation, association meeting planners who work exclusively for an association, or independent meeting planners who contract out their services to both associations and corporations. Association management companies as well as travel agencies are also becoming more active in planning meetings,

Figure 1-4 Los Angeles, California—the downtown skyline is an urban mix of hotels, nightclubs, restaurants, and home to the $485 million expansion of the Los Angeles Convention Center. (Courtesy: Los Angeles Convention and Visitors Bureau.)

conventions, and expositions. (See chapter 7 for a complete description of planners.)

Host venues provide sleeping rooms, meeting rooms, and food and beverage as well as a number of other services for groups attending meetings, conventions, or expositions. Types of host venues include hotels, conference centers, resort hotels, universities, bed and breakfast inns, and so on. (For a complete description of host facilities, see chapter 5).

Services refers to all those individuals and organizations that provide support for the meetings, conventions, and expositions segment of the industry. Service suppliers include, but are not limited to, ground handlers, destination management companies, entertainers, decorators, transportation companies, attractions, and tour guide companies.

Exhibitors are financially intertwined with all segments of the meetings, conventions, and expositions industry. They provide much of the revenue needed for planners to hold meetings, conventions, and expositions. Exhibitors are individuals working for a company and may be called many names other than exhibitor, such as advertising director, communication director, or director of marketing, who is involved with the corporate exhibit program. Exhibitors select expositions to attend based on their ability to provide qualified leads and to introduce their products, both new and old, to an interested audience.

Summary

This chapter has briefly introduced the reader to the exciting and lucrative industry of meetings, conventions, and expositions. It has carefully outlined how this segment of the hospitality industry fits into the overall scope of the hospitality or tourism industry and has begun to familiarize the reader with some of the major components of the industry.

References

Fridgen, J. 1991. *Dimensions of Tourism.* East Lansing, Mich.: Educational Institute of the American Hotel & Motel Association.

Gartrell, Richard B. 1988. *Destination Marketing for Convention and Visitor Bureaus.* Dubuque, Iowa: Kendall-Hunt.

Lofft, Virginia. 1992. Hip-hip hooray! *Successful Meetings.* New York: Bill Communications, Inc.

McIntosh, R., and C. Goeldner. *Tourism: Principles, Practices, Philosophies,* 6th Edition. New York: John Wiley & Sons, Inc.

McNabb/DeSoto & Company. Successful Meetings' 1991 Industry Study.

Mill, R. 1990. *Tourism: The International Business.* Englewood Cliffs, N.J.: Prentice Hall.

Ridenour, J. 1990. The nation's parks—resource issues for the 1990's. Keynote address presented 29 March 1990, at the outdoor Recreation Trends Symposium III, Indianapolis, Ind.

Rutherford, D.G. 1990. *Introduction to the Conventions, Expositions, and Meetings Industry.* New York: Van Nostrand Reinhold.

Discussion Questions

1. How has the development of meetings, conventions, and expositions been closely tied to the development of tourism?
2. Discuss the impact you see tourism having on your own community. Give examples of hospitality operations you are familiar with and how tourism—specifically meetings, conventions, and expositions—affect them.
3. How do the four components of tourism relate to meetings, conventions, and expositions?
4. Based on what you have learned about the history of tourism and meetings, conventions, and expositions, speculate about what you believe the future holds for this industry.

Key Terms

tourism industry
hospitality industry
tourist
convention bureau
convention service manager
attractions

transportation
convention
meeting
exposition
host facility

2

Convention and Visitors Bureaus

Learning Objectives

1. To understand the history, general purpose, and organizational structure of convention and visitor bureaus.
2. To understand the methods of funding for a bureau and appreciate the complexity of the taxation issue, as it relates to bureau funding.
3. To realize the different services that a bureau offers to members, tourists, and meeting planners.
4. To understand how bureau members can best work with their bureau.
5. To become familiar with the International Association of Convention and Visitor Bureaus and overview its services to member bureaus.

Introduction

The first convention bureau was established in Detroit in 1895. What led this city to form an agency whose sole purpose was to promote the city of Detroit for business expansion? Several factors led to the increasing industrialization of America and the aggressive pursuit of business development. These factors included: (1) population increase, (2) the Industrial Revolution, (3) railway and communication improvements, and (4) The Depression of 1893.

First, America was growing rapidly. The decades after the Civil War saw a surge in population, due to a higher birth rate and an influx of immigrants. The labor force grew larger, making it possible for industries to grow and expand. Businesses wanted to find new markets and develop new divisions and offices.

The Industrial Revolution, considered by some experts as the single most important economic development of the latter part of the eighteenth century, began replacing human labor with machine labor. Productivity, efficiency, and profit increased as a result of increased machination. Businesses could expand because they had more capital, and the nation was eager to grow so that it could compete with European countries, some of which were still economically superior to America.

The Industrial Revolution also led to improvements in the nation's railway and communication systems. Large cities were connected by a network of railroads by the mid–nineteenth century, allowing for increased traffic between industrial centers. Telegraph, mail, and telephone all appeared by 1890. With their appearance, industry could effectively communicate and interact with businesses and customers in other cities.

Finally, the Depression of 1893 alerted businessmen to the importance of actively recruiting industry and business. Although this Depression was not as severe as the Depression of the 1930s, economic hardship did hurt the business development. Industrial leaders in Detroit realized that to counteract the damage caused by the Depression, they would have to pursue business development more aggressively.

Prior to the establishment of the first official convention bureau, some city and business marketing was already occurring. Traveling salesmen tended to stay in the same large, luxurious hotels in industrial cities along the railway circuit. These hotels, some of which became famous, promoted themselves and their locations and served as sites for conventions and meetings. The hotels also worked with city merchants to market the city to businessmen considering expansion.

In 1895, some enterprising businessmen and city officials in Detroit hired a traveling salesman to "sell" the city. This new method of business marketing caught on and, by the early 1900s, nearly 3,000 such organizations existed nationwide. Initially, most bureaus were designed to primarily sell and service conventions, but, as time went on, more of the bureaus began promoting tourism. To accomplish this goal, many of the convention bureaus added the words "and visitors" to their names.

Purpose

According to the International Association of Convention and Visitors Bureaus (IACVB), a convention and visitors bureau is "a not-for-profit umbrella organization which represents a city or urban area in the solicitation and servicing of types of travelers to that area or city. . . whether they visit for business or pleasure or both" (*IACVB General Information* 1990, p. 2). The convention and visitors bureau is the organization that coordinates the efforts of the various factions within a community. These factions include city government, civic and trade associations, and individual suppliers, such as hotels, motels, restaurants, and attractions. Today's bureaus act as the intermediary between potential visitors and local business.

Specifically, a bureau has four primary responsibilities:

1. To encourage groups to hold meetings, conventions, and trade shows in the area it represents;
2. To assist those groups with meeting preparations and to lend support throughout the meeting;
3. To encourage tourists to visit the historic, cultural, and recreational opportunities the city or area has to offer; and
4. To develop and promote the image of the community it represents.

In other words, the convention and visitors bureau was designed for the sole purpose of selling a city. Richard Newman, President of the IAVCB states, "People go where they have been invited. It's the job of the convention and visitors bureau to invite them." Figures 2-1 and 2-2 are examples of how bureaus "invite" people to a location.

The techniques used to sell a city may vary from bureau to bureau, but the end result should be the same—an increase in revenue generated by visits to the city. Many bureaus take part in national trade shows designed to allow CVBs to sell their cities to interested groups. At these trade shows the convention and visitors bureau generates a list of prospective clients, such as associations, corporations, or travel agents. After the show, sales representatives from the bureau's marketing department visit the

Orlando/Orange County
Convention & Visitors Bureau, Inc.

Orlando/Orange County
Convention & Visitors Bureau, Inc.

Orlando/Orange County
Convention & Visitors Bureau, Inc.

Orlando/Orange County
Convention & Visitors Bureau, Inc.

Orlando/Orange County
Convention & Visitors Bureau, Inc.

Orlando/Orange County
Convention & Visitors Bureau, Inc.

Orlando/Orange County
Convention & Visitors Bureau, Inc.

Orlando/Orange County
Convention & Visitors Bureau, Inc.

Orlando/Orange County
Convention & Visitors Bureau, Inc.

Orlando/Orange County
Convention & Visitors Bureau, Inc.

Orlando/Orange County
Convention & Visitors Bureau, Inc.

Orlando/Orange County
Convention & Visitors Bureau, Inc.

Figure 2-1   One of the jobs of the local CVB is to invite people to come visit their community.

prospective clients. If the group is sincerely interested in the city as a possible site for their meeting or convention, the bureau develops a familiarization trip (FAM trip) to introduce them to the many services and facilities their city has to offer (see figure 2-3).

A *FAM trip* is "a hosted trip to assess facilities, locations or service" (*The Convention Liaison Council Glossary* 1986, p. 24). During these FAM trips the convention and visitors bureau acts as the coordinator, bringing together all of the suppliers in a city. The bureau's sales manager will determine the needs of the groups and then pair the group with hotels that can meet these needs. These suppliers are then asked to act as hosts for the potential clients. The suppliers provide rooms, meals, and entertainment for

Figure 2-2 The state tourism boards are also in the business of attracting visitors.

Figure 2-3   Familiarization trips allow the host city the opportunity to show off all that it has to offer to potential group business. (Courtesy: Athens CVB.)

the representatives of the groups interested in coming to their city. This allows them to put their best foot forward and to "wine and dine" prospective clients.

Another method of soliciting visits to the city is through listings in trade journals, such as *Tradeshow Week* or *Successful Meetings*. The readership of these magazines and journals consists of independent meeting planners, association directors, corporate meeting planners, and any other individual interested in the meetings and convention market.

Once the bureau has sold a prospective client on its destination, they still play an important role in providing service to the group. The bureau can make the meeting planner's job easier by recommending reliable sources for services, supplying information on facilities and prices, assisting in securing hotel commitments, helping with tour planning, putting the planner in touch with leading businessmen, and acting as a liaison between the organization and local government officials and assisting with program planning (*IACVB General Information* 1990, pp. 2–3).

The third responsibility of a convention and visitors bureau is to assist in developing the individual and group tour business. The bureau works closely with the suppliers in the tourism industry, including tour operators and wholesalers, airline carriers, and retail travel agents. The bureau uses marketing strategies, such as direct mail solicitation, trade show participation, and sales calls to meet prospective clients. The goal of these strategies is to alert persons associated with individual and group tour business to all the attractions in the area, as well as special events, such as festivals, celebrations, and parades.

Another function of the bureau's tourism faction is responding to written and telephone inquiries from individuals seeking information about their destination. Many bureaus include inserts in popular magazines, where readers can request information on different locations.

The key to successful destination marketing relies upon the perceived image of the location. For this reason the convention and visitors bureau must be very active in the development and promotion of this image. The reputation of a destination as an excellent host city of conventions and meetings or as a wonderful tourist location is just as important as the actual facilities and services provided by the community. For example, if potential visitors perceive New York City as extremely expensive, they will avoid the location, even if in reality it is competitively priced. Therefore, it is important that convention and visitors bureaus nurture an image that leaves a favorable impression of their locations. Convention and visitors bureaus develop such an image largely through the media. They sponsor attractive advertising and solicit favorable media exposure. Image campaigns, such as "Virginia is for Lovers," also create a positive popular perception. Figures 2-4, 2-5, and 2-6 are promotional scenes that evoke images of the locations they represent. These types of photographs are often used by local convention and visitors bureaus to help market their locations.

Organizational Structure

The organization chart seen in figure 2-7 is of the New York Convention & Visitors Bureau, Inc. This bureau is organized in much the same way as all bureaus are organized. As stated earlier

Figure 2-4   The only vehicles of their kind in the world today, cable cars are over a century old. This nationally designated moving landmark climbs Nob Hill at 9$\frac{1}{2}$ miles per hour. (Courtesy: San Francisco CVB.)

in this chapter, bureaus are comprised of member businesses that are located within the communities they are serving. From this membership base, a board of directors is appointed. This board acts as the governing body for the bureau and works in conjunction

Figure 2-5 The famous Hollywood sign is an international beacon for sunshine and glamour. (Courtesy: Los Angeles Convention and Visitors Bureau.)

with the chief executive officer and their staff. The professional staff is usually divided into three divisions: the sales and marketing department, the operations/administration department, and the communication department.

The sales and marketing department is responsible for identifying potential clients in the areas of meetings, conventions, and expositions. They are responsible for identifying new business as well as servicing the business. Services provided can be, but are not limited to, housing, registration, assistance in the development of pre- and post-conference tours, as well as support in the development of spousal programs. They also provide promotional material for the various tourism sites in their community. The amount of services provided is related directly to the funding provided to the bureau.

The operational or administrative arm of the bureau deals with financial issues and membership development. This department is

Figure 2-6   Anaheim's 42-mile coastline is said to be the "American Riviera," with more pleasure boats and yachts than any other U.S. harbor. (Courtesy: Anaheim Area Visitor and Convention Bureau.)

responsible for generating funds and keeping track of these funds as well as for promoting membership drives. Information services provide all of the printed material for the bureau. Depending on the size of the bureau, they may have their own in-house advertising agency and printing department. If the agency is smaller, they contract out much of this work and limit their in-house staff to a graphics specialist.

Funding

The IACVB states that most bureaus are classified as independent 501(c) organizations under the Internal Revenue Codes. According to the Internal Revenue Codes, a 501(c)6 is a not-for-profit organization. This means that the organization cannot engage in regular business activities that are normally conducted on a for-profit basis. The revenue generated through bureau activities must be spent on programs sponsored by the bureau.

The economic health of a city or community is closely related to its ability to make full use of its resources, such as attractions, historical sites, hotels, meeting and convention space, and restaurants. Convention and visitors bureaus can increase the profitability of their communities by promoting all of their assets. Those communities that have invested adequate funds in their convention and visitors bureaus and who have held them accountable for those funds see a tremendous return on their investment.

The funding for these privately operated, not-for-profit organizations comes from various sources. In the United States an accomodations tax, or hotel room tax, accounts for the largest portion of the funding (see table 2-1). It can be broken down into local sales tax, city hotel tax, and state hotel occupancy tax. Other funding sources are general state and local taxes, state matching funds, membership dues, cooperative investments, publication revenues, convention services, sponsored events, and trade shows (Gartrell 1988, p. 44).

The accommodations tax is a tax levied on each room sold within the city. The tax was originally designed to generate funds for

Table 2-1 *Room Tax as percent of total budget for Convention and Visitors Bureaus (1993 figures)*

Total Budget ($US)	Percent
Up to 200,000	87.88
200,000–450,000	88.44
450,000–750,000	78.46
750,000–1,250,000	80.24
1,250,000–2,000,000	81.76
2,000,000–5,000,000	71.23
Over 5,000,000	59.16

Adapted from the IACVB 1993 Bureau Funding and Expenditure Survey.

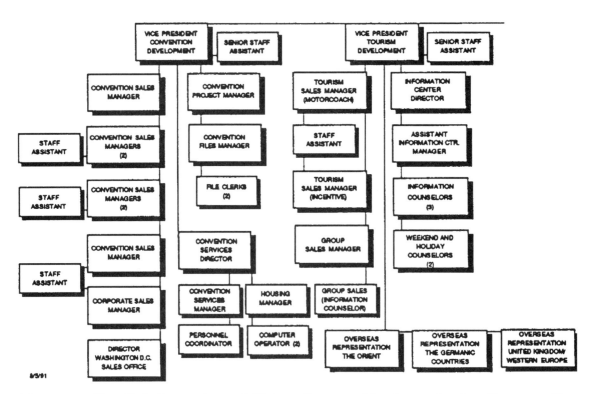

Figure 2-7   New York Convention and Visitors Bureau table of organization. (Courtesy: New York Convention and Visitors Bureau.)

visitor attractions and to increase funding for destination marketing without burdening the local people. The hotel room tax varies from city to city; currently, total taxes range from as low as 3 percent in smaller cities to as high as 19.25 percent + $2.00 in New York City (1993 figures).

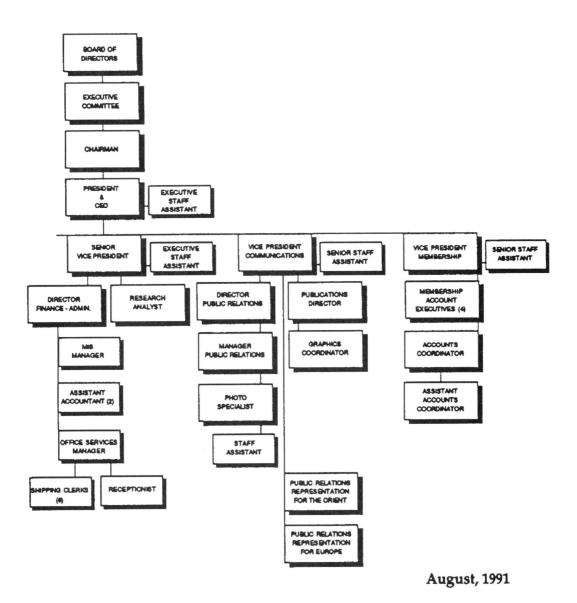

August, 1991

Figure 2-7   (Continued)

Although this tax still provides a large portion of the convention and visitors bureau's funding, recently there has been a growing trend for cities to direct these funds towards other expenses. For instance, some cities have directed room tax money towards such expenditures as sports facilities, convention facilities, arts and sciences, school boards, subsidized housing, and the general fund (Butler 1990). Tough economic situations have put tremendous pressure on local governments to generate revenue to meet the needs of the community. An easy solution appears to be to use the revenue generated from the accomodations tax. This tax has become an excellent source of revenue for legislators, since it does not directly affect their constituents. Therefore, not only do many municipalities use room tax for purposes other than bureau funding, but they also continue to increase the tax rate.

This tendency has begun to cause concern among the hospitality industry because of its long-term effect on the industry's marketability. A reduction in funding to the bureau ultimately translates to a reduction in the number of meetings and conventions brought into the community. Since conventions are booked approximately 3 to 4 years in advance, this quick-fix solution will begin hurting a city some years after the bureau funding is reduced and will continue to hurt it for years. Therefore, the use of the hotel room tax for expenditures other than for public safety, convention facilities, or the convention and visitors bureaus is deemed a misappropriation of this tax and is being opposed by many national associations representing the meetings and convention industry (Rutherford 1990).

Another major portion of a convention and visitors bureau's funding comes from membership dues. Typically, members are hotels, motels, restaurants, attractions, and other visitor-related businesses. Because the convention and visitors bureau coordinates all the various components of the meeting and visitor industry, it is vitally important that those businesses associated with the hospitality industry be members. Their membership allows them to take part in cooperative advertising, trade shows, and familiarization trips, as well as receive bureau publications and reports about conventions and shows coming to the city. These reports include the history of the groups' spending practices, as well as size requirements, preferred activities, and time schedule. It will also provide demographic data about the groups' participants.

Another source of funding for the convention and visitors bureau that has become increasingly significant is miscellaneous and general city, county, or state taxes that have been appropriated as part of the legislative process. These funds need to be renewed yearly and generally require an annual presentation to the legislature, reporting the use of previous funds as well as justifying the uses of new funds. Grants or matching funds are frequently available from the local government to support specific programs or visitor services.

There are many other avenues for convention and visitors bureaus to provide income for their operations. For instance, bureaus have developed special advertising publications that generate funds through the sale of advertising space within the publication. Other sources of revenue include special events; educational programs; fees for such services as registration, housing, and convention management; and event assistance (Hosansky 1986; Milner 1987). By necessity, convention and visitors bureaus often display great initiative and creativity in generating revenue for their programs.

Services

Generally speaking, the local convention and visitors bureau should be the first stop for any visitor or meeting planner who is considering a stay in the area. The convention and visitors bureau is designed to warehouse all of the information about a city's visitor-related services. For the tourist, as figure 2-8 suggests, these services include city maps, restaurant guides, shopping guides, hotel guides, and brochures on local attractions. For meeting planners who are considering a city as a possible destination for their group, the bureau can provide a host of different services. For example, bureaus may assist in the site selection process by providing a list of properties that can handle the meeting, by recommending reliable sources for services, by suggesting possible ground transportation, by coordinating familiarization trips, and by acting as a convention management consultant to the meeting planner.

If the meeting or convention is large enough to require several hotels, the convention and visitors bureau may act as a coordinator of housing. The association hosting the conference or meeting will provide its participants with a form listing the possible properties. The participant completes the form and mails it to the convention and visitors bureau for processing. The bureau then makes the reservations at the selected properties. Many bureaus have a computerized operation to facilitate this process.

Figure 2-8 Los Angeles Convention and Visitors Bureau Visitor Information Center—downtown. (Courtesy: IACVB.)

Upon arrival, the bureau may further provide such services as registration assistance, tour guides, and brochures. They may also act as coordinator for local support services, such as photographers, caterers, audiovisual companies, florists, and decorators.

How CVB Members Can Work More Effectively With Their Bureaus

Within the next decade the hospitality industry will face competition as it has never seen before. Those who wish to be successful in this competitive environment must make use of all available resources. To this end the convention and visitors bureau can become a powerful ally for hotels, motels, restaurants, attractions, and other visitor-related businesses.

Success lies in the ability of a business to form a strong partnership with the convention and visitors bureau. Griffin Miller (1990) states in "CVBs: Partners With Punch" that the formula for success is "bureau + hotels/suppliers + cooperation = a win-win situation" (p. 42). The teamwork necessary for a successful partnership includes keeping the bureau updated on any new improvements or developments that take place in the establishment, cooperating with the bureau when it sponsors site inspections and FAM trips and working together to support the community as a whole (Miller, 1990 p. 44).

Often, members of convention and visitors bureaus forget that they are equal partners in this cooperative effort. A member business should consider the bureau an extension of its own sales and marketing department. Thus, it is important that the businesses not only expect leads to be sent to them from the convention and visitors bureau, but that they also send any potential leads they might encounter in their day-to-day activity to the bureau. This enables the bureau to play a supportive role in its members' activities.

Another way members can foster a better relationship with their convention and visitors bureau is to develop a joint selling effort with the bureau. Members should be as interested in selling the city as they are in selling their individual properties. Sales and marketing individuals should understand the importance of being fully versed in the many amenities the city has to offer. This enables the sales and marketing departments to work in conjunction with their convention and visitors bureau in selling the destination as a whole.

Richard Newman (1991) suggests that bureau members also get involved with all of the various activities provided by the bureaus. These activities range from familiarization trips to education of the local legislature. A bureau is only as strong as its members. Therefore, support of bureau activities is essential.

International Association of Convention and Visitors Bureaus

The International Association of Convention and Visitors Bureaus (IACVB) was founded in 1914 for the specific purpose of allowing existing convention and visitor bureaus to exchange information about solicitable meetings and conventions. The organization also had as its mission the improvement of the professional practices in the meetings and convention industry. Today, nearly a century after its inception, the primary purpose and mission remain the same.

As figures 2-9 and 2-10 indicate, the entire basis of IACVB is its international scope. As of 1991, IACVB membership consists of 389 CEOs of convention and visitors bureaus in 25 countries. Additional representatives of a member bureau other than the chief executive

IACVB ORGANIZATIONAL STRUCTURE

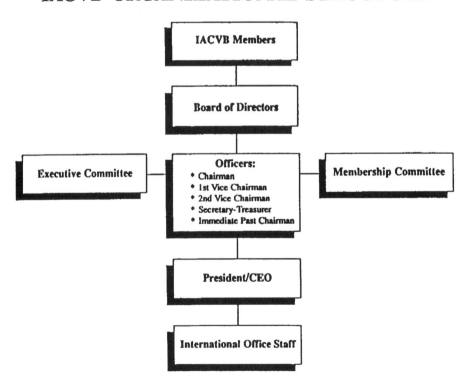

Figure 2-9   IACVB Organizational Structure. (Courtesy: IACVB.)

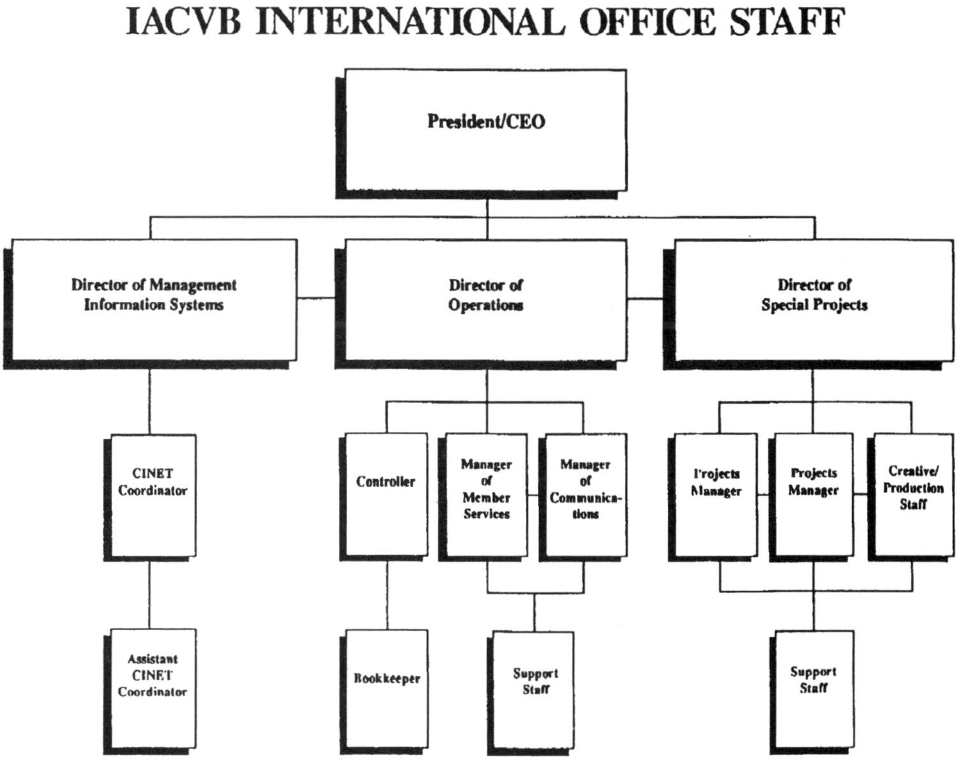

IACVB INTERNATIONAL OFFICE STAFF

Figure 2-10 IACVB International Office Staff. (Courtesy: IACVB.)

officer are categorized as "professional staff" members. Unlike many of the other associations related to the conference and meetings industry, the IACVB does not allow allied memberships for industry suppliers. This closed membership guarantees the opportunity to network and solve common problems.

In fulfilling its mission statement, the IACVB has developed numerous member services. The most important benefit for IACVB members is the CINET program.

Participation in this computerized information network enables member bureaus to exchange demographic and historical data on organizations holding meetings and conventions throughout the world. CINET's data files create one of the most complete, versatile convention lead services in the industry, allowing subscribers to "pick and choose" the exact information needed to maximize their ability to effectively solicit and serve convention-holding organizations (*IACVB General Information* 1990, p. 2).

The CINET program screens upcoming meetings and conventions that IACVB member bureaus may wish to host. To be included in the CINET program, meetings, or conventions must adhere to the following:

1. They must be transient and salable conventions, open to bidding from any city in the world.
2. They must include 50 or more rooms to qualify for a listing.
3. They must be recognizable associations or organizations, either regional, national, or international in scope (Gartrell 1988, p. 11).

IACVB members who make use of the CINET program are able to target specific meetings or conventions that they have the physical facilities to host. This enables them to then plan marketing strategies designed to solicit these groups.

Other services provided by the IACVB include educational opportunities, research, Destination Showcase, consultant services, and publications. The educational opportunities vary from seminars and workshops to certificate programs. IACVB's annual convention provides an arena for the open exchange of ideas and experiences. The annual convention also provides an avenue for sharing and solving common problems within the industry. The research arm of the IACVB sponsors studies on important facets of convention and visitors bureau management. This research is not only shared with members, but has become an important source of information for the industry.

The IACVB's consultant team provides counsel to existing convention and visitors bureaus. Additionally, the team has the expertise to do feasibility studies for cities that are considering establishing a convention and visitors bureau. These feasibility studies look at the ability of the existing city to organize and fund such a bureau.

Publications provided by the IACVB enable convention and visitors bureaus to educate the general population about the important role a CVB can play in a community's economic success. IACVB publications are also designed to educate and update their members. These publications include an annual membership directory, tour operator manual, monthly newsletter, bylaws with rules and regulations, legislative updates, and position available announcements.

The newest service provided by the IACVB is "Destination Showcase" (see figure 2-11). This is a mini–trade show, where the

Figure 2-11   Destination showcases at Javits Center, New York City. (Courtesy: IACVB.)

IACVB invites meeting planners and association executives involved in the city selection process to visit exclusively with member bureaus. Richard Newman, president of IACVB, stated that the first Destination Showcase in 1991 had 1,100 attendees. Attendees were extremely pleased, and the IACVB has made plans to expand this showcase to other parts of the country.

Summary

Convention bureaus were established around the turn of the century, largely as a result of increased industrialization brought about by the Industrial Revolution. These bureaus quickly became established and began catering to visitors as well as conventions; thus they changed their name to include visitors. Convention and visitors bureaus are not-for-profit organizations designed to solicit and service both business and pleasure visitors to a city. Hotels, restaurants, motels, attractions, and other visitor-oriented facilities belong to a bureau, and their active participation is vital to a bureau's success. Bureaus are funded largely through the city's accomodations tax, which the city sometimes also uses for expenditures other than visitor-related facilities and services. This use is considered a misappropriation by many associations in the meetings and convention industry. Other sources for funding include membership dues, other taxes, joint advertising efforts with members, and other services offered for a fee. The International Association of Convention and Visitors Bureaus (IACVB), founded in 1914 to encourage interaction and information exchanges between bureaus, offers many services to its member bureaus. Some of those services include the CINET (computerized information network) program, educational opportunities, research, consulting, and Destination Showcase.

Reference

The Convention Liaison Council Glossary. 1986. Washington, D.C.: The Convention Liaison Council.

Gartrell, R. B. 1988. *Destination Marketing.* Dubuque, Iowa: Kendall/Hunt Publishing Co.

Hosansky, M. 1990. *IACVB General Information and Membership Directory.* (November). Champaign, Ill.: IACVB.

Miller, G. 1990. CVBs: Partners with punch. *Hotel & Resort Industry,* (December) pp. 42–47.

Rutherford, D. G. 1990. *Introduction to the Conventions, Expositions, and Meeting Industry.* New York: Van Nostrand Reinhold.

Discussion Questions

1. Discuss the important role that a convention and visitors bureau can play in the economic well being of the municipality it serves.
2. Using the information available from your CVB, attractions, hotels, resorts, and restaurants, develop a "FAM" trip to introduce a meeting planner to your city.
3. Discuss various marketing techniques employed by different CVBs in your area. What differs between a successful marketing plan and an unsuccessful one?
4. Discuss the various forms of funding CVBs receive. What implications do these types of funding have on the operation of a CVB?
5. In your opinion, what services provided by a CVB are the most important?
6. Based on your readings, develop a strategy for groups to employ that would enable them to work more closely with their CVB.
7. Discuss the importance and purpose of IACVB.

Key Terms

industrial revolution	hotel room tax
convention and visitors bureau	CINET
familiarization (FAM) trip	destination showcase
IRS code 501 (c) 6	

3

Players in the Industry

Learning Objectives

1. To recognize the main participants in the convention and meetings industry and have a general understanding of their roles.
2. To understand the different types of associations.
3. To understand the purpose of convention centers.
4. To understand why conference centers developed and what they provide to the industry.
5. To differentiate between the different types of meeting planners and recognize their responsibilities.
6. To become familiar with tour operators and how they participate in the industry.
7. To appreciate the history and economic benefits of trade shows and expositions.
8. To understand the various roles of those involved in trade shows, including the trade show sponsor, the show manager, and the service contractor.
9. To become familiar with the role of the hotel and the convention service manager.
10. To recognize the convention and visitors bureau's role in the industry as a whole.

Introduction

The size of the convention and meetings industry has expanded to the point that it now encompasses a variety of players. To operate effectively in this segment of the hospitality industry, one must understand these players and their roles. This chapter will introduce the various players, including:

- Associations
- Convention centers
- Conference centers
- Corporate meeting planners
- Independent meeting planners
- Tour operators
- Trade shows and expositions
- Trade show sponsors
- Exposition or show managers
- Service contractors
- Hotels
- Convention and visitors bureaus

Associations

It is because of our system's (government's) complexity that associations have such a potentially useful role to play. They can educate and inform. They can improve the quality of decision-making by their expertise. They can be advocates for a position or an approach to an issue. They can support candidates they believe will best serve the nations. They can encourage good citizenship by promoting voter registration and getting out the vote.

—Ronald Reagan

An association may be considered an organized body that exhibits some variety of volunteer leadership structure, which may employ a staff and that serves a group of people who have some interest, activity, or purpose that they share in common. The association is generally organized to promote and enhance that common interest, activity, or purpose (Rutherford 1990, p. 14).

Modern associations find their roots in historical times. Ancient Roman and Oriental craftsmen formed associations for the betterment of their trade. Medieval times found associations in the form of guilds, which were created to ensure proper wages and to maintain work standards.

The evolution of associations in the United States began in the eighteenth century. At that time the Rhode Island candle makers organized themselves, and in Philadelphia Ben Franklin formed what is today called the American Philosophical Society. The oldest trade association still in existence was formed in 1786 in New York City to organize merchants. Today it is called the New York Chamber of Commerce (*ASAE Factbook* 1993, p. 4). The American Society of Association Executives states that there are currently 23,000 associations operating in the United States and 100,000 more at the regional, state, and local levels.

> The association industry is significant in many respects—total employees, payroll, and membership—but in one area it is the undisputed leader. It's *the* big spender when it comes to conventions and meetings. In 1991, the association industry spent $26 billion to hold 215,000 meetings and conventions and attracted 22.6 million attendees. (*ASAE Factbook* 1993, p. 24)

National associations operate with an average staff of 16 and a budget of $2.9 million annually. Although services provided by associations vary from organization to organization, 95 percent of them hold annual conventions and 80 percent host one trade show annually. Also, 73 percent have educational seminars as events separate from their annual convention (*ASAE Factbook* 1990, p. 14). Figure 3-1 graphically illustrates the activities in which most national organizations are involved.

There are two recognized categories of associations: trade associations and professional associations. Both exist primarily for the betterment of their members. A key activity for both types of associations is to gather and exchange information through publications, educational seminars, newsletters, and meetings.

Trade associations are not-for-profit organizations designed to address the needs of for-profit businesses. The members of these associations represent business firms, and they generally share a common focus. For example, the Professional Convention Management Association (PCMA) brings together people interested in the convention and meetings industry. Their members work together towards collective goals that will affect their particular industry. For instance, PCMA's commitment to the improvement of the con-

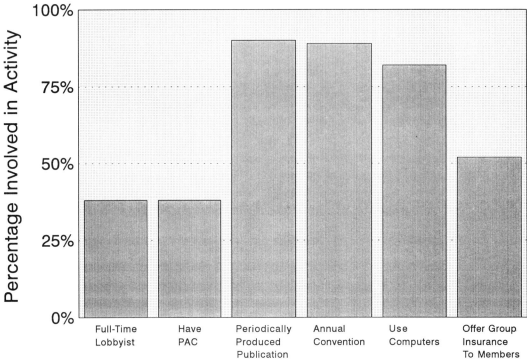

Figure 3-1   National association activities. (Courtesy: ASAE.)

vention and meetings industry is evidenced by its establishment of an educational foundation in 1985. This foundation was designed to develop a training pool of future industry professionals through supporting educational programs in colleges and universities.

Like trade associations, professional associations are also not-for-profit organizations. Professional associations, however, are not involved with business pursuits. Rather, they are designed to assist individuals in their pursuit of common goals and interests. There are three distinct categories of professional associations. The first category represents those with common personal interests, such as the American Association of Retired Persons (AARP). The second category addresses scientific, engineering, and learned societies, such as the Council on Hotel, Restaurant and Institutional Education (CHRIE). The last category is dedicated to religious, charitable, public service, or fraternal causes, such as the American Heart Association (*ASAE Factbook* 1993, p. 8–9).

Convention Centers

"A comprehensive convention center is a public assembly facility that is designed to host meetings and exhibits under one roof. It also has provision for banquet, food and beverage, and concession service" (Rutherford 1990, p. 78–79). Most convention centers are owned by the city, county, or state government and are operated by a designated board or authority. The Jacob K. Javits Convention Center in New York City (figure 3-2) is an example of one such facility. The Anaheim Convention Center (figure 3-3) is another example. In some cases these publicly owned facilities may be operated by privately owned management companies, such as Ogden Allied or Spectacon Management Company.

Convention centers offer large, flexible spaces to host trade shows as well as smaller rooms for banquets, meetings, and association parties. Generally, the convention and visitors bureau

Figure 3-2   The Big Apple's Convention Center. The Jacob K. Javits Convention Center, stretching along the Hudson River, can accomodate 85,000 visitors daily. Designed by I.M. Pei and Partners, this graceful steel and glass sheathed "tinker toy" skeleton encloses 900,000 square feet of exhibition space. More than 16,000 glass panels reflect the New York City sky. (Courtesy: N.Y. Convention and Visitors Bureau.)

helps market the convention center, although some centers have their own salespeople who solicit such business (*Professional Meetings Management* p. 132).

Although historically convention centers existed primarily to service the community, an analysis of recent trends indicates that there is increasing pressure for convention centers to be profit centers. Most of these facilities generate revenue through rental fees of exhibition and meeting room space. Other revenue sources include food and beverage catering, concessions, and vending. Convention centers have also begun to offer specialized services to the exhibitors who participate in shows held in the facility. According to a survey by Rutherford, the most common income-producing services are electrical; telephone; stage construction/lighting;

Figure 3-3   Anaheim Convention Center, the West Coast's largest convention facility, features a 27,000 square foot arena, three 100,000 square foot and one 150,000 square foot exhibit halls. The Center provides a total of 935,000 square feet of exhibit and parking space. (Courtesy: Anaheim Area Visitor and Convention Bureau.)

plumbing, air, and sound. (Rutherford 1990, p. 93). (For a detailed discussion of convention centers, see chapter 5).

Conference Centers

"By definition and design, a conference center is a specialized hospitality operation dedicated to facilitating and supporting conferences (small to medium size meetings averaging between 20 and 50 people)" (Haigh & Hudson 1989, p. 5). Conference centers differ from convention centers mainly in that most conference centers provide overnight accommodations for their attendees. Convention centers, although they usually are located near or even adjacent to a hotel, do not consider themselves in the housing market. Conceivably, visitors at a conference center would have no need to leave that center during the entire duration of their conference. All their needs, from meals to accommodations and leisure activities, would be provided by the conference center itself.

The conference center was created to meet the growing demand for specialized meetings. While many hotels were fairly successful in meeting these needs, most fell short of the demands of conference and meeting planners. Planners need a facility that focuses on the specific requirements of conferences, rather than conventions or tourist travel. Thus, conference centers evolved. Currently, there are over 170 conference centers within the United States and 49 outside of the United States (1993 figures).

The design of a conference center is one of its many points of distinction. Because meetings and conferences are their sole source of revenue, conference centers have been designed to fulfill the specialized needs of individuals attending meetings or conferences. Conference center design emphasizes comfort and privacy for the groups holding meetings in the facility. This attention to comfort manifests itself in all areas of the conference center, from meeting rooms to guest rooms. For example, conference center chairs and tables are manufactured specifically to keep the conference attendee comfortable and alert for long periods of time. Guest rooms are equipped with work study resources, including well-lit reading areas, desks, dictionaries, and computers.

"Conference centers generally offer a separate conference dining room. Usually, the dining room offers buffet breakfast and buffet lunch service, and a la carte or buffet dinner service" (Haigh & Hudson 1989, p. 11). Refreshment breaks are another unique feature of conference centers. Most conference centers provide continuous refreshment throughout the meeting, allowing the attendee to break at will. This food and beverage arrangement frees the meeting planner from having to make specific menu decisions.

Another point of distinction for conference centers is their ability to provide all audiovisual equipment for the conferees. The conference center can maintain control over the quality of their own equipment and can respond more quickly to attendee's needs than an outside rental agency can.

The conference center has a unique pricing system that allows a "one-stop-shopping" approach. Conference centers charge one price that includes meals, room rate, meeting rooms, audiovisual equipment, coffee breaks, and paper supplies needed by the conferees. This complete meeting package is advantageous because planners know exactly what the meeting is going to cost. There are no hidden charges for breaks, service charges, or other extras.

The concept of a conference center is fairly new. The need for a governing body to educate convention and meeting professionals about conference centers resulted in the formulation of the International Association of Conference Centers (IACC) in 1981. Not only does the IACC educate the industry about conference centers, but they have also developed sample conference plans (see figure 3-4) and criteria to standardize and protect the integrity of conference centers.

Conference centers must meet these strict criteria if they wish to be a member of the IACC. According to the IACC, conference centers fall into four distinct categories:

- Conference center
- Resort conference center
- Nonresidential conference center
- Ancillary conference center

There are significant differences among the various categories, but all types have some common characteristics (see Appendix I).

Growth trends in the conference and meeting industry support the need for more conference centers. To ensure the viability of these centers, careful attention must be given to location, design,

SAMPLE CONFERENCE PLAN
Per Person Per Night

		SINGLE	DOUBLE
Dinner	$18.00		
Breakfast	8.00		
Lunch	12.00		
Refreshment Break	10.00		
		$48.00	$48.00
15% Service Charge		7.20	7.20
Conference Department		25.00	25.00
Guest Room		119.80*	74.80*
PER PERSON PRICE		$200.00	$155.00

* With the CMP Plan, any change in the price increases or reduces the room allocation, and allocations to other departments remain constant.

SAMPLE DAY GUEST PLAN
Per Person Per Day

Lunch	$12.00	
Refreshment Breaks	10.00	**PER PERSON PRICE $50.00**
15% Service Charge	3.30	
Conference Department	24.70*	

* With the Day Guest Plan, any change in the price normally increases or reduces the conference allocation, and allocations to other departments remain constant.

VIII. WHAT MAKES A GOOD CONFERENCE CENTER SITE

The traditional location rule that applies to hotels and resorts is applicable to conference centers. When a conference center fails, usually location is a factor. Most often conference centers are suburban and the location elements that are generally important are:

1. Proximity to a major concentration of corporation headquarters and/or regional offices.
2. Proximity to a major airport (within an hour's drive).
3. Easy access to major highways (15 minutes to a major artery).
4. A setting that allows for a distraction free environment.

The location criteria is not applicable for not-for-profit or educational conference centers that are tied to universities. The key is to identify with the university and to be located on campus. However, if those facilities are self supporting, then it requires the location criteria listed above, in addition to, the campus location.

INTERNATIONAL ASSOCIATION OF CONFERENCE CENTERS

Figure 3-4   Sample conference plan. (Courtesy IACC.)

and marketing. Haigh and Hudson predict that future sites for conference centers will include conference centers tied to universities as well as conference centers that are owned by individual corporations (Haigh & Hudson 1989, p. 19–20).

Association Meeting Planners

As stated earlier in this chapter, associations are managed by professionals, one of whom is the association meeting planner. The planner's primary goal is to plan all association meetings. Of these professionals, 85 percent plan meetings on a full-time basis, averaging five meetings per year (Bernert 1990, p. 23). Association meeting planners are responsible for directing meetings dealing with member services, standards, conventions, trade shows, and publishing. Sales, training, and management meetings are also becoming an important aspect of the association planner's responsibility.

Corporate Meeting Planners

Corporate meeting planners are employed by a for-profit business or corporation, and their job includes, but is not necessarily limited to, planning meetings and conventions for that company. They range from a secretary who has been given the responsibility to plan one training session for the boss to an official corporate meeting planner whose sole responsibility is planning, organizing, and implementing meetings and conventions for the employees, managers, and owners of the corporation. Therefore, they often have titles other than "Meeting Planner." Of all corporate planners, 43 percent have meeting planning as their primary area of responsibility, averaging over five meetings per year (Bernert 1990, p. 23). Corporate planners are involved with a variety of different meeting types, such as management meetings, training meetings, sales meetings, incentive trips, and seminars.

Independent Meeting Planners

Independent meeting planners are entrepreneurs who specialize in planning meetings and conventions. Associations or corporations who do not have a full-time meeting planner may choose to contract with an independent meeting planner. With the downsizing of corporations' budgets, this is an economical way to have meetings and conventions professionally planned. Independent meeting planners may also work in conjunction with a full-time corporate or association planner. In this case the role of the independent meeting planner is that of a support person who lends his expertise to the project. For example, the independent meeting planner may only be involved with the site selection process or be in charge of a single event, or may act in an advisory role for the entire meeting or convention. (For a detailed discussion of the independent meeting planner, see chapter 6).

Tour Operators

According to the National Tour Association, a tour operator is "a person or company which creates and/or markets inclusive tours and/or subcontracts their performance. Most tour operators sell through travel agents and/or directly to clients" (*Partners in Profit* 1991, p. 67). In other words, operators arrange small group tours that provide a complete vacation package, including transportation, accommodations, some meals, sight-seeing, and a professional escort. These tours are offered to travelers for a single price.

Tour operators are playing a growing role in the convention and meetings industry also. They work with meeting planners in arranging tours and activities for the meeting attendees and their families who want to combine business with pleasure. Often, attendees stay in the convention city for a few days after their convention has ended, to sightsee, relax, or enjoy that city's entertainment. In addition, operators often create tour packages for the attendee's spouse/guest or children. Thus, while the participants are in a meeting, their spouses/guests may take a bus to a local museum or their children may go to the zoo. The operator works with area suppliers to arrange any necessary meals, accommodations, tickets, escorts, and transportation for these trips.

Meeting participants receive information about these "extra-curricular" events well in advance of the convention. Attendees' spouses/guests and children usually pay one registration fee, which includes the tour(s). Attendees who choose to stay in a convention city after their meeting ends usually register and pay separately for post-convention tours. There is a growing trend for attendees to bring their families with them, so the job of the tour operator is becoming more important in the meetings industry. Figure 3-5 provides a sample of a spouse/guest tour.

Spouse/Guest Tours

Spouse/Guest Programs are designed to provide planned activities while the members are participating in the Summer Meeting program. In addition, they offer opportunities for spouse/guest attendees to become better acquainted.
(Refer to the Spouse/Guest Programs section of the Meeting Registration Form enclosed in the Registration Info/Materials envelope in the portfolio for additional details and registration.)
(Spouse/Guest Tours are included in your Spouse/Guest Registration fee.)

FRIDAY, JUNE 7, 1991
8:00 a.m. - 5:15 p.m.
Tour A
Discover Colorado

Sponsors: **Colorado Springs Convention** **& Convention Bureau** Christine Bonati Convention Services Manager Colorado Springs, CO	**Chariot Travel** Brian Parker, Sr. President Colorado Springs, CO	**The Broadmoor Hotel** Perry Goodbar Assistant Director of Sales Colorado Springs, CO	**NAEM**

The day has "wonders to behold!" We begin with a picturesque drive south to the pride of the U.S. and Colorado, The United States Air Force Academy. Arrive at the Barry Goldwater Visitors Center where you can learn about the Academy and where you will want to pick up a memento of your visit. Following the Visitors Center, tour the famous Cadet Chapel, a breath-taking array of color in an inspiring atmosphere. The Chapel is one of Colorado's most visited attractions.

Depart the Air Force Academy for a drive-through tour of the Garden of the Gods Park. The wondrous and spectacular red rock cliffs, which tower into the sky, are over 200 million years old, and the park itself is home to a unique collection of plant and animal life. This is one of the most unusual parks you will ever visit and a great opportunity for pictures along the way.

Then it's on to the lovely Broadmoor Hotel. The resort is the one-and-only 5-star resort in Colorado and you must see it to believe it. We'll enjoy a fabulous lunch prepared by one of their award winning chefs. "Lunch where the rich and famous go."

On to Old Colorado City for that much desired shopping time. The old trading posts and watering holes now provide dining ambience and shopping alternatives found only in the Rocky Mountains. Make sure you bring your "stash of cash" for the treasures that await you in "them thar hills."

Buses Depart Promptly at 8:15 a.m. from: Radisson Hotel Denver, Lobby.
Hyatt Regency Denver hotel, Lobby

Maximum: 92 Participants

Attire: Casual, comfortable walking shoes, light jacket, and don't forget your camera.

Figure 3-5   Spouse/guest tours. (Courtesy: NAEM.)

The National Tour Association (NTA) is the largest trade association in the escorted group tour industry. NTA members include tour operators; suppliers, such as hotels, airlines, cruiselines, and sight-seeing services; and destination marketing organizations, such as state tourism offices and convention and visitor bureaus. Among the NTA's services are a spring convention for its members and educational publications. In addition, the NTA supports the National Tour Foundation, which awards scholarships to travel and tourism students.

Trade Shows and Expositions

Trade shows, expositions, exhibitions, and scientific/technical conferences are terms popularly used interchangeably in the conference and meeting industry. "Exhibition," historically a European term, has been adopted by Americans as we become more global, particularly in referring to traveling shows, such as art exhibitions. Expositions, as stated in the CLC *Glossary,* are public shows. Trade shows are historically private shows open only to those involved in the industry. They are "business-to-business." Although some trade shows do open themselves up to the public on their final days, most are still completely private.

All these terms basically describe an activity designed to represent a major industry marketing event (Mee 1988, p. 51). Trade shows provide a forum in which players associated with a particular industry can bring their wares together and exhibit in unity products that are desired by a single trade or industry. For example, the American Hotel and Motel Association sponsors its annual trade show every November in New York City. This trade show brings together all the suppliers associated with the hotel and motel industry. The forum provided allows attendees and exhibitors to exchange information about their products.

Trade shows have a very interesting history. The evolution of trade shows can be traced to biblical times. Evan St. Lifer, in his article "Trade Show Retrospective" (1990), states that trade shows or expositions started when caravans crossing the desert would meet and exchange wares. From an American perspective, the history of the trade shows traces back to 1876 when Alexander

Graham Bell showed his telephone at the Philadelphia Centennial Exposition, a show celebrating America's first 100 years.

"It was truly the forerunner of the modern day trade show," said Don Walter, executive director of the National Association of Exposition Managers. In fact, the Centennial Expo was the predecessor of industrial shows that would punctuate the next 60 years. "Just the way it was done, in a semi-booth style where products were displayed and used by the attendees and touched and felt, made it the fore-runner of today's shows," said Walter. (St. Lifer 1990, p. 10)

As the industrial era evolved, marketing of products became more important. During this time, salesmen found themselves spending the majority of their time on the road selling their products. Due to the impracticality of trying to call on customers individually, salesmen began to rent hotel rooms to display their wares. They would then invite their customers to stop by their displays. This practice profited individual companies.

Although hotels had served as the arena for the evolution of trade shows, with the industry expanding, they became inefficient to use. By the mid-1920s, industrious individuals developed an exhibit hall, thus allowing large groups of exhibitors who shared a common product or industry to showcase their wares together. This gave a new look and feel to the trade show. No longer were clients crowded into small hotel rooms and forced to endure overzealous exhibitors who refused to let them leave the room until they placed an order (St. Lifer 1990, p. 11). In exhibit halls, clients were allowed to roam freely from booth to booth.

"Currently, the trade show industry represents the most exciting, dynamic, and cost-effective means for marketers to achieve their sales goals. The over $21 billion industry is projected to expand at a rate of more than 8 percent through 1995" (Mee 1988, p. 56). In 1991 there were 6,118 trade shows held in the United States and Canada (TSB 1992). A Trade Show Bureau Research Summary reported that over one-third of the trade shows held in the United States reported attendance figures ranging from 1,001 to 5,000 attendees. In addition, over 13 percent of the trade shows hosted in the United States had over 10,000 attendees. When you consider the enormous numbers of attendees involved in trade shows, it is no wonder that cities are fiercely competing for the trade show business.

In the overseas market, approximately 3,300 U.S. companies participated in trade fairs and related events in 1989. This figure accounted for a 25 percent increase over the number of participants in 1988 and is projected to increase. With the evolution of the European Community as well as the free trade agreements between the United States and Mexico and between the United States and Canada, the U.S. Department of Commerce believes that international expositions will increase in their importance and become a major arena for trade.

Within the trade show industry there are several key players. These include trade show sponsors, exposition managers, show managers, service contractors, hotels, and convention and visitors bureaus. (For a detailed discussion of these and other players in the trade show industry, see chapter 6.)

Trade Show Sponsors

Trade show sponsors are generally trade or professional associations who use the trade show as an integral part of their meetings and/or conventions to generate revenue. For example, the National Restaurant Association is the sponsor for the NRA trade show that is held in Chicago each May (figure 3-6).

Because sponsorship of trade shows has become an extremely lucrative business venture, corporations have evolved whose sole purpose is to develop and market specific trade shows. For example, The Interface Group, the world's leading independent producer of trade shows and expositions, was developed for the sole purpose of managing the COMDEX trade show, a billion-dollar trade show designed to bring together major computer companies (figure 3-7).

Sponsors are responsible for procuring the physical facilities in which the trade show will be held. They are also accountable for managing the show. This management includes developing an exhibitor list, marketing the show to exhibitors and attendees, organizing suppliers, organizing move-in and move-out of the show, and overseeing all financial responsibilities and contracts involved with the trade show. Depending on the expertise of the sponsor and the size of the show, this management may be done in-house or it may be contracted out to an independent exposition or show manager.

Figure 3-6   The National Restaurant Assciation is the sponsor for the NRA trade show held each May at McCormick place in Chicago. (Courtesy: National Restaurant Association.)

Exposition or Show Manager

As stated above, an exposition or show manager may work directly for the sponsoring organization or for a corporation whose sole purpose is to manage trade shows. The show manager is responsible for all aspects of the trade show. Depending on the involvement of the sponsoring organization, the exposition or show manager may or may not select sites. Many of the largest trade shows do not move, but are held in the same exhibit hall in the same city annually. For example, the National Restaurant Association trade show is held every year in Chicago at McCormick Place.

Once the site has been selected, exposition managers are responsible for recruiting exhibitors and attracting attendees. To successfully do this, they must have developed a profile of prospective and/or past attendees. This profile should include demographic and psychographic information as well as past buying behaviors.

Figure 3-7   The Interface Group was developed for the sole purpose of managing the COMDEX trade show, a billion-dollar trade show designed to bring together major computer companies. (Courtesy: The Interface Group.)

Once a profile has been developed, the show manager will use this information to develop an exhibitor prospectus to send to potential exhibitors. This prospectus outlines all important information required by a prospective exhibitor to make an educated decision about whether or not to exhibit at the trade show. This information includes, but is not limited to, times and dates of the show, move-in and move-out information, cost of booths, payment schedules, details about the sponsoring organization, procedures for assigning booths, housing information, and the rules and regulations for the show.

The exhibitor prospectus plays a major role in the marketing of a trade show. Without it, a show manager has very little opportunity to sell the show. Therefore, it is very important that a show manager keep accurate records of attendance figures as well as implementing post-event evaluations to ascertain the success of the event from both the exhibitor's and the attendee's point of view.

The exposition manager is also responsible for attracting qualified attendees. This is done through advertising and marketing promotions and by providing exhibitors with free tickets that they may distribute to their clients. A trade show may also run educational seminars and meetings concurrently to attract the targeted market.

The trade show manager must also develop an application form and contract that provides for an agreement between the exhibitor and the organization sponsoring the trade show. Although the contract is between the exhibitor and the sponsoring organization, the manager acts as liaison between the two and is responsible for maintaining an open line of communication throughout the planning and implementing stages of a trade show.

Another very important charge of the exposition manager is to select an official service contractor and subcontractors. Managers are responsible for insuring that contractors are qualified to provide services for exhibitors and that contractors receive exposition management support in providing these services (NAEM report 1989).

The logistics involved with other services, such as housing, shuttle buses to and from the facility, and official airlines with their discounted airfares, are all very important aspects of a show manager's job. Registration for both exhibitors and attendees, signage, and exhibitor directories are also important duties that must be coordinated by the show manager.

The exposition or show manager is ultimately responsible for all activities during the trade show or exposition. From move-in to move-out, the show manager must be on hand to lend assistance as well as to settle disputes between exhibitors and contractors. Finally, the show manager's job is done when the evaluations of the trade show or exposition have been tallied. A report is then filed with the association or organization sponsoring the event and plans begin for future shows.

The premiere organization for exposition management is the International Association of Exposition Managers (IAEM). IAEM is a nonprofit organization that works towards the advancement of exposition management through education, information, and dissemination of knowledge.

Service Contractors

Service contractors, exposition service contractors, general contractors, and decorators are all terms that have at one time or another referred to the individual responsible for providing all of the services needed to run the facilities for a trade show. "A general exposition contractor is multi-talented, and equipped to serve all exhibit requirements and creative ideas" (*1991 Annual Guide to Exposition Service,* p. 8).

Services Provided by Exposition Service Contractors

1. Exhibit and material handling and storage.
2. Safe and timely drayage of exhibits and materials.
3. Proper and efficient installation, maintenance, and dismantling of displays.
4. Customized exhibit design and construction or rental of modern, eye-catching displays.
5. A full range of clean, functional furniture and equipment, plus carpets, drapery, special effects, and other display accessories.
6. Safe and immediate access to vital services, such as water, electricity, and gas. Each is installed by a trained technician in accordance with local regulations and codes.
7. An impressive array of signs and banners, each made according to your specifications for size and color.
8. Can provide or arrange for services such as complete audiovisual needs, lighting, sound systems, security, cleaning, photographic, or floral service.

Source: *1991 Annual Guide to Exposition Service* 1991, p. 8

The service contractor is hired by the exposition show manager or association meeting planner. In the case of some facilities, the service contractor is a part of the facilities management team and, in order to use the facility, the sponsor must use their service contractor. In other situations the facility may have an exclusive contract with an outside contractor, and they may require all expositions to deal with this contractor.

"The Exposition Service Contractors Association (ESCA) is the professional organization of firms engaged in the provision of materials and/or services for trade shows, conventions, expositions and sales meetings" (*1991 Annual Guide to Exposition Service,* p. 4). Like most trade associations, ESCA provides services to its members by acting as a clearinghouse for relevant information. ESCA has also developed guidelines to maintain progressive business standards and to promote cooperation and networking opportunities for its members. (For a detailed discussion of service contractors, see chapter 6).

Hotels

As mentioned earlier in this chapter, hotels played an important role in the conception and early establishment of the conventions and meetings industry. Today their role has changed, but it is no less important to the overall scheme of conventions and meetings. Wherever there are out-of-town guests for a meeting, convention, or trade show, there is a need for comfortable overnight accommdations. The San Francisco Marriott hotel (figure 3-8) is internationally renowned for its ability to provide exceptional accomodations for meeting attendees.

Additionally, many hotels provide meetings and conventions with meeting rooms, convention facilities, and small exposition halls. In fact, meetings and conventions have become a major source of revenue for a large percentage of hotels. This revenue is generated primarily through the rental of sleeping rooms, food and beverage, and meeting space rental.

Although a number of individuals are very important to the success of meetings and conventions for hotels, the most important is the convention service manager. This position is fairly new to the industry. "At hotels of 30 to 3,000 rooms, management is designating an individual to service—and, in an important sense, re-sell—groups: corporate, convention, incentive and tour" (Pearson 1982, p. 159).

Once the sales department has sold a group on their hotel, the convention service manager acts as the liaison between the meeting planner and the hotel. This position has increased the marketability of hotels as convention properties, since the convention service manager's primary focus is to service the meeting and/or convention. Meeting planners no longer must deal with several different department heads within the hotel; one person can help

Figure 3-8 Many major hotels provide meeting rooms and convention facilities. (Courtesy: Marriott, San Francisco.)

them with all their needs. (For a detailed discussion of convention service managers and hotels, see chapter 5.)

Convention and Visitors Bureaus

A convention and visitors bureau is a not-for-profit organization designed to solicit visitors and conventions to a community. Although some are housed within the state government, most are privately operated but funded through the hotel accomodations tax. The bureau is the organization that coordinates all activities surrounding meetings and conventions to include marketing the destination, providing information about possible host facilities, coordinating familiarization tours for interested meeting planners or association executives, and acting as a liaison between the group and the many suppliers within the community. (For a detailed discussion of convention and visitors bureaus, see chapter 3.)

Summary

There are a number of different organizations and individuals involved with the meetings and conventions industry. Associations, both trade and professional, are not-for-profit organizations that often host meetings or conventions. Convention centers are flexible facilities, usually owned by the government, that offer large and small spaces for shows, meetings, and banquets. Conference centers, a recent development, are facilities designed specifically to host smaller conferences. They include accommodations as well as food and beverage services and meeting areas.

Meeting planners, who have varying degrees of responsibility for organizing meetings, may work for an association or a corporation, or they may be independent entrepreneurs. Tour operators often work with meeting planners in arranging group tours for the meeting attendees or their families. These group tours are often offered before and/or after a conference. Trade shows, which are generally private, and expositions, which are generally open to the public, are a growing industry. They generate sizeable economic benefits for exhibitors, show sponsors, the host facility, and the host city. Trade show sponsors are associations or businesses who sponsor shows to generate revenue. The show manager, who may work for either the show sponsor or for an outside show management company, is responsible for all aspects of a trade show. The show manager works as a liaison between the sponsor and the exhibitors. Service contractors provide services and products needed for the show and are usually hired by the show manager or the meeting planner. Meetings are often held at a hotel, which provides a convention service manager to act as a liaison between the meeting planner and the hotel. The convention and visitors bureau is also instrumental in soliciting meeting and convention business for a city and then helping to service groups who hold events in that city. As the meetings and conventions industry continues to become more professional, more global, and more sophisticated, these industry professionals will need to have state-of-the-art education and training to remain on the cutting edge of this growing industry.

References

1991 Annual Guide to Exposition Service. 1991. Exposition Service Contractors Association–National Association of Exposition Managers.

ASAE Association Factbook. 1993. Washington, D.C.: ASAE.

Bernert, L. 1990. Meetings glorious meetings. *Successful Meetings (2),* (July) pp. 23, 25–26, 28–31, 41, 43–44.

Conlin, J. 1990. The challenge of the decade ahead. *Successful Meetings (2),* (July) pp. 7–9, 11–12.

Haigh, S., and R.W. Hudson. 1989. *Understanding Conference Centers.* Fenton, Mo.: IACC.

Mee, W. W. 1988. Trade shows: This marketing medium means business. *Association Management,* (July) pp. 50–56.

Pearson, J. A. 1990. How to service conventions. In *Convention Sales,* ed. M. Shaw, pp. 159–163. East Lansing, Mich.: Educational Institute of the American Hotel & Motel Association.

Rutherford, D. G. 1990. (1990). *Introduction to the Conventions, Expositions, and Meetings Industry.* New York: Van Nostrand Reinhold.

St. Lifer, E. 1990. 15). Trade show retrospective. *Meeting News,* (July 15) pp. 10–12.

Discussion Questions

1. Discuss the various roles of participants in the conventions, meetings, and expositions industry.
2. Discuss the different types of associations, and give examples as to local associations that fit each category.

3. Why could convention centers provide better services for meetings, conventions, and expositions than a resort or hotel?
4. Describe the different types of meeting planners and how their roles differ from one another.

Key Terms

associations
trade associations
professional associations
scientific, engineering and
    learned societies
convention center
conference center
association meeting planners
corporate meeting planners

independent meeting planners
tour operator
trade shows
expositions
exhibitions
trade show sponsor
exposition/show manager
exhibitor prospectus
service contractor

4

The Sponsor

Learning Objectives

1. To understand who meeting sponsors are and the value that meetings have for an organization.
2. To realize the necessity of goals and objectives in conceptualizing meetings.
3. To appreciate the process of meeting planning and management, including:
   a. Establishing the meeting's goals and objectives
   b. Targeting the population
   c. Designing the program
   d. Developing the budget
   e. Selecting the site
   f. Negotiations and contracts
   g. Marketing and promotion
   h. Food and beverage
   i. On-site management
   j. Providing services to attendees
   k. Evaluation

Introduction

There are many groups that are considered consumers of meetings and conventions. These groups vary from corporations to associations to religious groups. They sponsor meetings for numerous reasons dealing with the specific purpose of their organization. This chapter will look at the groups sponsoring meetings and expositions, their reasons and purposes in sponsoring meetings and expositions, and the specific types of meetings and expositions sponsored. This chapter will also address the process of meetings and exposition management. This chapter is not designed to be a "how to" source of information, but to provide an overview of the process.

What is a Sponsor?

Sponsors of meetings and expositions are as varied as the meeting or exposition itself. They may be groups or individuals. Sponsors of meetings or expositions can be:

- Associations
- Corporations
- Trade unions
- Independent companies who sponsor and operate trade shows
- Religious groups
- Tour groups
- Theater and arts groups
- Social organizations

These organizations decide to sponsor a meeting or exposition for many reasons. In the case of corporations, meetings may be designed to disseminate information, solve problems, train people, or plan for the future. Associations may sponsor meetings and expositions for the purposes of networking, educating members, solving problems, or generating revenue.

Meetings serve a valuable function within corporations and associations. The following list delineates just a few of the functions of meetings (Woods and Berger, 1988, pp. 101–102):

- Generate a spirit of unity and cooperation that contributes to the formulation of a collective identity;

- Enhance communication by creating a pool of shared knowledge;
- Provide a forum for the generation of new ideas;
- Afford management an opportunity to define and promote the collective aim of the organization;
- Obtain increased commitment to decisions by involving more individuals in the decision-making process; and
- Provide a setting in which company leaders can act like leaders on a very visible level.

Sponsors of meetings and expositions are responsible for the conceptualization phase of a meeting or exposition. This phase must occur before the logistics of a meeting are planned. In fact, without the proper conceptualization, a meeting is likely to be unfocused and unproductive. This phase involves, first of all, determining whether or not there is even a valid need for the meeting or exposition. Once the sponsor can justify holding this meeting, they can then attend to the other aspects of the conceptualization phase, such as establishing a list of potential attendees and developing the philosophy of the meeting or exposition.

Determining whether or not there is a need for the meeting is the first and perhaps most important step in planning a meeting, and yet this is the step most often overlooked. Meetings occupy 50 to 60 percent of the average manager's workweek, but many executives consider meetings an unproductive use of their time. There have been numerous surveys done to ascertain individual perceptions of the importance of meetings. These surveys report that "participants rate nearly one half of all the meetings they attend as 'a waste of time'" (Ashenbrenner 1988, p. 43). This is particularly distressing, considering that the average business meeting of ten to twelve managers costs about $1,000 in direct salaries for actual meeting time alone. Perhaps the reason so many of these meetings are considered unproductive is because many of the individuals charged with the responsibility of organizing meetings have never received any formal training in meetings management.

According to Ashenbrenner, a meeting should be viewed as a last resort. He suggests a number of questions that should be asked before a meeting is called (Ashenbrenner 1988, p. 43):

1. Do I need the resource capability of the group?
2. Will a meeting be faster, and can we accomplish more?

3. Can I gain commitment to ideas and decisions by having the group present?
4. Can I prepare for and conduct this meeting properly?
5. Will a meeting "tie up" people too long?
6. Will a meeting cost too much in terms of salary and lost productivity?
7. Will people have adequate time to prepare?
8. Will personality clashes or disagreements sabotage the meetings?
9. Will the meeting have solid leadership?
10. Do the advantages outweigh the disadvantages?

Once these questions are answered and a need for a meeting established, the individual responsible for the meeting must decide how to plan the event. Planning is often left to individuals who have little if any knowledge about how to plan, organize, and execute meetings. Therefore, it is no wonder that meetings appear to be poorly organized and the participants become frustrated with the apparent waste of time. Many sponsoring organizations find that it is much more practical to hire an individual whose primary responsibility is to plan, organize, and execute meetings. This in turn saves the sponsors money by avoiding some of the problems just discussed.

In the case of expositions, sponsors either take on the role of exposition manager or find someone else to fill that position. Exposition managers can be employees of an association or a show management company, or they can be private entrepreneurs who perform tasks such as conceptualization and development of trade shows (Rutherford, 1990 p. 51).

The Process of Meeting and Exposition Management

The process of meeting and exposition management starts well before the date of the meeting. There are a number of steps involved:

- Establishing the goals and objectives
- Targeting the population

- Designing the program
- Creating a budget
- Selecting a site
- Negotiating contracts
- Formulating committees
- Establishing a marketing and promotion plan
- Hiring subcontractors
- Designing food and beverage functions

The process continues on-site during the actual event. Activities involved include move-in/move-out, implementing the plan, coordinating the various participants in the event, and managing the overall meeting. Post-event activities include evaluation, feedback, and planning for the future.

Goals and Objectives

As stated in the beginning of this chapter, the goals and objectives of a meeting or exposition should be established by the sponsor. "One of the hardest jobs meeting planners have is to get their client to sit down and outline the purpose for the meeting," says Toni Sylvester, an independent meeting planner in Columbia, South Carolina. Sylvester explains, "Without an inherent understanding of the goals and objectives for a meeting, the meeting planner cannot move forward with the rest of the pre-event activities." Therefore, one of the first responsibilities of the meeting planner is to meet with the sponsor of the event to ascertain the reasons for holding the meeting.

To do this the meeting planner must first understand the goals of the organization and from these goals derive the objective for the meeting. "Objectives are specific and measurable. An individual meeting will have one and only one primary, or first-level objective that is measurable" (Hildreth 1990, p. 12). The meeting planner should understand whether or not the sponsor of the meeting or convention is interested in, for instance, providing a serious educational experience for the attendees, entertaining the attendees and their families, boosting the morale of the attendees, solving a specific problem, or some combination of these objectives.

Targeting the Population

Once the goals and objectives are determined, those involved with the planning stage of the meeting or exposition must determine who should attend. Often people are included in meetings that are not appropriate or relevant for them; they walk away from the meeting feeling like they have wasted their time. On the other end of the spectrum, many meetings come to a screeching halt when it is determined that a key player has been overlooked and the objectives cannot be reached without the input of this person. Therefore, serious consideration should be given to choosing the participants for each meeting.

In the case of expositions, the development of the exhibitor list as well as the target audience must be addressed. The sponsoring organization must attract exhibitors to their exposition. This is done by convincing the exhibitors that the show will provide an excellent marketing opportunity for them. To accomplish this they must provide the exhibitors with a prospectus outlining the proposed audience, thus allowing the exhibitor to determine whether or not the attendees are their targeted audience. Therefore, targeting the population is very important to both meetings and expositions.

Designing the Program

What is the program design? "It is the structuring, balancing, and pacing of the program by combining major topics and sub-topics, passive and active sessions, serious and fun presentations, and formal and informal times to provide professional and personal growth and networking opportunities for participants" (Price 1989, p. 11).

Included in the program design is the overall theme and the meeting or exposition agenda. In designing a theme for the meeting, convention, or exposition, planners should ensure that their theme takes into consideration the needs of the audience, flows from the objectives of the event, and provides continuity (Jedrziewski 1991, pp. 9–10). For example, the theme for the Council on Hotel, Restaurant and Institutional Education's 1993 annual conference was "Putting Theory and Application to Work"; included on the agenda were several keynote speakers who spoke to the issue of equipping students for the real world.

Budget

"A budget is nothing more than an estimate of income and expenses and a plan to adjust the anticipated expenses to the expected income" (Dotson 1988, p. 88). Budgeting is not a favored activity of meeting planners or exposition managers, but it is one that they must be intricately involved with. Overall budget figures are normally provided by the sponsoring organization, but specific guidelines are usually ascertained from previous conferences, meetings, or exposition budgets. For this reason it is imperative that impeccable record keeping be adhered to.

A budget includes fixed expenses, variable expenses, and sources of revenue. Fixed expenses are not dependent on the number of attendees. For example, some fixed expenses are administrative fees, postage and printing, advertising and promotion, staff travel, speaker fees, and contracts with certain suppliers, such as audiovisual firms.

Variable expenses are those that fluctuate depending on the number of attendees. Most expenses included in the budget fall into this category. Variable expenses may include food and beverage; hospitality programs; exhibition expenses; guest rooms; gratuities; registration materials; printed materials, such as programs, proceedings, and handouts; support personnel; and evaluation materials.

Once expenses have been determined, sources of revenue to support the activities must be developed. Sources of revenue are as varied as the creativity of the sponsoring organization. Registration fees are the most constant source of income for conferences. In the case of expositions, exhibitor rental fees and registration fees comprise the largest sources of revenue. Other forms of generating revenue are advertising, sales of cassette tapes and educational material from the event, sponsorship, grants, company funding, and funding provided by the sponsoring organization or company. Without these sources it would be impossible to host a meeting, convention, or exposition.

As stated earlier, figures for these expenses and revenues are usually provided by previous budgets. However, in the event that these figures are not available, example budgets are available through many different sources. Richard Hildreth (1990) cites a study that has computed budgets from approximately 1,000 corporate and association meetings.

Site Selection

The site selection process is an extremely important part of the sponsoring organization's activities. Regardless of the type of meeting, convention, or exposition, the site is a critical factor in the success or failure of the event. Convenience and cost are the two most important factors in the site selection process, according to Joseph Conlin (1990). Based on surveys done by American Express, U.S. Travel Data Center, and McNabb/DeSotto, Conlin concludes that, although exciting locations and popular pastimes such as golf, tennis, and free time are important in the site selection process, they rank well behind cost and convenience in the eyes of the meeting planner or exposition manager.

To begin the site selection process, the planner must first consider the goals and objectives that have been established for the meeting, convention, or exposition. Based on these goals and objectives, they develop a meeting plan or format. The next step is to develop a group prospectus that will enable the meeting planner or exposition manager to determine the physical requirements for the meeting, convention, or exposition.

A prospectus is a "formal document that profiles [a] group" (Price 1989, p. 28). The purpose of this prospectus is to provide a clear and concise document that outlines in detail the history of the sponsoring group and attendees as well as a proposal of the specific requirements for the meeting or convention. "All site requirements are to be included, such as preferred dates; number and type of guest rooms; number, size and usage of meeting rooms and estimated times required; range of acceptable rates; dates and types of food and beverage events; exhibits and any other special events or activities; and any related information such as complimentary requirements" (*Guide* 1990, p. 9).

Catherine Price suggests that the following sections should be included in a prospectus (Price 1989, pp. 27–28) :

Section 1—Introduces organization and specific conference or meeting in a general way.

Section 2—Addresses site requirements.

Section 3—Provides historical information about this group's behaviors and spending practices for this meeting or a similar meeting.

Section 4—Detailed day-by-day time-and-event specification.

This prospectus can be sent to the convention and visitors bureau of cities you are considering. Based on this prospectus, interested parties can bid on the meeting, convention, or exposition.

Site selection may or may not be the sole responsibility of the meeting planner. In the case of associations, often there will be a committee whose primary responsibility is the selection of the host city. Associations may also have their location dictated through the bylaws of their association charter. Location may be limited by the size of the exposition facilities needed to house the exhibition.

Within corporations, executives may have input into the location selection process. In these cases the meeting planner may serve as a resource for providing information about proposed sites. Those responsible for the site selection generally choose the city first and then the hotel. Generally, the selection of the host city is based on:

- Cost
- Convenience
- Availability of transportation
- Room availability
- Exhibition space availability
- Meeting space availability
- Recreational activities
- Drawing power
- Climate
- Popular image of city

Once the host city has been chosen, the specific hotel, convention or conference center, or exposition facilities must be chosen. In cities with convention and visitors bureaus, the selection of the host property can be made much easier. The active CVB provides a central point for the dissemination of information regarding the possible facilities that will meet the needs of the meeting, convention, or trade show. The meeting planner or exposition manager will mail the prospectus to the bureau, who will then pass the prospectus on to all member properties. Those properties that meet the physical requirements of the group will then submit a proposal of what their properties have to offer to the CVB. The bureau will organize this material and send a completed packet to the meeting planner or exposition manager, thus enabling the planner to review on paper all possible sites. The CVB will also organize familiarization trips to allow the planner to visit prospective sites and do on-site inspections. If there is not a convention and visitors bureau in the host city, the meeting planner or exposition manager must solicit proposals from individual properties.

During the site inspection there are many things that one must consider. The easiest way to guarantee that key factors involved in the site selection process will not be overlooked is to use a checklist developed prior to the visitation. The checklist can include the following areas: sleeping rooms, meeting and exhibit space, transportation (airport and ground), food and beverage, recreation (both on site and local attractions), and services (concierge, turndown, etc.).

When reviewing sleeping rooms, a meeting planner needs to consider number of rooms available, type of rooms provided, quality of furnishings, security of the room and corridors, accessibility for handicapped individuals, quality of lighting for reading, and adequacy of work surfaces. Faith Popcorn, founder of Brain-Reserve, has identified a new trend in customer preference called "cocooning." Popcorn states that ". . . people are cocooning, they want their room to be like their home—a small cocoon so they will feel safe" (Juergens 1989, p. 58). This tendency towards cocooning translates into customer preference for homier interior decorating, such as quilts and comforters on the beds as well as fresh flowers in the rooms, hairdryers, and coffee makers. Cocooning means providing basic amenities that make hotel rooms seem more like home.

Another area that needs to be closely inspected is meeting rooms. Points reviewed should include number, shape, and size of rooms; quality of furnishings; lighting; existence of barrier-free design; accessibility of audiovisual equipment; and suitability for exhibits. In reviewing exposition space the following points should be considered in the inspection: square footage of exhibit space, accessibility, union issues, limitations placed on such activities as move-in and move-out, utilities, policies regarding such issues as drayage, storage, and exclusivity of subcontractors. Figure 4-1 illustrates a useful tool that meeting planners often use—a meeting room checklist.

As stated earlier, transportation costs may account for one-third to one-half of a conference, meeting, or exposition's ex-

MEETING ROOM CHECKLIST

During Site Visit

1. Number of meeting rooms available
2. Size of meeting rooms
3. Cleanliness
4. Configuration (Any obstructions?)
5. Soundproofing
6. Accessibility to the physically challenged
7. Lighting
8. Control of heating and air (Is it centrally or individually controlled?)
9. Accessibility of restrooms
10. Proposed renovation schedule in or near meeting space
11. Esthetically pleasing
12. Adaptability of staff
13. Allowance for buffet tables for breaks
14. Media equipment accessibility(outlets, electronic switches)

Pre-Meeting Checklist for Meeting

1. Seating

   - Chart

   - Extra seats available

2. Decorations

   - Flower arrangements
   - Flags
   - Banners
   - Lectern

3. Electronic equipment availability

   - VCR
   - TV
   - Screens
   - Microphone
   - Slide projector
   - Teleprompter
   - Other

4. Visual aids

   - Blackboard
   - Easel
   - Bulletin board

5. Water pitcher and glasses

6. Pencils/pens/paper

7. Any relevant reading materials should be in place for attendees so as to avoid confusion at a later point.

Figure 4-1   Meeting room checklist.

penses. Given the fact that it is such a large portion of the budget, transportation issues warrant careful attention. Transportation is two-fold: (1) The planner needs to consider how to get the attendees to the geographic location, the actual host city, in which the meeting is being held, and (2) the planner needs to consider how to move them from location to location within the host city. The planner or exposition manager must also be concerned with the movement of cargo. For example, cargo may be exhibit materials, office supplies, or registration materials. Although moving this cargo is often referred to as "drayage," in its purest definition, drayage is the "transfer of exhibit properties from point of arrival to exhibit site" (*The Convention Liaison Council Glossary* 1986, p. 15).

Exhibitors are ultimately responsible for the transportation of their booths and supplies, but it is up to the sponsoring organization to ensure that exhibitors are able to transport their material with ease. This means that the sponsoring organization must have a thorough understanding of the facility's role. Before making the site selection decision, the sponsor should know who at the host facility receives the shipments, where the shipments are stored, how security is set up, how to get assistance with unpacking and repacking, and how the billing procedure works (*The Convention Liaison Council Manual* 1985, p. 36).

With regard to the movement of people, the planner must first consider how the attendee is going to get to the city being considered. In today's society most individuals attending meetings, conferences, or expositions either fly or drive, but there is also the potential for rail travel.

The sponsoring organization must also consider intra-city transportation. Attendees flying in should be able to travel from the airport to the host facility efficiently and safely. For those who are driving, city maps, hotel maps, and street signs should be detailed, accurate, and clear enough that the attendees do not get lost in an unfamiliar place. The sponsor must review all of this material before a final decision can be made.

The tone of the conference is directly influenced by the ease in which attendees can make the transition from home to host property. Therefore, the overall analysis of the ground transportation entails reviewing all possible means of transportation to include airport shuttles, taxis, city buses, rail transportation, city maps, and car rental.

If program design requires moving attendees from facility to facility during the conference meeting or exposition, ground transportation for the movement of large groups of people must be studied. This may require contacting a ground service operator. A ground operator is a "company or person in (a) destination city handling local transportation and other local travel needs" (*The Convention Liaison Council Glossary* 1986, p. 32). For example, a city-wide conference might necessitate the use of ground service operators to shuttle attendees to and from the convention facilities to their various hotels. On a smaller scale, ground transportation may be required to take attendees to special events held away from the host property. For example, at the 1991 Professional Convention Management Association's Annual Conference in Boston, attendees were shuttled from downtown hotels to see the Boston Pops perform at another location.

A final word about transportation concerns the importance of meeting the transportation needs of all the conference or meeting attendees. Many travelers today have special needs, such as the older traveler, those traveling with small children, and the handicapped traveler. While reviewing all forms of transportation, the meeting planner must be cognizant of those attendees with special needs.

The role of food and beverage in the overall scheme of a conference or meeting should not be underestimated, and so the planner should carefully evaluate a potential site's abilities in this area. As figures 4-2 and 4-3 illustrate, food and beverage functions meet more than just the physical need for food; they enable the planner to set and maintain the theme for the convention or meeting. They also provide an arena for networking, allow attendees to interact socially, provide an opportunity to recognize key players, and allow for a break from the formal program.

Not even the best planned meeting or convention can counteract the negative influence a poorly executed food and beverage function has on the overall perception of the quality of the convention or meeting. Food and beverage functions leave a lasting impression on the conference attendees. It is the planner's challenge to see that the impression is a favorable one.

When reviewing the potential host properties, the sponsoring organization must confirm that the properties have the resources necessary to service their group. An overall review of the property should include:

Figure 4-2   Food and beverage functions meet more than just the physical need to eat; they enable the planner to set and maintain the theme of the event. (Courtesy: Marriott San Francisco.)

- Restaurants
- Lounges
- Room service
- Banquet facilities
- Flexibility in menus
- Culinary skills of staff
- Cleanliness of facility
- Decor of dining areas
- Staff (overstaffed/understaffed)
- Refreshment break menus and service areas
- Ability to meet special dietary needs
- Availability of theme food and beverage functions

The individuals involved with the site selection should also pay close attention to the service attitudes of those who will be interacting with the attendees. In a recent survey, individuals involved with

Figure 4-3   Food and beverage functions provide an arena for networking and social interaction as well as providing a break from the formal program. (Courtesy: Stouffer Harborplace Hotel.)

the meetings and convention industry were asked, "Is the attitude of the service staff figured into the selection equation?" 95 percent responded yes. Of those responding affirmatively, 5 percent stated that the service attitude of the staff accounted for less than one-tenth of the selection equation, and 24 weighted the service attitude as one-tenth to one-half of their decision. Of those responding yes, 39 percent stated that one-quarter to one-half of their selection decision was made based on the service attitude of their staff. The remaining 32 percent felt that over half of their decision rested on the service attitude of the staff (Strick and Montgomery 1991).

As stated earlier, another area that must be reviewed during the site selection process is the ability of the host city and property to provide services and facilities for leisure time activities. Recent studies show that the four main leisure activities important to the success of meetings are golf, free time, tennis, and tours (Conlin 1990, p. 57). The sponsoring organization must understand which activities are important to their group and then ensure that these activities are available. Coleman Finkel (1980) succinctly sums up the site selection process by stating that there are eight separate environments within which different activities take place. These environments are (Finkel 1980, p. 32):

1. The principal meeting.
2. The area to which participants adjourn for breaks.
3. The areas in which participants work on team projects.
4. The sleeping rooms.
5. The areas available for socializing.
6. The rooms where meals are served.
7. The facility itself.
8. The areas provided for recreation and exercise.

Negotiations and Contracts

Once the site has been selected, the negotiation of price and services provided begins. Negotiations usually take place between representatives from the host property (director of sales and marketing) and the sponsoring organization (meeting planner or association executive). There are many negotiable areas involved with conventions, meetings, and expositions. These include guest sleeping rooms, function space, safety, security and accessibility, food and beverages, renovation and construction, contingencies, restrictions, and cancellations.

Once negotiations have concluded, a contract is written and signed. A contract is "a legal document defining responsibilities for all parties concerned" (*The Convention Liaison Council Glossary* 1986, p. 23). For a more detailed discussion of contracts and negotiations, see chapter 7.

Formulating Committees

Sponsorship of a meeting, convention, or exposition is a huge undertaking, and many times this requires the formulation of committees. Each committee will have a specific purpose and will establish its own goals and objectives. For example, if the sponsor of a conference is a professional association, the association's bylaws probably provide an outline of committee structure to plan, organize, and operate the conference. Each committee would have a chair and members whose goals and objectives, which are stated in the bylaws, are to handle specific tasks within the framework of the conference. These committees would then work in conjunction with the association's professional staff and with the membership at large. Examples of association committees would include, but are not limited to, site selection committee, program committee, social committee, and a host conference committee.

Marketing and Promotion

The most carefully selected site in conjunction with a well-planned, dynamic program or exposition will be all for naught if no one is there to see it. Therefore, the sponsoring organization needs to assure attendance. This is done through careful attention to the marketing and promotion of the event. The promotional and marketing materials provide the first impression a potential attendee has of the upcoming event. Therefore, this material is responsible for setting the tone of the conference, meeting, or exposition.

Obviously, marketing and promotion is less of an issue for corporations, who by their very nature can assure attendance at meetings. Therefore, this segment of this chapter deals specifically with those groups who have to encourage people to attend their functions.

In order to successfully market and promote an event, the sponsoring organization must:

1. Determine their break-even attendance figures.
2. Develop a marketing plan.
3. Develop a timetable.
4. Implement the program.
5. Evaluate the program.

Marketing procedures should start with determining the break-even attendance figures. The break-even attendance figure is the minimum number of paying attendees the event must have in order to *not* lose money. If this event is supposed to generate profit, the minimum number of attendees must, at the very least, create enough revenue to cover expenses. During the initial planning phase, the planner and the sponsor should establish the absolute minimum number of participants (Jedrziewski 1991, p. 235). Determining this number requires that the sponsors have a clear understanding of their budget.

Once the break-even figures are determined, the marketing plan must be designed. A marketing plan is a written blueprint of an organization's marketing activities with respect to a particular meeting, convention, or exposition. Although this segment discusses marketing for a specific event, one must always remember the impact that the marketing has on the overall reputation of the sponsoring organization. Marketing for a specific annual event also has carryover from year to year.

A marketing plan should begin with a clear and concise understanding of the goals and objectives for the marketing and promotion of the event. For instance, a sponsor may determine that the goal of the marketing plan is to increase awareness of the organization and its annual meeting or that the goal is specifically to increase attendance at said meeting. These goals and objectives should be explicit in nature and be easily measurable.

Next it is important to identify the target market. The sponsor must decide who they want to attend the event. In most cases this group has already been targeted and described in the prospectus. Once the sponsor understands their targeted audience, they must then develop appropriate marketing and promotional strategies.

In determining the market strategies for the marketing and promotional activities, the sponsor must keep in mind what strategies will effectively reach the intended market and hold their attention long enough to convey the message. The marketing strategy most often used for the transferal of information regarding meetings, conventions, and expositions is direct mail. "The most common methods—and things people most often responded to—are brochures, invitations, and personal letters" (Price 1989, p. 55). Direct mailing tends to yield the best results for the money spent.

Secondary marketing strategies might consist of advertisements in trade journals or magazines, flyers, paid endorsements, telephone calls, or word of mouth (Price 1989, p. 55). These strategies may or may not be cost effective when compared with the overall effect of direct mail.

Choosing the marketing or promotional strategy is just the beginning. The targeted audience probably receives large quantities of mail each day. The challenge becomes to create a mailer that attracts their attention and makes them want to open the envelope to read the contents. If they have solicited the information, they are very likely to read it. If the mailing is unsolicited, they are unlikely to read it, and so designing an eye-catching mailing that attracts attention is doubly important.

Once the marketing or promotional strategies have been determined, a timetable must be created. When do each of these strategies need to be implemented? Timing may be everything. Does the first suggestion of an annual conference appear in the previous year's program? How much lead time does each strategy require? For instance, it may require several months to shoot a commercial or to design and print a glossy brochure.

PCMA suggests that for an annual meeting the following timetable be used as a guideline for pre-conference marketing strategies:

52 weeks before the event is the best time to announce the date and location of the meeting.

24 to 36 weeks before the event, send out the first set of press releases. If budgets permit, a second mailing of press releases should follow with any key pieces of information, such as keynote speakers, educational seminars, and so on.

24 weeks before the event is the time to start advertising in key industry publications.

18 to 24 weeks prior to the event, mail first round or brochures to the targeted population. Include registration and transportation information.

14 weeks before the date of your event, mail a second round of brochures to your targeted audience.

8 to 12 weeks before the event, mail a final reminder to your targeted audience.

2 to 6 weeks in advance of the conference, meeting, or exposition, send out badges, final programs, and any other promotional pieces that attendees should bring with them.
(*Professional Meeting Management* 1988, pp. 282–283)

If budget or marketing strategies allow only one mailer to be sent to potential attendees, Dotson suggests that all of the relevant information concerning registration, transportation, housing, seminars, and so on, be sent six to eight weeks prior to the meeting, conference, or exposition (1988, p. 184).

Marketing continues once attendees are at the event. Promotional gimmicks, such as pins, balloons, mints, banners, programs, table tents, proceedings, and fliers, can all be used to continue the promotion of special activities taking place within the main event. On-site promotional activities also include the marketing and promotion of future events. This can be done through inserts in programs, handouts, fliers, and gimmicks. In developing the marketing plan, certain criteria should be followed. Alastair Morrison states that the criteria for a marketing plan should be (Morrison 1989, pp. 201–202) :

1. Based on fact;
2. Organized and coordinated;
3. Programmed;
4. Budgeted;
5. Flexible;
6. Controllable;
7. Internally consistent and interrelated; and
8. Clear and simple.

Implementing the marketing plan is closely tied to the timetable just discussed. Different parts of the plan need to be implemented at various times within the overall game plan. Timing is critical to the success of a marketing plan. Although evaluation is addressed last in this section, in reality it should be considered in every step of the marketing plan. The evaluation of a program must be based on the desired results, which are clearly stated in the goals and objectives for the marketing plan. These goals and objectives have been carefully written to provide easy forms of measurement. Often, in the case of conventions, meetings, and expositions, the success of the marketing plan is judged by comparing current attendance figures with previous years' figures. While this might in part reflect the success of the marketing plan, other areas must be reviewed also. For example, if the event is an exposition and the attendance figures are down, yet the exhibitors had a more successful exposition with more qualified leads and sales, then attendance figures would not be a good indication of the success of a marketing plan.

Food and Beverage

The food and beverage functions must dovetail with the overall program design and budget for the meeting, convention, or exposition. The sponsor is responsible for:

1. Determining the number of food and beverage functions needed for the conference or meeting
2. Determining the type of food and beverage functions needed for the conference or meeting
3. Determining the cuisine
4. Guaranteeing attendance figures
5. Developing a system for record keeping

When determining the number of food and beverage functions to be included in a meeting, convention, or exposition, the sponsor must remember the overall budget. Working within the budget, the sponsor can establish a food and beverage program that meets the needs of the attendees by recognizing the time restraints of the schedule, the abilities of the host property, and the perceived desires of the attendees.

Once the number of food and beverage functions is determined, the type of function must be established. There are many ways to provide food and drink for attendees. These are:

- Breakfast
- Lunch
- Dinner
- Refreshment breaks
- Receptions
- Hospitality suites
- Theme parties
- Late night suppers
- Recreational activities

Specifics for planning and organizing these various types of functions will be discussed in further detail in chapter 5.

In the past, choosing the cuisine for a meeting or convention meant choosing between chicken and beef. This is not the case for today's meetings and conventions. Attendees are savvy consumers of food and beverage. They expect quality. The sponsor is required to be knowledgeable about the desires of the attendees. Although there is a trend towards lighter menu choices, there are still those groups who demand heartier fare. Therefore, the planner must know his or her group and choose menus accordingly.

Once the number, type, and cuisine for the food and beverage functions has been determined, attention must be given to establishing attendance figures. Because food and beverage functions are very expensive, it behooves the sponsoring organization in conjunction with the planner to give special attention to the matter of guarantees.

"A guarantee is the minimum number of meals you want served and will have to pay for" (Price 1989, p. 100). Host properties generally will require a 24- to 48-hour advanced minimum guarantee. Additionally, it is common practice for the host property to be prepared to serve anywhere from 3 to 10 percent over the guaranteed number. This allows for both the planner and the host property to operate with a margin of safety.

The last area in food and beverage for the sponsor to be concerned with is record keeping. The sponsor, in conjunction with the host property, should develop a system for keeping track of the number of people served at the food and beverage functions. This can be done several ways. The most common way is by the collection of tickets. The sponsor will provide attendees with meal coupons or tickets in their registration packets. These tickets will then be collected at each food and beverage function. The tickets serve as the sponsor's record of how many people were served and verify the charges presented by the host property. These tickets can be collected by a representative from either the sponsoring organization or the host property at the door to the food and beverage event. The collection method should be determined by the planner before the event.

Other forms of record keeping include plate count, head count, and quantities consumed. These methods of record keeping are adequate for smaller functions, but become cumbersome with large numbers of people, thus bringing into question their accuracy.

Regardless of the type of record keeping used, it is important that both the sponsoring organization and the host property are in agreement. After the function is over, it is too late to question how much food and beverage was served. Therefore, a preexisting system for record keeping alleviates most potential problems.

The food and beverage portion of a meeting, convention, or exposition affects the other portions of the event. Attendees who are hungry or poorly fed are unproductive and unconcerned with the greater goals of the meeting. Meeting planners rarely have complete control over the content of speeches and presentations, but they do have control of the menu; food and beverage is one area in which planners can truly excel and make a name for themselves.

On-Site Management

On-site management involves overseeing every aspect of the meeting or convention from the moment that registration tables open until the last guest departs. Obviously, for larger meetings lasting several days, one person cannot attend to every activity. Therefore, the planner and sponsor need to have a good working relationship with the site staff and suppliers to ensure that things happen when they are supposed to (figure 4-4).

The planner should arrive a few days before the event to meet with the hotel staff, suppliers, personnel, and other key individuals. This pre-convention, or "pre-con," meeting allows all the separate parties to understand what each other's needs will be during the run of the event. Price recommends that the pre-con meeting should include each department that has unique responsibilities for the meeting, such as Front desk, Accounting, Security, Electrician, and Bell staff (1989, p. 310). In addition, the hotel sales manager, the convention services manager, and the general manager should also attend this important session (Price 1989, p. 153).

During the meeting, communication between the different parties remains crucial. Price suggests that the planner conduct personnel check-ins to make sure that all employees are at their assigned areas, pick up messages regularly from the staff office, and maintain other regular communications with suppliers and personnel through such devices as pagers, beepers, and walkie-talkies (figure 4-5) (1989, p. 381).

The planner also must monitor on-site attendance, because it is useful to know how many people attend each different function. Attendance figures should be noted on a form for this purpose. After the convention, the planner and sponsor can study the attendance results to decide how best to plan for next year's meeting.

Figure 4-4   A pre-convention meeting includes all parties responsible for making the events happen. (Courtesy: Professional Convention Management Association.)

For instance, if a certain meeting's attendees include many golfers, the afternoon sessions may draw low attendance as most people tee off on the greens. When arranging the next year's convention, the planner may decide to reduce the number of afternoon sessions or even eliminate them completely.

The planner should also conduct a "post-conference" meeting, as illustrated in figure 4-6. Here the staff has an opportunity to critique the meeting. Price explains, "The purpose is not to point fingers or place fault, but to seriously evaluate the process, the strengths and weaknesses, good and not so good, why certain things happened, and what was or wasn't done that did or didn't help" (1989, p. 155).

Other vital post-meeting activities include writing the appropriate thank-you notes, reviewing and paying bills, and tipping and gift giving.

Figure 4-5 Meeting planners should remain on-site during the event to assure that all activities run smoothly. (Courtesy: Marriott Corporation.)

Providing Services at Meetings

The site should be able to offer a broad range of services to the attendees. If some of these services are not already in place, then the planner and sponsor must make them available. General information about the types of services offered should be included in an early mailing. Attendees should also have the opportunity to make any special needs known to the meeting planner well in advance of the event (Price 1989, p. 310).

A sample of attendee services include (Price 1989, p. 312):

1. Honoring credit cards
2. Cashing checks
3. Valet cleaning/laundry
4. Laundromat
5. Barber shop/beauty salon

6. Interpreters (specify type, hourly rates, and advance notice required)
7. Child care
8. Special diets (specify advance notice required)
9. Medical emergency assistance
10. Spouse and children programs
11. Recreational facilities

Evaluation

A meeting is not over until it has been evaluated. The purpose of evaluation is to ascertain whether or not the goals that were laid out during the conceptualization phase were reached. During the initial planning stages, the sponsor and planner determined the reasons for holding a meeting in the first place. In evaluating the meeting, the sponsor and planner should return to these goals and decide if they were actually met.

For instance, if a particular meeting's main goal was to educate employees on how to use a new computer system, the evaluation must center on how effectively this information was conveyed. Attendees should be asked direct questions, such as "Do you understand the new computer system better?" and "Are you more likely to use this system now than you were before this meeting?" If this meeting had comfortable chairs, much publicity, and excellent food, but the employees did not learn the new computer system, then the meeting was not, strictly speaking, successful. In planning the next educational meeting, the sponsor and planner will want to make specific changes to make sure that the goals of the meeting are actually met.

There are a number of different ways that meetings can be evaluated. Smaller meetings can be evaluated through informal methods. Comment cards and informal conversations with the planner give attendees a chance to give general feedback. Sometimes after a meeting, a sponsor or planner will telephone a few attendees and ask for their impressions of the event. Another

Figure 4-6   A post-convention meeting gives the staff the opportunity to critically evaluate the meeting. (Courtesy: Professional Convention Management Association.)

method involves a focus group, which meets after the fact to share specific concerns or suggestions for improvement.

Formal methods, such as questionnaires or surveys, are more common ways of evaluating attendees's perceptions of the event. Questionnaires should be straightforward, short, and easy to understand. The most effective time to distribute the survey is onsite, immediately after a workshop or seminar. A representative from the sponsoring organization should emphasize how important the survey is and ask attendees to complete and return it before they move on to the next event. If immediate return is not practical, then attendees can be asked to return the completed survey in a postage-paid envelope.

Attendees usually appreciate the fact that their opinion counts and are often willing to give detailed suggestions for improvement. Many attendees, however, prefer to simply check off their answer in multiple-choice questions. Therefore, in order to increase the return rate, the survey should be designed so that it can be easily and quickly completed.

Formal surveys can be tabulated by a computer company or, in the case of a small sampling, by individuals. The results will indicate what portions of the program attendees enjoyed and, even more importantly, what portions they disliked. When the same complaint is repeated several times, then this may be an indication that a change needs to be made in that portion of the program. Thorough evaluation makes poor programs good and good programs excellent (Juergens 1988).

Summary

The sponsor of a meeting, convention, or exposition is the group, association, or corporation responsible for the event(s). These organizations choose to hold meetings for a variety of reasons. Some of these reasons might include generating revenue, educating/training of members, networking, and/or problem solving.

The sponsor is responsible for the event concept. Included in this conceptualization phase is the determination that a need exists for the meeting or show (much research exists to support the notion that far too many needless meetings are held). Once the need has been verified and the concept established, sponsors then proceed to plan the program. Frequently, sponsors hire a meeting planner or a show manager to plan, organize, and execute the event(s).

The process of meeting management starts well before the date of the meeting. There are a number of steps involved, such as:

- Establishing goals and objectives
- Targeting the population
- Designing the program
- Creating a budget
- Selecting a site
- Negotiating contracts
- Formulating committees
- Establishing a marketing plan
- Hiring subcontractors
- Planning logistics
- Designing food and beverage functions

Meetings management continues on-site during the event and also includes post-event evaluation.

References

Ashenbrenner, G. 1988. Planning effective meetings. *Business Credit,* (July/August) pp. 43–46.

The Convention Liaison Council Glossary. 1986. Washington, D.C.: The Convention Liaison Council.

Conlin, J. 1990. First priority. *Successful Meetings (2),* (July) pp. 57–58, 62–63, 67, 69.

Dotson, P. C. 1988. *Introduction to Meeting Management.* Birmingham, Ala. Professional Convention Management Association.

Finkel, C. 1980. The "total immersion" meeting environment. *Training and Development Journal,* pp. 32–39.

A Guide for Meeting Planning. 1990. Boston, Mass.: ITT Sheraton Corporation.

Hildreth, R. A. 1990. *The Essentials of Meeting Management.* Englewood Cliffs, N.J.: Prentice-Hall, Inc.

Jedrziewski, D. R. 1991. *The Complete Guide for the Meeting Planner.* Cincinnati, Ohio: South-Western Publishing Co.

Juergens, J. 1988. Good, bad or indifferent . . . how'd ya like the meeting? *Meetings & Conventions,* (June) pp. 40–44, 55.

Juergens, J. 1989. Kernels of wisdom. *Meetings & Conventions,* (December) pp. 56–69.

Morrison, A. 1989. *Hospitality and Travel Marketing.* Albany, N.Y.: Delmar Publishers, Inc.

The Professional Meeting Manager. 1988. Birmingham, Ala: The Professional Convention Management Association.

Price, C. 1989. *The AMA Guide for Meeting and Event Planners.* New York: Amacom/American Management Association.

Rutherford, D. G. 1990. Introduction to the Conventions, Expositions, and Meetings Industry. New York: Van Nostrand Reinhold.

Woods, R. H., and F. Berger. 1988. Making meetings work. *The Cornell H. R. A. Quarterly,* 29(2):101–105.

Discussion Questions

1. What is the role of the sponsor?
2. How does the sponsor interact with the supplier?
3. This chapter states that "determining whether or not there is a need for the meeting is the first and perhaps most important step in planning a meeting. . . " Discuss this statement and support your agreement or disagreement with examples from your own life.
4. The process of meeting and exposition management involves 11 steps. Using these steps, develop a hypothetical meeting or exposition.
5. Develop a checklist for a site visit that would help you thoroughly examine potential cities for your meeting, convention, or exposition.
6. Develop a checklist for inspecting potential host properties.
7. Why is it important for a sponsoring organization to determine their break-even attendance figures?

Key Terms

conceptualization phase	ground service operator
program design	negotiations
budget	contracts
fixed expenses	break even
variable expenses	marketing plan
theme	target market
prospectus	pre-convention meeting
site inspection	post-conference meeting
drayage	

5

Host Venues

Learning Objectives

1. To recognize the main functions of a host property.
2. To understand the various duties of the representatives of the host property.
3. To understand the different types of host properties.
4. To differentiate between the different types of host properties.
5. To recognize the role the host property plays in the overall execution of a meeting, convention or exposition.

Introduction

For the purposes of this book, the host property refers to any facility used to house a meeting, convention, or exposition. There are many types of facilities that host these types of events. These facilities fall into six broad categories: convention centers, conference centers, cruise ships, resorts, hotels, and multipurpose facilities. Each of these types of facilities is designed to meet the needs of different groups. This chapter will address the differences between these five categories as well as provide insight into the overall role of the host property.

Significance of Convention and Meeting Business

The meeting and convention segment of the hospitality industry is divided into two main sections: corporate business and association business. According to *Successful Meetings* magazine in its State of the Industry report, corporations spent $37 billion sending their employees to meetings. The average company spent $605,000 on meetings. *Meetings and Conventions* magazine reported that more than 706,000 corporate meetings are held annually in hotels and motels throughout the country.

On the association side of the equation, *Meetings and Conventions* magazine reported that more than 197,000 association meetings were held annually. Associations are also responsible for sponsoring numerous educational seminars. Estimates of the attendance for both meetings and educational seminars is over 31 million people annually. Government, social/fraternal, education, military, and entrepreneurial (such as COMDEX or traveling seminars), while not as large as the association and corporate segments, still make up a significant portion of the meeting and convention business.

These numbers speak for themselves. Clearly a hotel, motel, or resort that has the physical facilities to host meetings or conventions should review their marketing plan to ascertain the viability of attracting these markets.

Role of the Host Property

The role of the host property is to provide the facilities and services needed to assist in the execution of meetings, conventions, and expositions. In the past, when people thought about the role of the host facility, they thought of rooms and food. Today the host property is much more intricately involved with the overall planning and execution of the meeting. This involvement may include helping to design and market the program, assisting in the planning of hospitality programs, theme parties, and sporting events, and training new meeting planners.

Many of the major convention hotels actually go so far as to provide training seminars for the meeting planner. Hilton Hotels has designed a Host (Hilton on-site Training) program to improve communications between the host property and planner. This program gives the planner the insights into the inner workings of the hotel, thus stripping away any lines of miscommunication and ultimately increasing the efficiency from both sides (Tannenhaus 1986). Sheraton has a similar program called Sheraton Showcase, which "teaches planners the ABCs and XYZs of meeting planning" (Lieberman 1991, p. 33). Al Bonney, the general manager of the Crystal Gateway Marriott in Arlington, Virginia, summed up the attitude of the suppliers by stating that "an educated consumer is our best customer" (Lieberman 1991, p. 34).

Although the practices just discussed are good business, they are also just another sign of the growing emphasis placed on service. Service is the buzzword of the nineties. Increasing competition in an overbuilt economy has forced the hospitality industry to reevaluate its attitude towards service. This coupled with the recession has affected all areas of the industry, but none more than those hotels, motels, and resorts that gain a large percentage of their income from conferences and meetings. Because of the recession and the decrease of discretionary income, associations and corporations who typically host conventions and meetings are faced with decreasing revenues. Therefore, they are becoming very selective in the way they spend their extra money.

For the hospitality industry this means that they must work harder to gain their portion of this discretionary income. In the past, this has meant offering newer rooms and more amenities, but the industry is also facing their own revenue shortage, thus the quality of service has become the point of distinction. Since today's conference attendees are more selective in the number of conferences they are attending, suppliers must focus on providing a level of service that leads the guest to feel at home, well cared for, and anxious to return (Callan 1990).

This hospitable service attitude must be exuded by all those associated with the host property. Everyone from the general manager to the housekeeper must understand the importance of service in their daily activities. For this to take place, commitment to a positive service attitude must start at the top.

Key Players In the Host Property

There are a number of individuals within the host property who are responsible for servicing the group. As you can see by the organizational chart in figure 5-1, there must be a clear understanding of the delegation of authority. The **general manager**

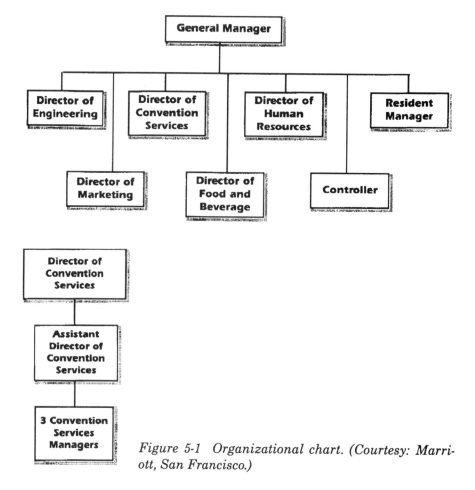

Figure 5-1 Organizational chart. (Courtesy: Marriott, San Francisco.)

is ultimately responsible for the success of any activity on his or her property. The role that general managers play in the conventions and meetings hosted on their properties depends on the importance of this market to their overall market mix. In those hotels that rely on meetings, conventions, and expositions for a large portion of their room nights, the general managers may play a vital role in servicing the groups. Regardless of their time investment, they are still committed to overseeing the overall orchestration of events. Often, general managers play a key role in the pre-conference meetings and are available for consultation during the events.

In many hotels the next person in the line of command is the **director of marketing.** "The director of marketing administers, coordinates, and supervises the activities of sales department executives who are responsible for soliciting and servicing conventions, sales meetings, tours, and other groups requiring public space and room accommodations. He or she also helps create and implement programs aimed at developing rooms, food, and beverage business from the individual business and leisure traveler" (Hoyle, Dorf, and Jones 1989, p. 153). They or their staff customarily are the first contact a group has with a property and therefore play a vitally important role in the meetings, conventions, and expositions market.

The active pursuit of meetings, conventions, and expositions must be the primary goal of the director of sales in those properties designed to service this market. To this end, many sales departments have individuals whose primary responsibility is to service various segments of the industry. For example, the sales department may have different divisions that focus on corporate sales, association sales, incentive travel sales, and leisure travel sales. Each of these individuals must be thoroughly schooled in the mechanics of their potential market. It has often been said that the meetings and convention industry is a relationship business. To sell a property, the sales department must know their markets inside and out. Meeting planners want to deal with people and therefore companies who understand them and their business. Building relationships is a long-term commitment that often times does not yield immediate, obvious results. Therefore, monitoring the sales staff's progress is a common practice that establishes sales quotas, which encourages productivity. These quotas may center on room night sales, number of sales calls, number of bookings, or any combination thereof. Although this is a strong incentive for the sales staff to increase their productivity, this practice may cause problems within the meetings and convention industry.

One must first understand that the sales department of a host facility is often plagued with extremely high turnover. This often means that the sales person who sells a meeting or convention may be long gone when the event comes to town. Therefore, the pressure to meet quotas coupled with the lack of accountability due to excessive job turnover may cause salespeople to make excessive concessions or promises to meet their quotas. These promises are then left to the remaining staff to fulfill. Promises such as these are often broken, thus leaving the meeting planner in a lurch. As this industry matures it will begin to solve this problem by focusing on the causes for such high turnover rates among salespeople and to introduce other methods of measuring success in the sales department besides the quota system. But for now, to protect the group from unkept promises, it is imperative that all special arrangements be clearly outlined in the contract, thus preventing any questions during the event.

In an ideal situation the salesperson who has taken such great care in developing a relationship with his or her clientele will not disappear from the picture once the business is booked. They will continue to play an important role in the servicing of the group to ensure that the client gets what the contract determined during the negotiation stage. Therefore, the salesperson becomes part of the service staff throughout the function.

Although the account executive remains a part of the servicing staff, once the contract is negotiated and signed, the **convention service department** takes over the reigns of command and is responsible for fulfilling the host properties' commitments. This transition generally occurs about 1 year before the convention. "The convention service manager has been referred to as 'the person who makes things happen.' He, or she, is the meeting planner's contact person, and so should be readily available to handle all of the convening group's on-the-spot needs" (Abbey 1988, p. 222).

In Ellen Muraskin's article "Convention Service Managers: The On-site Connection," she addresses the concept of "uniservice." "Uniservice" allows the meeting planner to experience one-stop shopping (Shaw 1990). In basic terms this means that the meeting planner no longer must deal with the individual departments, such as catering and rooms, and support departments, such as audiovisual and special events. They need only contact their convention service manager to have any of their needs met. The convention service manager is a fairly new position that evolved from the demands made by meeting planners for a central point of command. Meeting planners are often frustrated when there is not a member of management who is intimately familiar with their meeting and who has the authority to get things done. This person or department acts as the liaison between the host property and the group. The positioning of this department within the organization is a point of contention. One school of thought is that the convention service manager should report directly to the general manager. This insures that the convention service manager has the authority to carry out his or her responsibilities. The other school of thought believes that this position allows too much freedom on the part of the convention service manager and that they should act as another arm of the sales department. In most cases positioning of this department is directly related to the percentage of the properties business that is generated through meetings, conventions, and expositions—the higher the percentage, the higher the department is placed in the organization.

The convention service manager must be brought into the negotiation process as early as possible, thus allowing easy transition from the sales department to the convention service department. This guarantees a clearer line of communication between the group and the convention service manager once the meeting, convention, or exposition has been turned over to the convention service department. The department then develops a series of written communications with the meeting planner to ascertain all of the needs of the group.

The convention service manager is then responsible for communicating these needs to the hotel staff. This is done through booking the appropriate space, blocking rooms for the meeting, convention, or exposition, planning meal functions, and so on. Again, constant communication between this department and the meeting planner or association executive must be maintained to guarantee success.

The convention service manager is also responsible for overseeing the actual event. This is accomplished through a series of meetings with the appropriate departments within the host property. These meetings are designed to address all details of the upcoming event. Individuals involved in these meetings can range from the general manager (depending on the size and importance of the event) to the front desk manager.

Two or three days before the event, the convention service manager brings together all of the key players with the meeting planner or association executive to iron out any last-minute changes. This meeting, called the preconvention meeting, ensures that all players are playing from the same game plan.

The preconvention meeting should be directed by the convention service manager and should involve:

Sales person
General manager
Catering manager
Front office manager
Director of housekeeping
Director of food and beverage
Security supervisor
Meeting planner/executive vice president

The salesperson is there to provide contract clarification as well as to show continued commitment to the success of the function. The general manager is there to provide continuity and to ensure that all the needs of the group have been met.

The catering manager, armed with detailed function sheets, will address every food and beverage function, its menu, its layout, and its staffing needs. They will also verify counts and discuss any last minute changes.

The front office will address the preparations that have been made to handle check-in/checkout procedures. This includes discussing all possible heavy check-in/checkout times and how they will staff to ensure smooth service. Many a meeting or conference has gotten off to a bad start because attendees have had to spend too much time waiting to get checked in or waiting for their room once they are checked in. The front office manager must also address the issue of overbooking. If it appears that it is going to be necessary to walk any members of the group, the front office manager explains how this will be handled.

The director of housekeeping will discuss all special services for the group. This might include turndown service, special amenities to be placed in the room, and any special arrangements for the executive suites.

The director of food and beverage will discuss all of the food and beverage operations available to the group, including room service, coffee shops, informal dining, formal dining, specialty dining, and lounges. In many cases the host facility has made special arrangements for large groups, such as putting more staff on the floor to handle the large influx of patrons during group breaks.

The security specialist will outline all necessary security measures that will be taken by the host facility. Included in this discussion should be the number and function of the security guards on duty, their specific training (i.e., CPR and first aid), fire alarm systems and evacuation procedures, location of nearest hospital and medical assistance, as well as the hotel lock system and safe deposit boxes.

After the host facility's representatives make their presentations, the meeting planner or executive vice president will address any areas of concern. This is the final opportunity to clean up any possible misunderstandings, thus preventing last minute problems.

During the event the convention service manager is on hand for all functions. He or she often arrives over an hour before the event begins and leaves well after the last attendee. This provides a sense of security for the sponsors of the function. A quick fix to unanticipated problems is the most important factor involved with a meeting, convention, or exposition. Yet not even the most capable individual can anticipate everything. Therefore, ensuring that someone of authority is on hand at all times to address the problems as they arise is crucial.

The convention service manager's job does not end when the event does. He or she is then responsible for billing, evaluation, and the post-conference meeting. This meeting allows the major players (convention service manager, meeting planner, salesperson, and general manager) to discuss both the positive and the negative aspects of the event. These meetings convey a sense of commitment to the overall success of the association or corporation and any future events they might host. This meeting also provides a forum for rebooking.

Services

There are many services provided by the host facility. These services include guest rooms and amenities, meeting rooms, exposition space, food and beverage, and specialty programs. Each of these areas are designed to enhance the service provided by the facility as well as to provide revenue for the host facility.

Guest Rooms

If the host property is a hotel, motel, or resort, the primary source of revenue with regards to meetings, conventions, and expositions is derived from the sale of guest rooms. Within the negotiation process, the number of guest rooms proposed by the sponsoring organization is a powerful bargaining tool. The room rates, meeting space charges, food and beverage prices, as well as specialty amenities are all negotiated on the basis of the number of proposed room nights the sponsoring organization brings to the negotiation table. (For a thorough discussion of this process, see chapter 7.) Once the number of guest rooms has been agreed upon, a room block is established. This room block ensures that attendees will have a space at the hotel. The room block should include the specified number and classifications of rooms agreed upon. Types of rooms needed vary from group to group, but usually fall under the categories of singles, doubles, twins, or suites. When planning the types of rooms needed for a specific event, one needs to consider the requirements of VIP guests, such as board members, association executives, special entertainers, major exhibitors, and special guest speakers. In many cases during the negotiation phase, special complimentary rooms or suites will be provided free of charge by the host property. The meeting planner must provide a detailed list of all room requirements to the convention service manager. This list should include any special arrangements for VIP guests, such as upgraded amenities packages or services, including fresh flowers, robes, fruit baskets, turndown and so on. This will avoid any confusion during the check-in/check-out phase of the event.

The room block is established based on the group's past history and the projections for this event. Since the room block is often initiated up to 3 years in advance, the host requires a confirmation, usually 30 days prior to the event. Under the circumstances where the room block is not needed, the sponsoring organization should release the unneeded rooms as early as possible, thus allowing the host facility to sell the rooms. Once the room block has been released, registrants will be given rooms on a first-come/first-served basis.

Guest rooms are a very important component of a convention, meeting, or exposition. Today's conference and meeting attendees are more selective in the number of conferences they are attending. In a recently conducted survey, meeting planners were asked what in-room amenities were important for the site selection process. Respondents stated that their clients were very interested in hotels that provided rooms that were "homey," not sterile and impersonal. The personal touches of decorating a room are important, such as flowers, live plants, quilts, comforters, and warmer color schemes. One respondent stated that "it is more an ambiance, a look and a feeling that translates immediately when you enter a room."

Judith Sawyer, in her column "From the Supply Side," addressed the issue of personal amenities. She stated that travelers were more interested in cakes of soap than in liquid soap. They wanted larger bath towels, a few essential toiletries (with the option of receiving extra ones if needed), as well as bigger beds and more rooms with double-double beds (*Successful Meetings* September 1991).

As a sign of the times, other things that meeting planners consider when choosing a site are non-smoking guest rooms and the accessibility of the entire property for individuals with special needs. Considerations need to be taken for individuals with physical disabilities, such as impaired vision, wheel chair confinement, and hearing impairments.

Check-in/Check-out

Even the most well appointed rooms cannot compensate for poor check-in procedures. It is very important that all parties be alerted to arrival and departure times of the attendees. The meeting planner is responsible for alerting the host facility to heavy arrival times, thus allowing the host facility to staff accordingly.

To avoid long lines and impatient guests, many host properties have instituted preregistration for their conference and meeting attendees. This preregistration allows the conferees to register by simply signing for their keys. They may even be able to register at an area away from the main lobby, such as the airport (as is the case with the Opryland Hotel in Nashville, Tennessee), thus allowing them to receive express service.

When preregistration is not possible, many hotels have designed diversionary tactics to keep their guests occupied.

Two of the most noted are the Las Vegas Mirage (as depicted in figure 5-2) and its mesmerizing 20,000-gallon salt-water aquarium located along the wall behind the front desk and the Hilton Hawaiian Village, with their service of fresh tropical juices. Both of these establishments have attempted to make the wait less stressful.

Figure 5-2   Thanks to the careful selection of exotic coral reef fish from all regions of the world, the Mirage's 20,000-gallon saltwater tank and coral reef landscape is a visual delight. Located at the registration area, sharks, triggerfish, pufferfish, grouper, and rays are among the colorful sea life inhabitants who call the Mirage "home." (Courtesy: The Mirage, Las Vegas.)

Check-out is equally important. Typically, guests have a schedule to keep and therefore do not have the time for a leisurely check-out. The development of express check-out has facilitated this process. Different express check-out systems allow the guest to either check out with the television and have their bill mailed to them or to receive their bill under their door first thing in the morning. Obviously, if a group traditionally pays with cash, express check-out would not be appropriate. Therefore, the convention service manager must be apprised of the group's payment history.

Meeting Space

Paramount to holding meetings is the availability and design of the meeting space. Meeting space is a very negotiable item for the host property and the group. In the case of host properties such as resorts, hotels, and motels that make their revenue from the sale of sleeping rooms, generally the rental fees for function rooms are directly related to the number of guest rooms a group is booking. If the group is booking only a small number of guest rooms but requires a large amount of function space, the rental fee will be very high. This is done in hopes of keeping function space open to entice groups that will utilize both guest rooms and function space. The rental fee is also negotiated based on the amount of food and beverage service required by the group. Customarily, the more food and beverage services required by the group, the less the room rental fee. In the case of a convention center or conference center, their profit comes from the rental of function space, and therefore fees for said space are usually higher and less negotiable than function space at other types of host properties.

In discussing meeting space, one must remember that the space is not limited to the standard meeting or conference rooms, but includes space needed for exhibits, social functions, and banquets. Many host facilities provide multipurpose function rooms. This allows the property to respond to the needs of their various clients. Groups' needs vary; some require limited meeting space, while others combine exhibits, social functions, and meetings, thus requiring the entire spectrum of meeting facilities available.

Meeting rooms include everything from board rooms to multipurpose rooms to auditoriums. It is incumbent upon the host property to provide groups with "room specs," which are detailed descriptions and scaled drawings of all of their space. The meeting planner must then, in conjunction with the convention service manager, determine what space best suits their needs (see figure 5-3).

Meeting space should be designed so that nothing detracts from the exchange of information taking place in the room. Rooms should include capabilities for audiovisual equipment, ranging from high-tech interactive learning to low-tech audiovisual—equipment like flip charts and bulletin boards. Special lighting should also be devised to use a mixture of incandescent and fluorescent lighting that can be controlled from within the room. Once the physical space has been determined, the focus turns to room setup. There are many ways to arrange a room. The setup is decided based on the agenda or activities to take place in the room. One of the most common meeting formats involves a single speaker or panel addressing a group of individuals. In

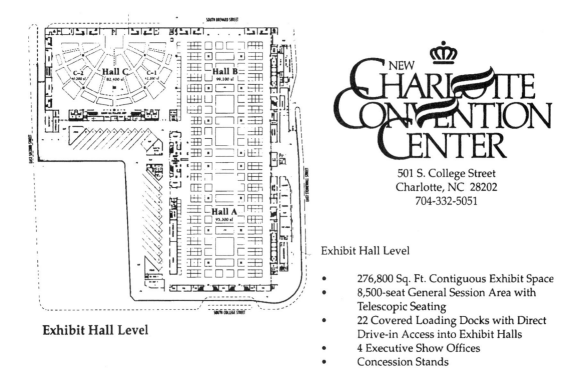

Exhibit Hall Level

NEW

CHARLOTTE
CONVENTION
CENTER

501 S. College Street
Charlotte, NC 28202
704-332-5051

Exhibit Hall Level

- 276,800 Sq. Ft. Contiguous Exhibit Space
- 8,500-seat General Session Area with Telescopic Seating
- 22 Covered Loading Docks with Direct Drive-in Access into Exhibit Halls
- 4 Executive Show Offices
- Concession Stands

Figure 5-3　The New Charlotte Convention Center.

this case, interaction among the audience is minimal, and therefore the seating arrangements should allow maximum viewing of the speaker. This can be accomplished in a number of ways. Auditorium or theater style is one of the most functional seating arrangements used for this forum, especially when the meeting involves large groups of participants. Auditorium or theater style seating involves placing chairs in rows, either straight or in a semi-circle. Chairs should be placed 4 to 6 inches apart, with approximately $2\frac{1}{2}$ feet from the back of one chair to the front of the chair behind it. More space is desirable between rows, but often times this is not practical. Although this format is excellent for the dissemination of information from speaker to audience, it does not allow for easy interaction between participants or for note-taking. In auditorium or theater-style seating, it is important to insure that the speaker or panel is easily visible to all participants. This may mean that the speaker or panel needs to be elevated on a platform. A platform may also be referred to as a stage, dais, or rostrum. Figure 5-4 illustrates an example of auditorium-style seating.

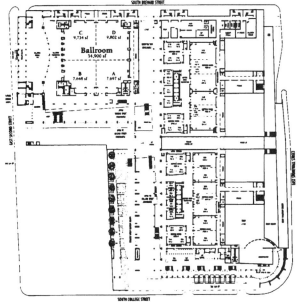

Ballroom & Meeting Room Level

- 34,900 Sq. Ft. Hotel Quality Ballroom
- Up to 46 Meeting Rooms
- Full Service Cafe & Lounge
- Central Taping & Remote Audio Recording Capabilities
- Closed-Circuit Television Capabilities

Concourse Level (not shown)

- 43,000 Sq. Ft. Registration Area
- Business & Visitor Service Centers
- 3 Exhibitor Suites
- 2 VIP Suites
- Press Room
- 3 Outdoor Plazas

Ballroom & Meeting Room Level

Figure 5-3 (Continued)

Figure 5-4   Auditorium-style seating. (Courtesy: Hospitality Franchise Systems.)

Another common format for speaker or panel presentations is school-room or classroom seating (as seen in figure 5-5). Classroom seating involves rows of rectangular tables (usually 18 inches wide), with participants seated on one side facing the speaker or panel. The classroom arrangement is conducive to participants taking notes, reading materials, or working on projects. This format can take several shapes, which include closed classroom, with no center aisle, open classroom, which has rows with aisles to provide easy access to seats, and V-shaped, which provides opportunity for participants to partially face one another.

When interaction among participants is an important function of the meeting, different seating styles will be used to facilitate this interaction. The style is usually dictated by the size and shape of the room as well as the number of participants. Some of the most common formats are U-shaped, hollow square, hollow circle, and semi-circle. Figure 5-6 is an example of a seating

Figure 5-5   Classroom-style seating. (Courtesy: Marriott, San Francisco.)

arrangement that allows face-to-face interaction among all participants. All of these shapes usually involve the use of 18-inch or 30-inch wide tables, with participants seated on one side of the table and with the tables facing each other. The boardroom-style utilizes a single column of two 30-inch tables placed side by side to provide a width of 60 inches. This is such a popular format that many host properties have permanent board rooms (figure 5-7).

Another common space requirement for meetings, conventions, and expositions is exhibit space. The exhibit space is usually a very large room that houses exhibits for the meeting, convention, or exposition. A properly outfitted exhibit hall among other things includes loading docks that are easily accessible to the exhibit space, adequate structural support that includes high ceilings, reinforced walls, and floors, and access to all major utilities (gas, water, and electricity), as well as adequate storage and security. The host property in conjunction with the meeting

Figure 5-6   Seating arrangements either facilitate or hamper communication. This arrangement is ideal for face-to-face interaction. (Courtesy: Marriott, San Franciso.)

planner or association executive needs to carefully review the requirements of the exhibitors to ascertain whether or not the physical facilities are adequate. In the event that the group does not require an exhibit hall, this space may be equipped with moveable walls enabling it to be converted to smaller breakout rooms.

The tone of the entire meeting is influenced by the comfort of the participants. Therefore, it is very important that the host facil-

Figure 5-7   Seating arrangement using the boardroom style. (Courtesy: San Diego LaJolla.)

ity pay special attention to the design of their meeting space. The design should include:

1. Temperature and lighting controls for each room;
2. Soundproof walls;
3. Barrier free (no pillars, columns, or other structural components that will obstruct the setup);
4. Comfortable tables and chairs;
5. Color schemes that enhance;

6. Flexibility to respond to a variety of audio and visual needs, including slide projectors, overhead projectors, video projectors, and sound systems;
7. Accessibility for the physically disadvantaged;
8. Flexibility, so as to accommodate platforms and dance floors.

Once they have determined the room requirements and the setup, the meeting planner in conjunction with the convention service manager should decide which services should be provided during the meeting. Minimum service requirements should include ice water for both the speakers and attendees. The water for the speaker should be easily accessible, either on the podium or in the lectern. A general rule of thumb regarding ice water for the participants is one pitcher for every ten people. In the case of classroom seating, glasses may be placed at each chair or at a central table in the case of auditorium- or theater-style seating. This water should be refilled and glasses replenished in between each session or at each break.

Other services may include:

1. Pads of paper and pencils
2. Mints or hard candy
3. Light snacks
4. Coffee, tea, and sodas
5. Ash trays if smoking is to be permitted

Food and Beverage

Not too many years ago, food and beverage associated with a meeting or convention were perceived poorly. Typical convention food left the attendees hungry and unsatisfied with the quality and quantity of items prepared. Food and beverage functions were considered a necessary evil, provided primarily to meet the attendees' basic need to eat. If an attendee had any special dietary needs, these would surely be met with substandard fare.

The banquet foodservice of yesterday barely resembles the food and beverage service of today. Many meeting planners report that the host facilities's ability to provide quality food and beverage service is significant in the determination of a meeting site. Today, food and beverage functions are inherent to the success of any meeting, convention, or conference. They provide the perfect environment for socializing with colleagues, meeting new people, networking, and revitalizing oneself from what may sometimes be an otherwise rigorous schedule of meetings. There are many types of food and beverage possibilities available. The ultimate choice is determined by the needs and objectives of the group, the group's budget, and the facilities and talents of the host facility.

For example, some groups are simply meeting to conduct a particular piece of business and do not wish to extend the length of the meeting by planning elaborate food and beverage functions. In this case, a working lunch of deli meats and cold salads may be sufficient. In other cases, part of the objectives of the group are to provide time for collegiality or networking, and therefore food and beverage functions are an integral part of the overall program. In this case, the requirements may include a combination of breaks, meals, hospitality suites, banquets, and special events. Regardless of the type of food and beverage functions required, quality food and service are imperative.

Although food and beverage prices are rarely quoted more than 3 to 6 months prior to an event, most host facilities have a standard set of menus and menu prices from which they work. Additionally, many of the food and beverage departments within these host facilities have the talent and capabilities to deviate from the standard menus and offer elaborate variations . . . for a price. All of these issues need to be discussed during the negotiation phase of planning a meeting, conference, or exposition and written into the contract between the host facility and the association or organization hosting the meeting, conference, or exposition (for a thorough discussion of contracts and negotiations, see chapter 8).

Frequently, the type of rooms available will determine the type of functions the food and beverage department can offer. For instance, functions hosted for several hundred people may prohibit sit-down banquet-style service simply because there are no rooms large enough to handle table seating for that many people. However, the same facility may be able to easily accommodate a stand-up reception for the same number of people. Therefore, the meeting planner needs to know what the capabilities and limitations of the food and beverage department are before the functions involving this department can be planned.

Armed with the information regarding the budget and objectives of the group, along with the knowledge of capabilities and limitations of the host facility, the meeting planner is now ready to plan the food and beverage functions. According to Joe Goldblatt (1990, p. 302), conventions generally include any combination of the following special events: opening reception, refreshment breaks, luncheon general session, the off-premise or themed event, and the final banquet. These special events would be included in the program, along with a variety of other breakfasts, lunches, dinners, and late-night suppers.

The main purpose of the opening reception is to welcome the attendees to the meeting or conference and to get them into the spirit of the conference. People attend the opening reception to see who else is there. They begin to establish their own personal agenda of who they need to see and what they hope to accomplish while at the meeting—in other words, the networking begins. It has become very common for meetings, conventions, or expositions to have a theme. If this is the case, the theme should be introduced at the opening reception.

In planning the opening reception or any other reception, *Meetings and Conventions* (1989) suggests that there are three basic areas that need attention. They are:

1. Physical surroundings
2. Foodservice
3. Beverage service.

When considering physical surroundings, be sure that the room fits the function, with square-shaped rooms being preferable to rectangular for the promotion of both service as well as interaction. If the room is too large, people will get lost; if it is too small, people may have difficulty maneuvering. The temperature of the room is important. Rooms warm up quickly when there are many attendees present, as well as food warmers, and so on; therefore, rooms need to be equipped with individual thermostats to ensure a comfortable climate.

Finally, the atmosphere of the room is critical to the success of a reception. Flowers are important, both at the entrance as well as on the buffet table, and background music helps to soften the noises inherent with food and beverage service. In an ideal situation a reception should offer both buffet and tray service. The buffet table allows the guests to serve themselves. Tray service serves several additional functions. First, it alleviates some of the congestion at the buffet tables, and secondly it allows guests to engage in conversations while still having something to nibble on. The general rule of thumb is one tray server for every 10 to 20 guests, depending on the menu.

When selecting food items for a reception, several issues need to be kept in mind. First of all, meeting planners need to consider the type of group. What types of foods are these attendees likely to enjoy? For instance, a group of all males would be more likely to prefer heavier foods than a group of all females. Secondly, meeting planners need to remember that many foods, though enjoyed by the group, are not appropriate for a reception. Foods that are too messy or that need to be kept frozen may not serve well during these functions.

Planning appropriate amounts of food can be somewhat tricky. While it may be forgivable to run out of some items being passed on trays, it is unsightly and annoying to guests to see empty chafing dishes on the buffet tables (particularly if they haven't had any of that item yet). Eight to 12 pieces of food per person per hour is the caterers' rule of thumb (*Meetings and Conventions* 1989, p. 45), leaning toward the lighter side for a group of all women and toward the heavier side for a group of all men and somewhere in the middle for a mixed gender group.

Beverage service is as important to the success of a reception as the food. The basic decisions here are whether or not to offer alcoholic beverages, and how extensive the offering should be. For instance, will wine be enough, or should spirits be included in the offerings? How extensive should the spirit selection be? The next decision will be whether to pay for liquor per person, by the drink, or by the bottle. If the group is small, by the drink seems to be more advantageous since it is more economical, and more choices can be offered. With large groups, purchasing by the bottle generally works best, since the per drink cost will be reduced substantially.

As mentioned above, another type of function that is generally included on a conference or meeting agenda is the refreshment break. As the name implies, these functions provide a break in the schedule to refresh and revitalize oneself. This break gives participants a chance to telephone the office (provided there are sufficient telephones available), engage in a little informal conversation, stretch their legs, visit the restroom, and consume a quick snack before reconvening for another meeting or educational session.

According to *Meetings and Conventions* (1989, p. 54), the biggest considerations when planning a refreshment break are menu, timing, and location. A few years ago a refreshment break menu consisted of coffee in styrofoam cups and danish. Today refreshment breaks have become much more elaborate. People want to see interesting foods and beverages presented in unique and colorful ways. Meeting planners are introducing themed breaks to provide more opportunity for creativity, and host facilities have recently begun to view refreshment breaks as a means to show off their talents as well as make a profit.

With the trends in nutritional dining, many meeting planners have focused on nutritional refreshment breaks by offering such items as granola bars, yogurt, and fruit juices. These meeting planners subscribe to the notion that eating healthy foods provides good thinking food for the attendees. Other meeting planners report that, despite lip service to nutritional food preferences, attendees prefer gooey, sugary foods. These are the meeting planners responsible for refreshment breaks with such themes as "a chocoholic break" and make your own sundaes (*Meetings and Conventions* 1991, p. 50). Whatever the menu choices, meeting planners work closely with the host facility food and beverage department to assure that the choices made will be popular with the attendees, as well as within the abilities of the host facility staff.

Timing of refreshment breaks is an important consideration in the overall success of the meeting or conference. The average meeting attendee has an attention span of $1\frac{1}{2}$ to 2 hours. Therefore, if meetings are planned to last an entire day, several breaks may need to be scheduled to include a lunch break of anywhere from 1 to 2 hours.

Although a 15-minute break is generally considered sufficient time to refuel and revitalize, it is frequently very difficult to actually keep the break to 15 minutes. Therefore, most meeting planners schedule 30 to 45 minutes for each break, thus allowing attendees sufficient time to return to their seats.

A common problem with refreshment breaks is the location of the setup itself. Frequently being set up in the back of the meeting room or in the hallway outside the room, breaks result in congestion and setup noise that distracts from the meeting. By planning the break in an adjoining room or foyer (figure 5-8), host facility personnel are free to set up the break before the meeting adjourns (it should be completely ready for service 15 minutes before scheduled meeting adjournment) and can break down and clean up after the meeting has reconvened.

A luncheon general session is another type of special event that is frequently included in a meeting's program. This is usually a sit-down luncheon with a minimum of three courses. In addition to the food itself, this function generally includes a speaker or other formal program with the topic being one of interest to all of the attendees.

Figure 5-8 A refreshment break gives participants a chance to refresh and revitalize. (Courtesy: Stouffer Concourse Hotel Los Angeles International Airport.)

Lunches other than the general session are usually either plated, sit-down meals, or buffets. Frequently, the length of time allotted for the lunch, as well as the menu and budget, will help the meeting planner in making this choice. For instance, meals served buffet-style tend to take longer than pre-plated banquet-style service. Also, it is generally true that buffets are more expensive than pre-plated service, because portion sizes cannot be controlled when guests are free to serve themselves. One big advantage to offering buffet-style service is that it allows the attendees to choose from among several menu items. For some groups, especially those with a varied membership, this may be an overriding consideration.

While buffets and pre-plated lunches are the most common types of service of the midday meal, there is evidence that meeting planners in conjunction with the host facility are putting their creative heads together and coming up with some unique deviations from the standard fare. For example, box lunches seem to be gaining in popularity. These are lunch meals preportioned and served in disposable boxes (some of which are quite unique). These lunches can offer everything from gourmet-type sandwiches to standard school lunchbox-type fare. Box lunches provide several advantages in that they are cheaper and easier to prepare and serve, cleanup is much simpler, and guests are free to eat at their own pace and to move about.

The off-premise or themed event is frequently found on meeting or conference agendas, especially if the attendees will be attending sessions for several days. This gives the attendee an opportunity to see outside the walls of the host facility and take advantage of some of the unique attractions of a particular destination. For instance, at the 1990 CMAA conference held in Orlando, the off-premise event was a trip to the MGM Studios at Disney. This was not only a memorable event, but also an opportunity that many attendees would not otherwise have had. The major drawback to these off-premise events involves the logistics of transporting large numbers of people. However, if reliable transportation is secured, off-premise events are usually very well received by the attendees.

The final banquet is usually a dinner event held on the last night of the conference or meeting. It is an opportunity to bring to a close the events that have taken place over the last few days, to say good-byes to colleagues, perhaps present awards, and otherwise set the stage for next year's conference.

Final banquets can take many different forms, from black-tie affairs complete with dancing and champagne toasts, to hoe downs complete with cowboy hats, barbeque, and comedians. The final banquet, as with all other functions, is determined by the likes and dislikes of the group (are they an adventuresome crowd?), budget, and the talents and facilities available from the host facility.

Aside from the final banquet, there may be other opportunities to plan and prepare dinners for the attendees. In regard to lunch, creative ideas may be utilized by the planning staff. However, buffet and pre-plated service are the most common. During a buffet dinner, guests would perhaps be more likely to expect some amount of service, as compared to a luncheon buffet. A common example is having a server carve a meat item and place it on the guest's plate as he or she walks by. For pre-plated banquet service, dinner would be served in a manner similar to lunch, with the exception of more courses potentially being added.

Apart from the standard food and beverage events, there are many other opportunities for the meeting planner and the food and beverage department to create functions for the enjoyment of the attendees. Some examples of these may be hospitality suites or late night suppers. A hospitality suite is set up in a suite in the host facility and generally takes the form of a very informal gathering. Although the menus may vary with the theme of the event, foods should be placed on trays on nicely appointed tables, leaving the guests free to help themselves. Hospitality suites may offer continental breakfast, such as that shown in figure 5-9, midday snacks such as soft drinks, tea, and munchies, or late night dessert buffets. Hospitality suites may be scheduled for a specific time of the day or evening or may be open continuously throughout the day or throughout the event. Late night suppers are welcomed events at the end of a long evening work session or other late night event. These suppers can take many forms, from hors d'oeuvres to full meals to desserts only. They may be stand-up/drop-in–type events or formal sit-down affairs. Again, creativity, budget, skills, and available facilities are the factors that determine the success of these events.

Throughout the planning stages, the meeting planner needs to keep in mind that while a variety of food and beverage functions are desirable, it is not necessary to fill every meal slot on the attendees schedule. Frequently, there are meal times left "open"

Figure 5-9   There are many opportunities to create food and beverage functions for the enjoyment of the attendees. Hospitality suites are informal, and guests are free to help themselves. (Courtesy: Marriott San Francisco.)

on the program to allow attendees free time to explore or to spend with family or to just relax by the pool. A listing of local restaurants is generally provided in the guest registration packet.

Once the meeting planner and host facility have agreed on the number and types of food and beverage functions and the menus have been determined, prices need to be established and attendance will need to be estimated. Prices are negotiated along with the many other aspects of the meeting, conference, or convention and are written into the contract signed by all parties. For a thorough discussion of contracts and negotiations, see chapter 7.

Estimating and guaranteeing attendance can be tricky. Generally, host facilities require only a minimum guarantee, with a 48-hour confirmation on exact attendance figures. The organization or association is then responsible for payment based on the number of attendees confirmed for that meal function.

To forecast the attendance figures, meeting planners will look at past meal attendance history as well as registration numbers to see how many people have paid their registration fees. To these figures, most meeting planners will add 10 percent to assure that any latecomers can be easily accommodated. The host property and the group will agree on a procedure to ascertain the number of individuals actually served. The most common measures used to arrive at the final number are head count, ticket count, plate count, and food consumed.

As mentioned above, food and beverage plays a vital role in the overall success of the meeting, convention, or exposition. For this reason it is imperative that the meeting planner work closely with the host facility's food and beverage department to assure that plans are accurately made and that execution of those plans is expertly done.

Hospitality Programs/Spousal Programs or Special Events

Today's conference attendee is a new breed. With the rising cost of travel and lodging, the graying baby boomers are judging the value of meetings and conventions against their own set of business and personal criteria (Conlin 1990). No longer do they use conferences as an excuse to get away from the family; now they use conferences as an excuse to take a mini-vacation with their families. The host facility that has the services and amenities in place to service the guests of the attendees is one step ahead of the competition.

The programs for the guest(s) of conference participants are commonly labeled hospitality programs or spousal programs. Hospitality programs are designed to entertain the guests of the conference attendees. These programs range from having a very extensive itinerary that keeps participants continuously busy the entire time, to a program that just provides suggestions for individual activities. The host property that provides help to the meeting planner in developing the hospitality program will insure increased profits for themselves. Hospitality programs increase the attendance at conferences. This in turn increases revenue for the host property because guests of attendees will eat in the restaurants, shop in the stores, and make use of the numerous other services offered by a full-service host facility. For this reason, many host properties include in their bids examples of programs designed for the entertainment of conferences participants and their guests.

Hospitality programs have come a long way from the standard fashion show, shopping spree, or ladies' luncheons designed for housewives accompanying their husbands. Today's hospitality program participants are more likely to be male than ever before and/or a professional themselves. Therefore, their wants and desires are different from those of past participants. The addition of children as hospitality program participants is also another trend that must be addressed when planning hospitality programs. Although the meeting planner and association executives or one of the associations' committees are ultimately responsible for planning the hospitality program, the host property should play an integral part in the planning.

Design of Hospitality Programs

The history of a group must be carefully reviewed before plans are made for a hospitality program. Program evaluations from previous years should be analyzed to ascertain the groups likes and dislikes. Although it is not a good idea to repeat an entire program, sections of past programs that have been very successful can be used in conjunction with new programs.

In combination with the historical review, the meeting planner together with the host property should survey the participants in advance to determine the interest of this group. This survey would address the following areas:

1. Hobbies
2. Sports they enjoy
3. Ages of participants
4. Gender of participants

A list of the local sites and attractions as well as services provided by the hotel should also be included. Upon reviewing the sites, attractions, and host property services, the participants should be surveyed to determine whether or not there is interest in any of the suggested activities. Once this information is compiled, the meeting planner in collaboration with the host property can plan a program that is tailor-made for the participants. Since the host property is involved with the design of the program, they can ensure that the property is properly staffed for all activities.

When designing the program, meeting planners may make use of destination management companies. Destination management companies provide local on-site coordination of the hospitality program and any other special events necessary for the meeting planner. This service is especially helpful if the meeting planner is unfamiliar with the surroundings and/or does not have the time or resources available to visit often. The destination management company knows the location well and can provide excellent insight into the unique qualities of the area. They are also familiar with all of the local contacts and are able to work as a liaison for the group in developing the hospitality program.

Tour companies may also provide services for the meeting planner or group. Local tour companies may provide not only transportation needs for the group, but may also offer services such as planned tours around the state, staffing for the hospitality room, theme parties, and airport greetings (Hoyle, Dorf, and Jones 1989). The host property can provide an invaluable service by placing meeting planners or groups in contact with the local businesses that service conventions, meetings, and expositions.

The actual design of the program will vary from group to group, and within groups their programs will vary from year to year, but some components are present in most hospitality programs. These components are the hospitality suite, planned social activities, food and beverage activities, and free time.

The hospitality suite is provided to allow hospitality program participants a place to gather to meet new friends, reacquaint themselves with old friends, meet for tours, ask questions, or just to relax. The hospitality room should be located near the meeting rooms so as to provide easy access to the attendees. It should be comfortably appointed with furniture conducive to conversation. The hospitality suites are generally staffed by either a host property employee, a volunteer from the community, or a member of the association's local chapter. The attendant provides information about the community and should be well versed in the group's itinerary so as to be able to provide important information to the program participants.

Planned social activities for the hospitality program may include:

- Tours
- Plays
- Concerts
- Sporting events
- Tournaments
- Guest speakers
- Shopping trips
- Demonstrations
- Cooking lessons
- Craft activities
- Movies

These activities are chosen based on the interest of the group as well as the budget for the hospitality program. Programs are financed in a number of ways. Some groups pay for the programs out of registrations fees; others get corporate sponsorship. Another way to finance hospitality programs is to have the participants pay the cost. Social activities can also be financed by combining some of the above options.

The care and feeding of the hospitality program participants is also another area of concentration within hospitality programs. Food and beverage takes various forms in a hospitality program. This plan may include food in the hospitality suites. Some groups have continental breakfast, afternoon tea, evening cocktails, and late night snacks all served in the hospitality suite. Others may just provide sodas and coffee—again, the degree of service depends on the funding for the program. Other food and beverage functions may encompass the full range of functions to include breakfast, lunch, and dinner. If the funding is not available for an extensive food and beverage plan within the hospitality program, a recommended dining guide should be provided for the participants and the means of transportation to these establishments should be addressed. The concierge is an excellent resource for information in this area, and participants should be encouraged to make full use of the information services provided by the host facility.

Although a hospitality program should be structured, there should be free time built into the program. This free time enables participants to sightsee, relax, or visit with friends. Further, it enables the participants to fully enjoy their free time, by having information already provided in regard to major attractions, prices for the activities, and transportation options to and from the activities.

Another area that hospitality programs should address is children's programs. Children's programs are designed to entertain the young guests of program attendees during critical times on the agenda. These programs can be as elaborate as providing all-day activities, in the form of day camps, as well as supervision during the evening functions, or they can be as simple as a trip to the zoo. Programs can be fashioned to include both parents and children, or they can be designed to entertain children while their parents attend other social functions. Children's programs are very popular in many host facilities. Many full-service hotels and resorts have preexisting programs that can be used for the group. The inclusion of children's programs is becoming very popular with a number of groups. Individual or group baby-sitting might be provided through the hospitality program. If the hospitality program does not provide baby-sitting services, many host properties will offer baby-sitting services for a fee.

Once the program is developed, it is very important that the itinerary be marketed properly to assure adequate participation. This usually entails at least two mailings of the itinerary and various brochures describing the events to potential program participants. The host property should make sure that a full-color brochure of their property as well as a detailed description of all of their amenities be included in the first mailing.

Marketing of the hospitality program should continue on-site once the guest arrives. This can be accomplished through posters in the lobby, brochures and itineraries being placed in the registration packet, and fliers strategically placed throughout the host property. If the host property has a television information system showing the conference agenda, the hospitality program itinerary should be included on the daily calendar.

Servicing the participants requires careful attention. Again, as Callan said, you want the participants to feel comfortable, well cared for, and anxious to return (1991). The primary goal of any hospitality program is to ensure the well-being of its participants.

Types of Host Facilities

Convention Centers

According to the *CLC Glossary,* convention centers are facilities for meetings and expositions without sleeping rooms (1986). They are generally funded by the local government and are used to generate revenue for the city and the local hoteliers and merchants. Convention centers became popular civic projects during the 1960s and 1970s, when communities were trying to revitalize their economies. "By the late 1960's most major cities either had a convention center or desperately wanted one. After all, a center meant conventions, and conventions meant visitors and money" (Migdal 1991, p. 78).

The evolution of the convention center includes changes in architecture, services offered, and the overall square footage of the facilities. The first convention centers were nothing more than concrete blocks and steel beams. They were designed for function, not beauty. Today's convention centers are concerned with blending into the architecture of the community.

> Some centers, such as the Los Angeles Convention Center (figure 5-10), have become vital architectural additions to sky-lines in the destinations they serve: in San Diego, sail-like material covers a portion of the roof, adding a nautical touch; in Portland and Denver, thin steel and glass towers reach skyward; and in Seattle and San Francisco, the centers' beauty lies in their unobtrusiveness. (San Francisco's Moscone Center was built partially underground, while Seattle's Washington State Convention Center was constructed over a highway.) (Migdal 1991, p. 84).

Convention centers are generally housed in close proximity to hotels or other housing facilities, thus providing easy access to sleeping rooms for attendees. For example, the John B. Hynes Veterans Memorial Convention Center in Boston has 360,900 square feet of meeting space, 5 exhibit halls, an auditorium, a ballroom, and 41 fully equipped smaller rooms and is just a short walk from more than 5,000 luxury hotel rooms.

The typical center's services include space for exhibits, various types and styles of meeting rooms, food and beverage service for meeting and conference attendees, and concessions for exposition attendees and exhibitors. Because convention centers are designed for the specific purpose of hosting meetings, conventions, and expositions, they are devised with registration areas throughout the property to allow easy registration for different groups using the facility on the same day. There are also common areas for breaks and relaxing in between sessions.

Conference Centers

Conference centers are facilities designed to provide an environment where people can exchange ideas with a maximum of ease and comfort (Anthony 1987). Conference centers differ from convention centers in that they provide sleeping rooms for their guests. The conference center was created to meet the growing demand for specialized meetings. While many hotels were fairly successful in meeting these needs, most fell short of what conference and meeting planners demanded. Planners needed a facility that focused on the specific requirements of conferences rather than tourist travel. Thus, conference centers evolved. Currently there are over 150 conference centers within the United States and 30 outside of the United States.

Conference centers vary from location to location, but most have (Crystal 1989):

1. Dedicated single-purpose meeting space;
2. Superior audiovisual capabilities;
3. Oversized guest rooms with well-lit workspaces; and
4. Conference service personnel.

John Marenzana, a conference center developer and past president of IACC, thinks that "all forward-thinking conference centers need to have a new perspective that they are really in the education business, not just the facilities business" (Sanger 1990, p. 86). Therefore, conference centers are focusing more on understanding how the adult learner learns and concentrating on providing an environment that facilitates this learning.

Conference centers provide individual event coordinators or conference coordinators who fulfill the same duties as the convention service manager in a hotel. This individual provides the one-stop-shopping approach for the meeting planner by being intimately familiar with the group's needs and by having the authority to see that their needs are met.

Figure 5-10   Los Angeles Convention Center transforms L.A. skyline. (Courtesy: Los Angeles CVB.)

Growth trends in the conference and meeting industry support the need for more conference centers. To ensure the viability of these centers, careful attention must be given to location, design, and marketing. Haigh and Hudson predict that future sites for conference centers will include conference centers tied to universities as well as conference centers that are owned by individual corporations (1989, p. 19–20).

Hotels

The majority of meetings, conventions, and expositions are held in hotels, primarily because of their vast numbers. Theoretically, hotels have everything necessary to host a meeting or conference; therefore, with slight modifications, they could potentially host conventions and expositions.

Hotels are capable of providing sleeping rooms, meeting rooms, and food and beverage services as well as many other amenities sought by groups. In many areas, hotels are counting on a larger percentage of the room nights to come from the convention and meetings industry than ever before. Because of the overbuilding in the late 1970s and 1980s, meeting planners are finding that hotels are very anxious for business and that they will work very hard to be accommodating to their groups.

Limited Service Hotels

Limited service hotels are not perceived as typical meeting or conference sites. But there is a sizeable portion of the meeting's market that operate on very tight budgets and therefore are very interested in the product offered by a limited service hotel. The limited service hotel market has been segmented and now it offers something for everyone. "Traditionally, economy lodging has been defined to include properties with modern, fully furnished rooms, without food and beverage facilities on the premises and with rates 20 to 50 percent below the average market rate" (Braus 1989, p. 77). Limited service properties come in all shapes and sizes—there are budget hotels, limited service hotels, luxury budget hotels, mid-priced hotels, and so on (Braus 1989). These properties provide varying degrees of services that can meet the needs of many groups and therefore should not be discounted. The limited service hotel segment of the industry generally offers smaller properties; consequently, smaller groups don't feel lost.

Resorts

"The 1980's was the decade of resorts. Aided by favorable tax laws, a burgeoning meetings market, and a dramatic leap in airline travel, real estate developers and hoteliers reshaped a small, seasonal, upscale segment of the lodging industry—resorts—into a year-round hospitality product" (McGee 1990, p. 37). With the increased emphasis being placed on mixing business with pleasure, many groups are opting to hold meetings, conventions, or expositions at resorts to allow their attendees to get the best of both worlds. They can attend their meetings, but they can also have a nice mini-vacation.

Resorts understand the tremendous potential for increased revenues through providing services for group business and therefore have undergone restructuring to include small conference centers on their property. By focusing on providing excellent conference facilities and services, the resort industry has positioned itself to provide not only all amenities associated with conferences, meetings, and expositions, but also with vacations.

Florida resorts are perfect examples of resorts taking an active position in servicing meetings. Disney resorts have moved into the meetings arena and have quickly helped to make Florida the number one destination for meetings and conventions. The largest convention resort in Florida is the Walt Disney World Dolphin, operated by Sheraton and located in the new EPCOT Resort Area. This facility has over 200,000 square foot in meeting and banquet space, a 51,000 square foot exhibit hall, a 56,000 square foot ballroom, 10,000 square feet in outdoor function space, and 28 meeting rooms. Its amenities include 1,509 guest rooms and suites, a number of restaurants and lounges, tennis courts, access to 3 championship 18-hole Disney golf courses, 3 pools, including a themed swimming grotto, and a white-sand beach.

Nontraditional Host Facilities

Nontraditional host facilities have become quite prominent in the meetings and conventions arena. Today groups are holding meetings and conferences on cruise ships, on trains, in bed and breakfast inns, and at universities. The cruise lines have actively pursued the meetings and conventions industry because they understand how lucrative this business is. The facilities provided by various cruise lines equal that of many fine resorts. The pricing structure is also a positive aspect for the group because the quoted price includes everything from audiovisual equipment to round-trip airfare and ground transportation.

Cruise lines have made changes in the ships' design so as to make the ships ammenable to group business. They now have ships being built with meetings in mind (Letich 1991). No longer are the ships being built with low ceilings and slender walkways; today's ships truly look like fine resorts. Unfortunately, using cruise lines for meetings or conferences is still relatively cost prohibitive, and many groups may miss an outstanding opportunity because of the rather high cost.

Trains as host properties are another unique option for groups. The train provides an atmosphere that is conducive to meetings. Business executives, for example, can take advantage of the "captive atmosphere of the train to conduct meetings in relative seclusion" (Adams 1991, p. 112). The American-European Express Railway Company, which has routes between Chicago, Philadelphia, New York, and Washington, D.C., provides services that are perfect for small meetings of 100 people or less. They can provide the meeting space necessary, as well as sleeping quarters and food and beverage service. Trains provide a perfect solution for meetings that need to take place en route. For example, if a group of businessmen in Seattle need to make a presentation in Washington, D.C., and need to prepare for the presentation together prior to the meeting, a train would provide them the needed space and time.

Another segment of the hospitality business that has just recently started seeking meeting business is the bed and breakfast establishment. These inns were founded as strictly leisure and tourist housing facilities, but as the economy has shifted, many innkeepers have been looking for new ways to bolster business. Hosting small meetings is an excellent solution. "The stress-free atmosphere and historic architecture, decor and furnishings helps restore fresh thinking and encourages creative solutions" (Greco 1991, p. 48). Inn owners interested in this market segment have to make changes, so as to provide meeting space, allowing groups special seating during meals, and provide more business support systems, such as phones in every room and fax machines.

Colleges and universities are also wanting a piece of the meetings and conventions pie. Meetings and conventions provide an excellent source of revenue in the summer, a traditionally quiet time on many campuses. With the decrease in government funding, many campuses are beginning to rely on meetings and conventions to alleviate budgetary burdens.

Campuses can provide a wonderful change from the standard meetings and conventions atmosphere. Dorm living as well as campus dining can provide an environment that enhances team building. Those campuses that recognize their potential as a host facility are concentrating their efforts on providing upscale services for those groups that are interested and willing to pay for these services. "Many schools now provide full-service conference planning and coordination, hotel-quality food, special events planning, destination management services and more" (Letich 1991, p. 35).

Summary

The role of a host property is very important to the overall success of a meeting, convention, or exposition. Host properties have become integrally involved in the meetings, convention, and exposition industry and now are considered more of a partner with than a supplier to the industry. Host properties provide training for new meeting planners, as well as services beyond that of providing rooms and food and beverage. They now service the group by being involved in the design of the overall program, the hospitality program, and the food and beverage program. They have altered their meeting space to provide areas more conducive to adult learning.

There are many types of host properties, some traditional and some nontraditional. The traditional properties include hotels, convention centers, conference centers, and resorts. Newcomers to the meetings and conventions arena are trains, cruise lines, bed and breakfast inns, and universities. All of these categories have their own unique ambiance and services that they provide to a group. As the meetings, conventions, and exposition industry has become more professional and more sophisticated, host properties have had to respond to the challenge by taking a more active role in providing quality facilities and services to meet the growing demand of this vibrant segment of the hospitality industry.

References

Abbey, Astroff. 1988. *Convention Sales and Services,* Second Edition. Cranbury, New Jersey: Waterbury Press.

Adams, M. 1990. Hooked on Disney. *Successful Meetings,* (September) pp. 48–55.

Adams, M. 1991. Luxury express. *Successful Meetings,* (March) p. 112.

Alonzo, V. 1991. Boom time for the box lunch. *Meetings and Conventions,* (October) pp. 61–62, 66.

Anthony, C. 1987. Conference centers fast changing concept. *Hotel & Resort Industry,* (November) pp. 67–70.

Brause, P. 1990. Repackaging the conference center. *Successful Meetings,* (March) pp. 55–57.

Brause, P. 1989. Hold the frills: meeting at economy hotels. *Successful Meetings,* (June) pp. 77–81.

Callan, Roger J. 1990. Hotel award schemes as a measurement of service quality—an assessment by travel industry journalists as surrogate consumers. *International Journal of Hospitality Management,* 9(1):45–58.

Conlin, J. 1990. The challenge of the decade ahead. *Successful Meetings,* (January) pp. 74–78.

Coulton, A. 1989. Instant meetings. *Lodging Hospitality,* (November) pp. 59–60.

Crystal, S. 1991. Squeezed for time. *Meetings & Conventions,* (December) pp. 48–58.

Crystal, S. 1989. Conference centers reach out. *Meetings and Conventions,* (February) pp. 94, 100–109.

Dolan, P. 1990. The bottom line. *Successful Meetings,* (July) pp. 13–21.

Feiertag, H. 1991. Target corporate travelers and small meetings. *Hotel & Motel Management,* (March) pp. 15–16.

Feiertag, H. 1987. Back yard bookings help in boosting group business. *Hotel & Motel Management,* (202) 16.

Ghitelman, D. 1988. Good-bye to the concrete box. *Meetings & Conventions,* 23(8):62–76.

Greco, G. 1991. The inn places. *Meetings & Conventions,* (May) pp. 46–50, 56.

Grimaldi, L. 1991. It ain't just java. *Meetings & Conventions,* (October) pp. 49–52.

Haigh, S., and R.W. Hudson. 1989. *Understanding Conference Centers.* Fenton, Mo: IACC.

Hoyle, L.H., Dorf, D.C., and T.J.A. Jones. 1989. Managing conventions and group business. East Lansing, Michigan: The Educational Institute of the American Hotel & Motel Association.

Jurgens, J. 1989. Kernels of wisdom. *Meetings and Conventions,* (December) pp. 56–69.

Lieberman, G. 1991. Educational programs, what's in it for you. *Meetings & Conventions* (February) pp. 33–34, 41.

Letich, L. 1991. When small meetings happen in big places. *Meetings & Conventions.* (November) pp. 67–73.

Letich, L. 1991. Meetings ahoy. *Meetings and Conventions,* (September) pp. 80–83.

Letich, L. 1991. Convening on campus. *Meetings and Conventions, (July).*

Lodging. 1987. Turning the right faucets on and off. (June) 55–57.

McGee, R. 1990. Transformation of resorts. *Successful Meetings,* (January) pp. 48–52.

Meeting & Conventions. 1989. Planners and suppliers face off. (April) pp. 63–69.

Midgal, D. 1991. The boom goes on. *Meetings & Conventions,* (August) pp. 78, 84, 89.

Ramsborg, G. 1991. Educational is vital to the professional planner. *The Meeting Manager,* (September) pp. 20–21.

Salomon, A. Crowne plazas tackle meetings. *Hotel & Motel Management,* pp. 2, 45.

Sanger, K., and T. Sanger. February. Conference centers: brain power for planners. *Meetings and Conventions.*

Sawyer, J. 1990. Gods for day. *Successful Meetings,* (September) pp. 294.

Shaw, M. 1990. *Convention Sales.* Michigan: Educational Institute.

Successful Meetings. 1991. State of the industry. (July) pp. 7–63.

Tannenhaus, N. 1986. Hilton hotels take meeting planners behind-the-scenes. *Hotel & Resort Industry,* (May) pp. 82–83.

Zack, D. 1989. Reception rules. *Meetings & Conventions,* (March) p. 45.

Zack, D. 1989. The coffee break. *Meetings & Conventions,* (March) p. 54.

Discussion Questions

1. What are the main functions of a host property?
2. How do the key players in a host facility interact with one another? Why is this interaction important to the success of the meeting, convention, or exposition?
3. What are the benefits in having a convention service department and providing "uni-service" to prospective sponsors?
4. Why is a preconvention meeting important? Who should be involved with this meeting?
5. Design an agenda for a preconvention meeting.
6. How does room format affect the overall success of the meeting?
7. A tremendous amount of emphasis is placed on the comfort of the participant. What can a host facility do to ensure the comfort of its guest during meetings, conventions, and expositions?
8. Develop a food and beverage program for a two-day mini-conference.

Key Terms

convention center	check-in/check-out
conference center	auditorium style seating
cruise ships	classroom seating
resorts	opening reception
hotels	refreshment break
multipurpose facility	off-premise event
host property	themed event
director of marketing	final banquet
convention service department	hospitality suite
preconvention meeting	spousal/hospitality program
room block	limited service facility
cocooning	non-traditional host facility

6

Trade Shows

Learning Objectives

1. To understand the purpose and marketing benefits of trade shows.
2. To appreciate the economic benefits that trade shows bring to the host city.
3. To identify the six major players in the trade show industry, including the show manager, the general service contractor, the specialty contractor, the exhibitor, facilities, and the attendee.
4. To understand the role each of these play and how they inter-relate with one another.
5. To become familiar with the Trade Show Bureau.
6. To understand how selling at trade shows compares with making sales calls, as far as cost-effectiveness is concerned.
7. To become familiar with how EC 1992 may affect the international trade show industry.

Introduction

As discussed in chapter 3, trade shows are designed to bring together individuals associated with a common business or activity for the purpose of reviewing materials and products related to their common interest. In this chapter we will examine the various players and their roles in trade shows. We will also address the marketing aspects of trade shows. Finally, we will discuss the economic implications of trade shows and how the globalization of the world will affect this industry.

Purpose of Trade Shows

The primary purpose of a trade show is to provide an arena for the exchange of information between companies and potential clients. Trade shows are quickly being recognized as a major segment of a company's marketing mix. Trade shows present the state of the art for an industry to both the exhibitors and the attendees (see figure 6-1). Exhibitors can compare their products to those of their competitors, while attendees have the ability to closely examine competitive products.

The trade show forum is also ideal for introducing and testing new products, thus allowing for feedback about the potential success of these products in the marketplace. Therefore, trade shows not only serve as part of the marketing mix, but also provide a medium for research and development.

Trade shows are an extremely lucrative business venture and serve as a source of revenue for the show sponsor (see chapter 3 for a more thorough discussion of trade show sponsors). In the case of an association-sponsored trade show, "the revenue received from the rental of booth space is second only to the annual membership fees as a source of income to the association" (Hoyle, Dorf, and Jones 1989, p. 318).

Not only are trade shows profitable for the sponsoring organization, but they also provide revenue for the host city and all related businesses. For instance, revenue from a trade show begins with hall rental and includes the employment of all those involved in the setup and move-in of a trade show. Carpenters, plumbers, electricians, florists, and drayage companies are usually hired from within the host city, thus increasing the employment oppor-

Figure 6-1　Anderson windows at the National Association of Home Builders Show held in Chicago at the Sherman House in the early 1950s. The demonstration draws interested prospects and highlights how an Anderson window operates. (Courtesy: Kitzing Inc.)

tunities within cities that host major trade shows. The Trade Show Bureau estimates that an average of 1.8 jobs are created for each delegate (attendee) that attends a trade show.

Exhibitors also have an economic impact (see figure 6-2) through their use of hotels for hosting hospitality suites for their clients and using restaurants to entertain potential customers. Delegates add to the revenue by renting rooms from local hotels as well as spending money in restaurants and shops. Any time an exhibitor or delegate simply buys a local newspaper, catches a cab, or picks up a toothbrush from a drug store, the host city has benefited economically from the trade show. Overall, the economic impact tradeshows have on a community is very significant and underscores the reasons for cities becoming involved in the trade show industry.

	Spending Generated Per Delegate Stay			**Spending Generated Per Delegate Day**		
Trade Show Delegate						
Delegate Expenditure	$518.65	$540.12	$584.95	$126.50	$131.74	$142.67
Association Expenditure	54.40	56.65	61.35	13.27	13.82	14.97
Exhibitor Expenditures	274.33	285.69	309.40	66.91	69.68	75.46
Expo Srv Contractor Exp	19.11	19.90	21.56	4.66	4.85	5.26
	------	------	------	------	------	------
	$866.49	$902.36	$977.26	$211.34	$220.09	$238.36
	------	------	------	------	------	------
Breakdown of Delegate Expenditures						
Hotel Room & Incidentals	$264.56	$275.51	$298.38	$64.30	$66.96	$72.51
Hotel Restaurant	56.87	59.22	64.14	13.87	14.43	15.63
Other Restaurant	59.08	61.53	66.63	14.41	15.01	16.26
Hospitality Suites	26.86	27.97	30.29	6.55	6.82	7.39
Entertainment	25.95	27.02	29.27	6.56	6.83	7.40
Retail Stores	42.44	44.20	47.87	10.35	10.78	11.67
Local Transportation	22.39	23.32	25.25	5.46	5.69	6.16
Other	20.50	21.35	23.12	5.00	5.22	5.65
	------	------	------	-----	-----	-----
TOTAL	$518.65	$540.12	$584.95	$126.50	$131.74	$142.67

Figure 6-2   IACVB Economic Impact Chart. (Courtesy: IACVB.)

Show Manager/Show Organizer/Show Producer

The show manager or exposition manager is an employee of an association or a show management company, or is a private entrepreneur, who performs tasks such as conceptualization and development of shows, their sales, marketing, advertising, and promotion to qualified attendees. The show manager's job is concerned with the infinite details of selling the show, moving in the show, setting up the show, executing the show, and moving the show out of the convention or trade show facility. (Rutherford 1990, p. 51)

The show manager's top priority has traditionally been to sell the floor space to exhibitors. Chapman, in fact, says show managers could be considered "real estate people who rent an exhibition hall" (*Exhibit Marketing* 1987, p. 257). There is a tremendous amount of behind-the-scenes work included in a show manager's job. They are responsible for marketing the show to potential exhibitors, selecting the show site, making hotel arrangements, developing educational programs, arranging for preshow and/or postshow activities, and overseeing all logistical planning. The show manager's job is made even more complicated by new demands on the position. As the trade show industry evolves, show managers are being required to develop more expertise in managing a marketing medium, "just like the publisher of a newspaper or a radio station manager" (p. 257).

The procedure by which a show is created and implemented varies. Sometimes a show manager develops a new idea for a potential trade show, books a facility to host it, and then sells the show to potential exhibitors. In the case of associations, a manager could be hired by an association to oversee its annual trade show or the association could have an in-house show manager. In any case, one of the manager's first priorities is to recruit potential exhibitors. In order to do this, show managers send out a show prospectus to potential exhibitors. A good prospectus will include the dates and location of the show, past attendance figures, past exhibitors, floor rental prices, and other basic information. A potential exhibitor should be able to make an informed decision about participating in the show based on the prospectus.

After an exhibitor decides to take part in a show, communication between the exhibitor and the show producer begins and will continue until the show ends. The producer keeps in constant communication with each exhibitor for the months preceding the show. One of the first and most important pieces of communication the manager mails out is the *exhibitor manual* (or *service kit*), a packet containing "the rules of the exposition organizer and exposition hall, along with a set of contracts and promotional pieces offering products and services from the official service contractor" (Chapman, *Expositions Work* 1989, p. 30). The exhibitor kit also includes information on payment expectations and insurance coverage provided (Chapman, *Exhibit Marketing* 1987, p. 16). (For more discussion on the service order forms included in the Exhibitor Manual, see the "General Service Contractors" section in this chapter.)

Perhaps the most important part of a show organizer's job is to market the show to the intended attendee base. Without attendees, the show fails. The attendee base may be a fairly specific segment of the population or, in the case of consumer shows, it may be the general public. The manager must know how to reach the intended audience as well as oversee the logistics of ticket sales and registration. Most show attendees register in advance, but some shows may allow people to walk into the facility, literally "off the street."

The show manager must also evaluate the show and verify such facts as attendance and exhibition presence. In the case of annual shows, the manager uses this evaluation to improve the next year's show, as well as to provide needed demographic information to exhibiting companies. (For more discussion on show managers, see chapter 3).

Contractors

The general service contractor is a major behind-the-scenes player whose function is to provide all major services to exhibition management and exhibitors for a trade show. Contractors actually service two levels of customers: (1) show management and (2) the individual exhibitors. These two customers have different needs during the setup and run of the show, and the general service contractor is responsible for working with both sets of needs.

When show managers begin planning a show, they send out requests for proposals to the sales departments of general contracting firms. The managers provide the contractors with detailed information about the show and its needs. Based on this information, the contractors then present the managers with two proposals for services. One proposal outlines the services provided for the management and what they will cost, and the other outlines the services provided for the individual exhibitors and what they will cost. The show manager typically selects one contractor to become the "official general" service contractor for that event. Figures 6-3a and 6-3b illustrate some of the activities performed by general service contractors.

(a)

(b)

Figure 6-3 (a) Building a booth. (b) Decorators at work. (Courtesy: The Freeman Company.)

Below is a list of services most general contractors provide their two levels of customers:

Show Management Services

General decorating—Registration, offices, entrance ways

Pipe and drape setup

Booth setup

Carpet rental

Furniture rental

Signage and graphics

On-site coordination for show

Advance planning for show

Labor and union contracting and management

Cleaning service

Drayage and material handling

Exhibitor Services

Rental exhibit options

Hospitality suite setup

Booth signage

Labor union contracting and management

Carpet rental

Furniture rental

Signage and graphics

Installation and dismantling services

There are other services that demand a high level of specialized expertise, such as floral arranging. If a need for one of these services arises, the general service contractor or show manager arranges for a specialized company, considered a "specialty contractor," to provide this service. Speciality contractors provide services either directly to exhibitors or sometimes as a subcontractor to the general service contractor. In the case of the Sands Expo Center in Las Vegas, Nevada, it has its own in-house florist, catering service, badge making shop, cleaning service, and so on, but the individual exhibitor is not required to use them. Below is a list of specialty services usually subcontracted out:

Specialized Services Provided by Specialty Contractors

Floral

Catering

Photography
Over-the-road transportation
Telephone/fax services
Modeling/supplemental booth personnel
AV rental
Security and security boxes
Electrical
Plumbing, air, and water
Exhibit design and construction

Some of these services may already be provided by the facility hosting the show. For instance, most facilities provide plumbing, air, water, and often electrical service. In that case, the facility itself acts as a specialty contractor.

"Drayage" refers to local material handling. Drayage includes shipping the booth from the local warehouse to the exhibition hall, transporting it from the truck to the booth site, and then returning it to the truck after the show. In addition, some exhibitors ship their booths to the general contractor a few weeks in advance of the show date. The contractor will then store the booth for the exhibitor and have it delivered to the hall for setup. Drayage also includes storing empty crates during the run of the trade show (Rutherford p. 207).

The exhibitor services department of a general service contractor sends order forms listing the many services an exhibitor may want or need to order. These forms are included in the exhibitor manual, which is mailed to exhibitors well in advance of the show. The exhibitors complete the forms and return them to the general service contractor, who processes these orders. This process is extremely complicated and demands constant, detailed communication between the show manager, the facility, the general service contractor, specialty subcontractors, and the exhibitors.

Once the show begins, representatives from the sales department (known as account executives) become staff members for the show manager and usually are present for the entire event to ensure that it runs smoothly. The account executives oversee the often-confusing setup of a show. During setup, the freight arrives, material is unloaded and delivered to the correct booth space on the floor, signs are hung, utilities connected, carpet is laid, and booths are put up. (Figures 6-4a, 6-4b, and 6-4c illustrate the stages of trade show setup.) All this activity occurs in a very concen-

(a)

(b)

(c)

146

trated, short amount of time and demands detailed planning and competent on-site management.

During the run of the show, the account executives mediate any labor disputes that arise and make sure the specialty subcontractors provide the expected services. The general service contractor signs the contract with the union.

After the show, the account executives are responsible for overseeing the move-out of the show. They also invoice the show manager and the exhibitors. (Exhibitors rent floor space from the show manager, but they buy other services and materials, such as signage, booth rental, or special decorating, from the general service contractor or exhibitor appointed contractor [EAC].)

Contractors can become very familiar with a particular show's needs and offer more efficient service if they service the same show year after year. Therefore, many managers who plan annual trade shows prefer multiyear contracts with their general service contractors. With multiyear contracts, as soon as one year's show ends, the contractor and the manager begin planning for the next year's show.

Exhibitors

According to the *CLC Glossary*, an exhibitor is simply the "company or organization sponsoring [the] exhibit booth" (1986, p. 16). Chapman (1987) further explains the responsibilities of the position: "Exhibitors rent space, purchase an exhibit, have it transported and set up, all in return for an opportunity to sell and are ultimately responsible for making a decision to participate at any show" (p. 254). For example, at a restaurant industry show, exhibiting companies might include food distributors, restaurant machinery distributors, restaurant and cooking schools, and companies that produce specialty cooking ingredients, such as spices or cooking oils. Figure 6-6 shows a food distributor serving up helpings of "Southern Style Chicken Chili" at the International Poultry Show in Atlanta. In between servings he dishes out information about the products.

Who serves as the exhibit manager for a company? According to Chapman (1987), there are basically two categories of managers.

Figure 6-4   (a) Trade show setup—Stage 1. (b) Trade show setup—Stage 2. (c) Trade show setup—Stage 3. (Courtesy: The Freeman Companies.)

```
Ellen Beckert
Director of Corporate Development
The Freeman Companies
```

The Freeman Companies, one of the nation's largest general service contractors, is composed of five individual companies who provide different services for trade shows and conventions. The Freeman Companies employs over 17 major convention city locations in the United States and Canada.

As The Freeman Companies' Director of Corporate Development, Ellen Beckert is experienced in all aspects of the general contracting industry. "The advantage of the industry is you get a lot of satisfaction in being able to produce something yourself," she explains. "What's interesting about trade shows is you're seeing the cutting edge of every industry. You get a sneak preview on life."

Beckert, a former teacher, has solid advice for hospitality students. She recommends that they try to learn about the industry "from the ground up" and work in the convention services side rather than just the sales side. "You have to know how it works before you can get into the management of it. You have to understand what you're selling. Work the service side of the industry so you'll know what it is you will be purchasing if you go into meeting planning or show management."

Figure 6-5   Interview with Ellen Beckert. (Courtesy: Freeman Companies.)

The first group includes company managers, business owners, sales managers, sales staff members, or corporate communications employees, all of whom coordinate their company's exhibits as an added job responsibility. These people are "part-time exhibit managers" because their involvement in trade shows is just part of a larger job. The second group of exhibitors are "full-time exhibitors," who consider themselves professional exhibit specialists. For these people, trade show and exhibition management is their career (p. vii-viii). These professionals are only found in the larger corporations, where their title may be Corporate Exhibit Manager, reflecting their exhibition responsibilities (p. 272).

Exhibit managers have several key duties (See "Ten Steps to Trade Fair Success" p. 150). First, they may help their company

Figure 6-6 *Exhibitors sell their products to interested attendees. (Courtesy: Kitzing inc.)*

select which trade shows to participate in. Once a show has been decided upon, managers are in charge of the logistics of moving their displays in and out of the facility. They recruit, train, and supervise their booth staff. Managers are also responsible for making sure that the exhibiting company sells as desired during the show. They are there to make a profit, and so it is the manager's responsibility to do everything possible to make sure that sales can and do happen. For instance, managers oversee transactions with potential customers visiting the booth, evaluate orders placed, and keep the display looking professional and inviting throughout the run of the show. They are responsible for effectively integrating the trade show activity or event into the overall market plan.

TEN STEPS TO TRADE FAIR SUCCESS

The following steps are crucial for show managers in planning a successful outcome for any trade show program:

1. Secure management support.
2. Set specific and realistic objectives.
3. Do a market analysis and adequate research.
4. Select a specific trade show that coincides with your market targets.
5. Plan an adequate budget.
6. Develop preshow promotion.
7. Create professional staff for the booth.
8. Learn how to sell and effectively negotiate during the exhibition.
9. Follow up trade show leads carefully and immediately.
10. Evaluate and measure the performance and results of a trade show.

Source: Trade Show Bureau, "Reaching Export Objectives through International Trade Fairs," 1991.

Attendees

Those people who attend trade shows and expositions to buy from the exhibitors and/or learn more about their industry are called the show attendees or delegates. The attendee's perspective of shows is very different from the show manager's and the exhibitor's. We will look at how the attendee views a show as well as examine the show manager's and the exhibitor's views on the attendees.

There are several different kinds of attendees at trade shows, including serious, qualified customers, trade show press, and what Miller (1990) calls "lookie-loos" (p. 18). Lookie-loos, as the name implies, are just curious people, often members of the general public, if the show is open (versus closed to trade only), who have no qualifications or intentions to buy. If you are an exhibitor, your goal is to politely excuse yourself from prolonged conversation with these nonbuying attendees in order to identify and spend time with serious customers.

Trade show managers hold a different view of such attendees. Managers are often interested in having as many attendees as possible, because high attendance figures make marketing future shows easier. An exhibitor will be more interested in participating in a show with 3,000 attendees than one with 2,000, even though half of those 3,000 attendees may not be serious buyers. In fact, there are now a few "private" shows that actually open themselves up to the public on their last day, in order to increase their official attendance count. Managers point out, however, that exhibitors can benefit from public attendance in indirect ways. Having greater public attendance helps promote and market the exhibiting companies, almost like "free" advertising. Therefore, exhibitors can benefit from having a certain number of "lookie-loos" view their booth, even if they don't buy.

However, a true business-to-business trade show is geared towards serious, qualified delegates. These attendees are *the* targeted audience. Any number of people from a particular company might serve as the show attendees, including CEOs, middle managers, sales managers, or buyers (see table 6-1).

Table 6-1 *Trade Show Attendees*

Job Function	First Time Attendees, %	Previous Attendees, %
Top management	15	25
Middle management	11	9
Engineer, R&D	21	20
Production	4	2
Sales & marketing	11	11
Purchasing	3	2
Data processing	7	7
Professional	9	10
Consultant	1	3
Educator	1	1
All others	12	8
Undefined	5	2
	100%	100%

Source: Trade Show Bureau research publication, *Understanding and Influencing Your Audience*, 1991.

Historically, trade shows have been viewed as a social event with no accountability for time or purchases. Thirty years ago 90 percent of the shows were produced by associations who had "no selling" clauses in their show contracts. This is no longer the case. Attendees now have specific plans and goals to make the most of their time on the trade show floor. Today's companies have invested a great deal of time and money to send representatives to trade shows, and many of these visitors have traveled long distances to attend the show (see figure 6-7).

Buying and selling at trade shows have become serious, professional ventures. According to 1991 figures from the Trade Show Bureau, 76 percent of the show visitors arrive with an agenda. "Fifty-seven percent of first-time attendees and 64% of previous attendees have made buying plans based on what they saw at the show" (Trade Show Bureau 1991). While at the show, these visitors dedicate a great deal of time to viewing the products and services featured. "Over a two-day period, more than one-third of trade show visitors spend over 8 hours at exhibits. The average visitor spends 13 minutes at each of 26 exhibits" (*Trade Show Bureau Composite Data* 1991, p. 16).

Trade Show Bureau

In 1978, twelve industry groups realized that a neutral, non-issue-oriented organization was needed to address the trade show industry. They founded the Trade Show Bureau for the sole purpose of "promoting trade shows as a bona fide marketing medium—a vital

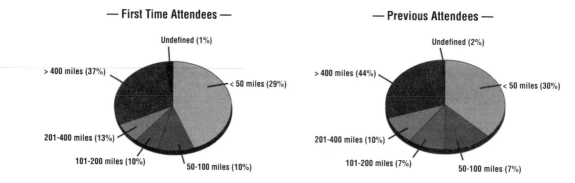

Figure 6-7   Miles they travel to show. (Courtesy: Trade Show Bureau.)

component in the marketing mix that could match or exceed comparable investments in other marketing venues" (TSB 1991). (See interview with TSB President, Jane Lorimar, figure 6-8.) To achieve this end, the Trade Show Bureau researches studies pertaining to industry trends and effective marketing practices. Corporate thinking regarding trade shows has traditionally been less than positive, but the Trade Show Bureau has managed to give the industry both credence and respect. Today, there are 17 sponsoring organizations and over 700 subscribing members of the Bureau. The mission statement of the Trade Show Bureau sums up their purpose: "To position trade shows and expositions as the primary marketing medium used to promote and sell products and services."

Marketing

As the trade show industry becomes more sophisticated, those responsible for the marketing of products or services will start to recognize what the trade show industry already knows. In a 1990 report by the American Business Press, trade shows were ranked as the second most useful advertising medium (see figure 6-9). The only medium perceived as more successful was specialized business publications.

Traditionally, the trade show has been separate from the typical marketing mix, because executive decision makers have not been educated on the marketing value of trade shows. Consequently, their lack of involvement has diluted credibility from the importance of trade shows as a marketing option. It has been an uphill battle for organizations such as the Trade Show Bureau to educate not only CEOs but also the business community about the effectiveness of trade shows as part of the standard marketing mix.

Due to the efforts of trade show associations, successful companies are starting to understand the importance of the trade show as a marketing tool, not just the social event it used to be. These companies are hiring and training exhibit managers who understand the importance of trade shows as a primary sales tool. A trade show specialist is a professional who is able to manage a booth that welcomes prospective buyers, qualifies those customers, and provides vitally important information about the product or services sold. A review of industry figures reveals the cost effectiveness of trade shows. According to a Trade Show Bureau

E. Jane Lorimar
President
Trade Show Bureau

Lorimar, President of the Trade Show Bureau, has had a great deal of experience in the trade show industry. In fact, before joining the Trade Show Bureau, Lorimar established and managed a major corporate exhibit program for a large American brewing company that participated in over 200 shows annually.

Lorimar has insight regarding all the different players in the industry. For example, she describes the job of a show manager as "playing matchmaker between the attendees (the buyers) and the exhibitors (the sellers)." Locating the right exhibitors and locating the right attendees are equally important in the show manager's job.

She also understands the important role of the trade show attendee. "Generally, the end user of the trade show is the attendee. If they are not satisfied, they will not come back or they will not stay. That means you lose the exhibitor, and when you lose the exhibitor you have no event. In addition, it's important to realize that the attendee of today is far more sophisticated than people realize."

How have trade shows evolved over the years? Lorimar explains that in the 1950s trade shows were primarily social events, and 90 percent were sponsored by associations. Exhibitors went to trade shows to maintain good client relations and to keep up with trends in their industry. Most trade shows, in fact, contained a "no-selling" clause in the exhibitor contracts. Lorimar explains, however, that now "the opportunity to sell at shows has increased. The mix has changed and the purpose has changed." Today, 60 percent of trade shows are produced by associations and 40 percent are produced by independent show organizers.

"The wonderful trend that I see is that trade shows are becoming recognized as a selling/buying opportunity, and the relationship between the seller and the buyer is becoming stronger on the trade show floor," Lorimar says.

Lorimar suggests that hospitality students decide which aspect of the industry they want to be in: the logistics side or the marketing side. "It's great if they have the talent to do both, but most people don't. People need to recognize that it is hard to be all things to all people. I would urge students to take, at a minimum, an introduction to marketing course and some business courses. Students need an understanding of how businesses, either for-profit or not-for-profit, make money."

Figure 6-8 Interview with Jane Lorimar. (Courtesy: Trade Show Bureau.)

Research Publication, it costs an average of $1,114 in personal sales calls to close a deal, compared to trade shows, which cost an average of $349 to close a deal. These figures further reflect the fact that it takes an average of 4.3 personal calls to close a sale in the field as opposed to 0.8 follow-up calls to make a sale that has been initiated at a trade show (Trade Show Bureau 1991).

One of the most difficult aspects of marketing is the identification of new sales leads. It is very hard for a sales staff to devote a large portion of their time to identifying potential customers, especially when the sales force works on commission. A trade show brings prospective customers to you. These prospective clients have taken an average of 30 hours out of their busy schedules for the specific purpose of reviewing and comparing products that they are interested in purchasing. "Exhibitors meet new people, uncover unknown buying influences (see figure 6-10), and also discover that 83% of their visitors have not been seen by one of their salespeople in the preceding twelve months" (Trade Show Bureau 1990).

Another unique aspect of trade shows is the ability for hands-on demonstration of existing and new products (see figure 6-11). It is very difficult for salespeople to carry anything but the most recent

Ranking media in terms of usefulness on a scale of 1 to 10 — with scores indexed to 100 — trade shows come up second.

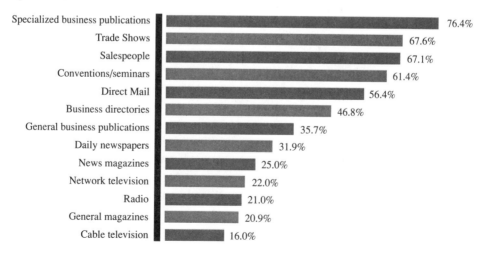

Figure 6-9   Trade shows rated second most useful ad medium. (Courtesy: American Business Press.)

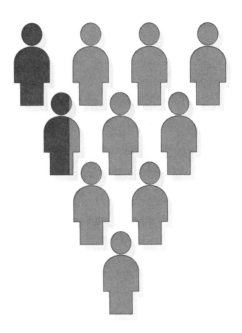

Exhibitors meet new people, uncover unknown buying influences, and also discover that 83% of their visitors have not been seen by one of their salespeople in the preceding twelve months! This statistic has remained constant for ten years.

Figure 6-10 Trade shows reach unknown prospects. (Courtesy: Andrews, Bartlett & Associates, Inc.)

samples (assuming their product can be carried) to their customers. It is as equally difficult for printed material to give a complete representation of a product to a prospective customer. Therefore, the introduction of new products is often difficult. In a trade show, many of a company's major products can be exhibited for consumers to examine (see figure 6-12). This is extremely important for companies that sell large equipment or rely on sensory stimulation to pique interest.

Economic Impact

Trade shows are not an American phenomena. European trade shows are extremely successful. In fact, the top 100 shows in Germany average 77,000 attendees, compared to 22,000 for the top 100 U.S. trade shows (Trade Show Bureau 1990). With the recent political, social, and/or economic developments in Europe, Asia, the former Soviet Union, Canada, and Mexico, the arena in which trade shows operate has increased tremendously in size. The movement towards a global economy has serious implications for the trade show industry.

In 1992, a single European Economic Community (EC) became a reality. This removed trade barriers between 12 of the Western European countries, allowing for the free flow of goods and services from country to country. It created a single market of 325 million people and a gross domestic product worth $4.7 trillion, a figure that is just slightly less than that of the United States (Conlin 1989, p. 33).

The U.S. Department of Commerce is fostering international relationships through the development of a division of experts,

Figure 6-11   In-booth trade show demonstrations are popular in specialty equipment market association shows. Demonstrations help sell the product. (Courtesy: Specialty Equipment Market Association.)

Figure 6-12   This exceptional trade show exhibit allows exhibitors to perform "hands-on" demonstrations which enhances the sensory perceptions of the attendees. (Courtesy: Display Systems, Ltd.)

whose sole purpose is to provide counseling on specific countries and/or industries within these countries. Their expertise allows American companies to research not only the products but also the protocol of countries they wish to do business with. Exports currently account for 4 percent of the gross national product. It is the hope of the Department of Commerce that this new division will enable the United States to participate in more overseas trade shows. This will bring foreign buyers to U.S. shows, thus increasing the demand for American-manufactured products, and therefore playing an important role in decreasing the U.S. trade deficit.

All of the implications of the EC 1992 are unknown. However, based on the breakdown of trade barriers, the trade show and exposition industry is facing a new frontier, one that will change forever the concept of trade shows.

Craig Smith
Senior Vice President
Andrews, Bartlett & Associates, Inc.
Hudson, Ohio

Craig Smith joined Andrews, Bartlett as a Senior Vice President in May 1981. Andrews, Bartlett is one of the country's largest general service contractors. The company includes five divisions: (1) an exposition service contractor, which designs, produces, and furnishes trade shows, (2) an A/V production division, (3) an independent service contractor offering installation and dismantling, (4) a communications/advertising/marketing division, and (5) a carpet rental division.

Smith points out the uneven nature of the industry. "Producing a trade show has tremendous peaks and valleys. You need a great number of people to start a show, very few people while it's running, and then a great number of people to close it down." Having enough people to put the event together is crucial, since, as Smith says, "There is nothing more absolute than the deadline for a trade show."

Smith explains that, furthermore, the industry is cyclical in nature. "In October, you can't get enough people for equipment to produce the business you have. In July, you could cut your work force in half. However, you have to maintain a core of knowledgeable, dedicated, committed people, and you have to keep the equipment on hand for when you need it. You have to carry overhead during times when it makes no sense on paper."

What is in store for the future of contracting? "I perceive a shift to where the specialty contractor will have a more direct relationship with the exhibitor," Smith says. "There are some specialty contractors, such as a modeling agency, who focus their marketing efforts specifically on companies who happen to participate in trade shows. This specialty contractor will accompany that exhibitor to all its shows and treat the exhibitor professionally, Exhibitors are demanding to be treated like a customer. That's why these specialty contractors have been able to become a bigger part of the industry."

Smith captures the essence of the trade show industry by describing it as "planned chaos." He continues, "On the surface, trade shows appear to be magic. But it is hard work, a major dose of common sense, and logistics. The harder you work in advance and the more you plan, the more successful you are. It's one of the most exciting industries you can be a part of."

Figure 6-13 Interview with Craig Smith. (Courtesy: Andrews, Bartlett & Associates, Inc.)

Elwood H. Hasemann
Vice President—Exhibitions
The Association for Manufacturing Technology (AMT)

Elwood H. Hasemann has been with The Association for Manufacturing Technology (AMT), founded in 1902 as the National Machine Tool Builder's Association (NMTBA), since 1968. As Vice President—Exhibitions, he oversees the association's biennial trade show, called the International Manufacturing Technology Show (IMTS), as well as AMT overseas shows and pavilions. The IMTS is held in even years in Chicago's McCormick Place, filling nearly 1 million net square feet. It is the preeminent exhibition for this industry in the United States. The IMTS in 1990 attracted over 16,000 visitors and 1,200 exhibiting companies.

How do you define an association trade show producer? "The member of the association staff who is designated to organize, market, and implement the show or shows," answers Hasemann, although he emphasizes that other duties vary widely, depending upon the size and purpose of the association and its trade show.

Hasemann talks about the goals of association trade show managers. "The show is one of the most visible activities of an organization, so you strive to make it the most important of all the shows in the industry your association represents. Secondly, because your members are also your exhibitors or attendees, you want to make sure the show survives. We are representing just our industry. We don't have the option to try something different if a show runs its course, unlike an independent show manager."

Like many associations, AMT considers its trade show its most important and most visible single event. However, the show is not exclusive. "It's a major member service," Hasemann explains, "But nearly two-thirds of our exhibitors are not even members." The association also considers its other activities, such as political activism, as important and necessary services.

Association trade shows have changed over the past few decades. Hasemann explains, "Historically, at least in the United States, shows weren't perceived as a place to do serious business, but a place to socialize. However, as marketing has become more sophisticated and the cost of participating in shows has gone up, trade shows have had to deliver. They have become more sophisticated and market-driven at all levels, and I think the industry will be better for it."

Hasemann has many suggestions for students interested
in getting into the trade show business. There are
numerous options in entering the industry. And they
can give experience that can apply to most career
goals. "Some of the areas that show managers are
weakest in are the handling and shipping of freight
and dealing with foreign exhibitors, so get some
experience in those areas. Communication skills and
general business skills, such as budgeting and accounting, are important. When it comes down to it,
however, on-the-job training is the bottom line."

"People have asked me how I can do the same show time
after time," Hasemann says. "I tell them that it's not
the same show. Every one is different. Each event
takes on its own personality and set of problems."

*Figure 6-14   Interview with Elwood Hasemann. (Courtesy:
The Association for Manufacturing Technology.)*

Summary

Trade shows, a growing marketing medium, provide a forum for
companies to display and sell their product to a specialized audience. They are cost-effective for exhibiting companies and provide
economic benefits for the hosting city. There are several key players in the trade show industry, all of whom must communicate and
work together to make shows run smoothly and successfully (see
figures 6-13 and 6-14). The show manager is the overall director of
a trade show. Managers oversee all aspects of planning and implementing trade shows, including selling floor space to exhibitors.
The manager signs a contract with a general service contractor,
who provides all the services to the manager and to the individual
exhibitors. Services include providing drayage (material handling), decorating the exhibit hall and the booths, and contracting
with labor unions. The general service contractor may also subcon-
tract specialized services, such as photography, to a specialty
contractor. The exhibitors are companies who sponsor booths at
the trade show. Some larger companies who attend many shows
have "Corporate Exhibit Managers," whose main responsibility is
to oversee all aspects of that company's trade show participation.
The attendees or delegates are those people who attend trade
shows to buy or learn more about their industry. Other attendees
include the press and the general public. The Trade Show Bureau
has been active in promoting this medium to businesses and the

general public, and their research reveals the tremendous cost-effectiveness of the shows. With the formation of the EC in 1992, Europe became a unified market and new trade show opportunities were created. Due to this expansion, it is predicted that American participation in international shows will increase.

References

Chapman, E. A. 1987. Exhibit marketing. New York: McGraw-Hill, Inc.

Chapman, E. A. 1989. *Expositions work*. East Orleans, Mass.: Trade Show Bureau.

Conlin, J. 1989. Breaking the trade show barriers. *Successful Meetings*, pp. 33, 35–36, 39–40.

The Convention Liaison Council Glossary. 1986. Washington, D.C.: The Convention Liaison Council.

Hoyle, L. H., D.C. Dorf, and T.J.A. Jones. 1989. *Managing Conventions and Group Business*. East Lansing, Mich.: The Educational Institute of the American Hotel & Motel Association.

Miller, S. 1990. *How to Get the Most Out of Trade Shows*. Lincolnwood, Ill.: NTC Publishing Group.

Rutherford, D. G. 1990. *Introduction to the Conventions, Expositions, and Meetings Industry*. New York: Van Nostrand Reinhold.

Discussion Questions

1. Discuss the marketing benefits of trade shows. How can trade shows enhance a corporation's marketing plan?
2. Discuss the economic impact that trade shows have on your city.
3. This chapter discussed the fact that trade shows are a cost-effective means of marketing. Explain why.
4. How will the EC 1992 affect the international trade show industry?
5. Develop a hypothetical exhibitor kit.

Key Terms

trade show	exhibitor services department
show manager	account executives
exhibitor manual/service kit	multi-year contract
general service contractor	exhibitor
specialty contractor	exhibit manager
drayage	trade show specialist

7

Meetings Management

Learning Objectives

1. Recognize the evolution of meeting planning as a profession.
2. Understand the definition of a meeting.
3. Understand the responsibilities of a meeting planner.
4. Recognize the various types of meeting planners.
5. Understand the parts of a meeting from the meeting planner's perspective and how responsibilities vary accordingly.
6. Understand how a meeting planner can influence meeting attendance.
7. Become familiar with the issues involved in the site selection process, from a meeting planner's perspective.

Introduction

This chapter will introduce the reader to the concepts and procedures associated with the management of meetings. According to *The American Heritage Dictionary,* a meeting is "An assembly or gathering of people as for a business, social, or religious purpose." Meetings are designed to bring together people who have a common purpose or bond.

The individuals or groups who sponsor meetings generally appoint a single individual or committee to coordinate the meeting. The person coordinating the meeting is called a variety of names: planner, meeting planner, meeting manager, coordinator, and meeting director, to name a few. For the purpose of this text, we will refer to this person as a meeting planner. The meeting planner analyzes the situation and then plans in a cost-conscious manner a meeting that meets the purpose of those who are attending. This chapter will address the responsibilities of the meeting planner.

Meeting Planners

Today's meeting planners must be experts in the area of adult education and effective communication. They must possess strong administrative and leadership qualities and be able to serve as consultants for the sponsoring individual or organization. In a recent study done by Strick and Montgomery (1991), 615 members of the Professional Convention Management Association (PCMA) were asked to rank ten personality characteristics associated with successful meeting planners. They ranked them as follows:

1. Organized
2. Efficient
3. Responsive
4. Attentive
5. Intelligent
6. Prompt
7. Courteous
8. Hardworking
9. Friendly
10. Hospitable

Meetings management is a stressful job requiring a special kind of individual. This chapter will introduce the reader to the overall scope of meetings management. Meeting planners are perhaps the most diversified group of players in the industry. Therefore, it is very difficult to find a succinct definition that applies to all meeting planners. In theory, a meeting planner is anyone who is involved with planning meetings—one meeting or many. Planning meetings may comprise only a small segment of an individual's job description, as is the case with many administrative assistants, or it may be the sole purpose of an individual's occupation, as it is with association meeting planners, corporate meeting planners, and independent meeting planners.

Although history has continuously recorded meetings of individuals with one another, the job description of the meeting planner has just recently begun to evolve. Meeting planners' primary responsibilities 25 years ago were simply to make lodging arrangements and organize the meeting rooms. They did not need special knowledge regarding audiovisual equipment, negotiation techniques, subcontracting, or education of adult learners. Today's meeting planners must be much more sophisticated and knowledgeable in these areas.

According to *Successful Meetings'* 1992 "State of the Industry Report," most corporate and association meeting planners are between the ages of 35 and 55. Over 50 percent of the meeting planners are women, 66 percent have a college education, and over 40 percent earn more than $35,000 per year. Most have an executive title, although often the title doesn't specifically refer to their meeting planning responsibilities. The executive titles stem from the fact that over 65 percent of corporate and association meeting planners are seasoned pros. They have over four years of experience in the field (Conlin p. 9). Although this composite gives a general idea of who the typical meeting planner is, the demographics continue to change and diversify.

Association Meeting Planners

Associations are managed by professionals. Depending on the size of the association, the planning of meetings and conventions may fall under the direction of the association's executive director or they may have a specific department or person who is responsible for the planning of meetings, conventions, and expositions. Top association executives usually spend their time working with association program committees, discerning what topics should be covered and how they should be covered. The actual nuts-and-bolts of the meeting planning is left up to the association meeting planner.

Meetings are big business for associations. In 1991 the average association hosted approximately four conventions/trade shows and six professional/technical seminars (*Successful Meetings* 1992). The breakdown of meetings sponsored by associations are:

Committee meetings	33.06%
Seminars	32.50%
Board meetings	21.81%
Training sessions	6.74%
Other	5.89%

Of these meetings, 63 percent had an average attendance of over 50 people (Convene 1992). In 1991 associations spent an average of $99,680 on travel to meetings, $90,530 on hotel accommodations, $74,840 on food and beverage, $17,250 on meeting space, $21,500 on trade show service, and $21,500 on exposition space (*Successful Meetings* 1992).

The planner's primary goal is to plan all association meetings. They may be responsible for regional, national, and international meetings. Most national or international associations are divided into regional groups to enhance interaction between the members. The regional chapters generally meet anywhere from biannually to monthly. Regional chapters meet to attend to business and to provide educational opportunities for local members. The association meeting planner is responsible for coordinating regional meetings as well as the Board of Directors' meetings. The number of board meetings held per year varies with the association, but the average association has two board meetings per year. Association meeting planners are responsible for directing meetings, dealing with member services, standards, conventions, expositions, and publishing.

A considerable amount of the association meeting planners time is spent planning the annual convention. The association meeting planner generally works in conjunction with a committee of association members in planning the convention. The planner's responsibility is to provide guidance as well as the leg work for the planning. They oversee the budget development, site selection, entertainment, transportation and on-site management of the conference. Promotion of the meeting is a very important function of the meeting planner. As was stated earlier, although association meetings and conventions are designed to provide services to the membership, they are also a primary revenue generator for the association. The yearly convention generally generates a large portion of the association's yearly revenue; therefore, high conference attendance is a very important factor. Large associations actually have a marketing department that works in conjunction with the meeting planner in promoting the annual convention. They are also responsible for the evaluation of the conference. Association committees plan the meeting agenda, educational sessions, and business meetings.

Corporate Meeting Planners

These planners are employed by a for-profit business or corporation, and their job includes, but is not necessarily limited to, planning meetings and conventions for the company. Corporate meeting planners range from a secretary who has been given the responsibility of planning one training session for the boss to an official corporate meeting planner whose sole responsibility is planning, organizing, and implementing meetings and conventions for the employees, managers, and owners of the corporation. Therefore, they often hold titles other than "Meeting Planner," such as administrative assistant and executive secretary. Of these corporate planners, 43 percent have meeting planning as their primary area of responsibility, averaging over five meetings per year (Bernert 1990, p. 23).

Corporate planners are involved with a variety of different meeting types, such as management meetings, training meetings, sales meetings, incentive trips, and seminars. Many of the meetings will be repetitious in nature and include many of the same people year after year; therefore, the corporate meeting planner must be very diligent in making the meetings new and exciting to the attendees. Unlike the association meeting planner, the corporate meeting planner does not have to spend as much time and energy promoting the meetings or conferences because atten-

SUMMARY OF ASSOCIATION MEETINGS CHARACTERISTICS
1991 vs 1990

MEETING CHARACTERISTICS	**CONVENTIONS/ TRADE SHOWS		PROFESSIONAL/ TECHNICAL SEMINARS	
	1990	1991	1990	1991
Percentage of Planners Who Planned	38%	29.7%***	18%	24.7%
Average Number of Meetings	1.7	3.9 (base 40)	6.2	6.1
Average Number of Attendees	1,004	687.8 (base 38)	121*	150.8
Average Days Duration	3.7	3.3	2.8	2.5
Lead Time for Signing Hotel Contract (in months)	18.3	N/A	8.9	8.5
Average Number of of Hotel Rooms	512	300.3 (base 40)	147	113.2

  * Adjusted to remove responses that inflate overall average.

  ** In 1990, those who said they were trade show or exposition
managers were counted.
In 1991, only those who planned conventions *and* acted as
convention managers were counted.

 *** Base: Of the 29.7% (or 54) convention planners, only 74.1%,
(those who had exhibits at conventions booked,) are counted
in remaining categories.

Overall Base: 1990=177, 1991=182

Figure 7-1   Summary of Association meeting characteristics.

dance is usually required by management. Although this removes one burden from the corporate meeting planner, it places another one on them. People are more likely to enjoy participating in meetings they feel they chose to attend; required meetings are therefore often viewed as a necessary evil and are more difficult to plan. Corporate meeting planners must be masters at orchestrating meetings that meet the needs of management as well as the attendees by providing an enjoyable atmosphere that is conducive to conducting business.

Independent Meeting Planners

Independent meeting planners are entrepreneurs who specialize in planning meetings and conventions. Associations or corporations who do not have a full-time meeting planner may choose to contract with an independent meeting planner. "In the 1990s it appears that a great many independent meeting planners will help fill the ranks of the world's growing number of consultants" (Bastian 1990, p. 30). Over the past decade, independent meeting planners have not only increased in number, but also have become more sophisticated and knowledgeable. Experts predict that the independent meeting planner field will continue to grow. With the downsizing of corporations' budgets, contracting experts presents an economical way to have meetings and conventions professionally planned.

Independent meeting planners may be solely responsible for a meeting, or they may work in conjunction with a full-time corporate or association planner. If the independent is working in conjunction with a corporate or association meeting planner, the role of the independent is that of a support person who lends their expertise to the project. For example, the independent meeting planner may only be involved with the site selection process or be in charge of a single event, or they may act in an advisory role for the entire meeting or convention.

In a recent study done by Strick and Montgomery, 152 members of the Independent Meeting Planner Special Interest Group of Meeting Planners International were surveyed to enable the researchers to develop a profile of the independent meeting planner. According to this research the average independent meeting planner is a female between the ages of 36 and 45. Their salaries ranged from $25,000 to $55,000 per year. Independent meeting planners are an educated group. Of the respondents, 65 percent had some college education, with over half of the sample being college graduates. The average independent meeting planner has been in the conference and meeting planning industry for at least four years. Their professional backgrounds were varied, with many having reached the independent meeting planner status through working in many different areas of the industry. One-third did corporate meeting planning, while one-fourth did association meeting planning. Only 20 percent of those responding to the survey have been independent meeting planners their entire meeting planning careers.

The average independent meeting planner spends their time planning a variety of meetings, with the average meeting planner planning between 6 and 15 meetings per year. Primarily they focus on sales meetings, management meetings, training seminars, and incentive trips. Also they are heavily involved with the planning of major conventions.

Government Meeting Planners

Government meeting planners are meeting planners who work exclusively for the government. They function much as corporate meeting planners do and can be found in all segments and ranks of

Figure 7-2   Independent meeting planners have recently formed a special interest group within their professional association of Meeting Planners International. (Courtesy: Meeting Planners International.)

the government. Like corporate meeting planners, government meeting planners are facing tough economic times and must be masters at managing the budget as more and more budgetary constraints are being placed on government employees regarding travel and overnight stays.

Travel Agencies

Travel agencies are new players to the meeting planner segment of the industry. Historically, travel agencies worked hand in hand with meeting planners to provide support in the site selection process, transportation needs, and housing information. Currently, there are a number of travel agencies that offer the one-stop-shop approach to sponsoring organizations by having trained meeting planners on their staff. This enables travel agencies to provide the expertise necessary for planning meetings while also taking care of the specific needs regarding rooms and transportation.

Responsibilities of Meeting Planners

The duties of meeting planners are as diversified as the meeting planners themselves. "While more than two-thirds have clear-cut responsibility for the logistical aspect of planning, a sizeable percentage shoulder more than half the burden for strategic and tactical goals: setting objectives, creating the agenda, and budgeting" (Conlin 1990, p. 11). The role of the meeting planner varies from meeting to meeting and organization to organization, but in general meeting planners are responsible for the following areas:

Pre-meeting Activities
Plan meeting agenda
Establish meeting objectives
Attendance
Set meeting budget
Select meeting site
Select the meeting facility
Select the hotel
Negotiate contracts
Plan exhibition
Exhibitor correspondence and packet
Marketing plan
Plan travel to and from site

Arrange ground transportation
Organize shipping
Organize audiovisual needs

On-site Activities

Pre-event briefing
Execute plan
Move-in/move-out
Management of people
Troubleshoot
Invoice approval

Post-meeting

Debriefing
Evaluation
Thank-yous
Shipping
Plan for next year

This list provides an overview of the many responsibilities of meeting planners as a whole. Such responsibilities may vary due to the nature of the association, corporation, or group the planner is representing. Association and corporate meeting planners are generally involved from the beginning stages of meeting management. They may be responsible for all aspects of the meeting, including the agenda, whereas the independent meeting planner may only be responsible for certain aspects of the meeting, such as site selection, agenda planning, budgetary concerns, and negotiations. The extent to which an independent meeting planner is involved is entirely up to the group sponsoring the meeting.

A brief overview of these responsibilities is necessary for the reader to fully understand the complex nature of meetings management. This discussion will be broken into three sections: pre-meeting, on-site activities, and post-meeting.

Pre-meeting Responsibilities

Before a meeting planner can start planning the meeting, he or she must first determine why the meeting is being held. Meetings can be and often are a tremendous waste of time and money. It is estimated that in 1992 Americans spent over 300 million days in meetings, over half of which were unproductive. Considering the cost of meetings, the number of unproductive meetings translates into millions of dollars lost every year through lack of productivity and surplus expenditures associated with meetings. Therefore, it is incumbent upon the meeting planner to help the sponsor determine whether or not the meeting is really necessary. The easiest way to accomplish this is to do a simple needs assessment exercise. The information derived from this exercise should address the following questions: What issues will the meeting address? What do the people involved think about the need to have a meeting? What is the intended impact of the meeting? (Letich 1991) Once the necessity of the meeting is determined, the meeting planner can work with the sponsors to ensure that the meeting is a productive one.

The key to a productive meeting is the **meeting agenda**.

Although the meeting agenda is not always the responsibility of the meeting planner, he or she must be intimately involved with both the written and hidden agenda of the meeting. Meetings and conventions are often designed for a number of stated reasons (training, problem solving, brainstorming, planning, networking, team building, etc.), but there may also be a hidden agenda. Many corporations use meetings as a way of rewarding top producers. Although the meetings are designed to provide education or training, there is also a lot of weight placed on providing recreational activities that will allow the participants to combine business with pleasure. Since conventions provide a large percentage of the operating budget for many associations, the annual conference must be designed to entice the membership's attendance. Often, the motivation necessary to attend a meeting or conference is closely linked with a destination that enables the participants to bring their families and combine business with a family vacation. The meeting planner must understand precisely what the sponsors are trying to accomplish so as to be successful in the management of their meeting or conference.

The agenda may be planned in conjunction with the meeting planner, or the planner may be given a copy of the meeting agenda. If the meeting planner is involved with the meeting agenda, he or she should advise as to the proper handling of specific types of meetings. For example, if the group sponsoring the meeting desires team building experiences, the meeting planner would provide insight into how this could be accomplished through room setup, educational opportunities, and recreational activities. The meeting agenda provides the groundwork for the establishment of **meeting objectives**. The establishment of meeting objectives is again something that the meeting planner may or may not be involved with. Regardless of the role that he or she plays in the establishment of meeting objectives, the planner must allow the entire plan for the meeting or convention to be driven by the objectives. The meeting's objectives provide the framework from which the meeting planner will set the budget, select the site and facility, and plan the overall meeting or convention.

Setting the **budget** for the meeting is a difficult task. It is successful if the meeting planner is consulted prior to the finalized edition. A working budget should be established and used as a guideline for making decisions, with the understanding that budgets change for different sites and various activities that are planned. The planner should always be kept aware of the budget and be consulted when changes in the budget are being made. Although control of the budget is generally left to the sponsoring organization or corporation, a successful meeting or convention cannot be planned without the planner being intimately aware of the budgetary constraints.

The budget should communicate income and expenditure estimates as thoroughly as possible. Many meeting planners have lost clients or jobs due to their inability to deliver the event within the established budget. Therefore, it is extremely important that the planner ensure that every possible expenditure is included in the budget prior to the event. Some meeting planners build in a "slush" fund to allow for correction of any items missed on the budget, but this is not a practice suggested by most planners because of the negative connotations associated with "slush" funds.

Income for a meeting, convention, or exposition could include, but is not limited to:

Registration fees
Exhibitor fees
Company or sponsoring organization monies
Advertising revenues
Revenues from the sale of educational materials
Event sponsor contributions

Registration fee interest
Grants or contributions

Expenses for a meeting, convention, or exposition could include, but are not limited to:

Meeting planner fees
Marketing expenses
Printing and copying expenses
Mailing
Shipping
Support supplies, such as office supplies and mailing
Support staff
Audiovisual equipment
Signage
Speaker fees, honorarium, and expenses
Entertainment and recreational expenses
Mementos for guest and attendees
Tours
Ground transportation
Spousal programs
Food and beverage events
Gratuities
Interpreter
On-site personnel
Rental fees for meeting and exposition space

The meeting objectives and budget will help determine the targeted attendees. **Attendance** can either be an important focus of the meeting planner, or it can be relatively unimportant. In the case of an association meeting planner or an independent meeting planner who is working for an association or another form of sponsoring organization, attendance is paramount to the success of the meeting or convention. In the case with corporate meeting planners or independent meeting planners working for corporations that will require attendance, the issue becomes unimportant.

Attendance is directly related to the type of marketing that the sponsoring organization in combination with the meeting planner does. Groups who solicit attendance from either their association or from the general public must develop a marketing plan. To develop a marketing plan, the planner must consider what they are marketing (convention, meeting, exposition, etc.) and what is their potential market (i.e., who the prospective attendees are). A great deal of information is needed in this step. If the meeting planner is familiar with their membership or has an established list of attendees and has demographic, psychographic, and historical data regarding past conference or meeting participation, then this task is much easier. If the planner is unfamiliar with the group, they must develop a profile of the potential attendee through detailed discussions with the executive directors of the association or corporation. The planner must then develop questionnaires designed to ascertain the needs and desires of the group that can be administered prior to the event, so as to give the planner some perspective as to the group's expectations. A wonderful source of information for planners new to the organization is the hotels which have previously accomodated groups. Hotels maintain detailed records of a group's activities, expenditures, and so on, and would be able to provide the planner with this information.

The meeting planner should then determine what marketing strategies would best suit the target market. There is an abundance of marketing strategies available, and the meeting planner is only limited by time and budgetary constraints. Successful meeting planners must understand the importance of marketing their meetings, and they must place adequate time and financial resources into successfully marketing meetings.

Site, meeting facility, and **hotel selection** are based primarily on the purpose of the function. The importance of selecting the proper host site and meeting facilities cannot be taken lightly. The success of a meeting, convention, or exposition rests heavily on the site and facilities chosen. The services provided by the site as well as the personnel and ambiance all greatly influence the attendees' perception of the event. Unfortunately, all too often the site is selected by committees or by individuals other than the meeting planner and then the meeting planner is expected to make the best out of what they have been given. However, when the meeting planner is included in the site selection process, 74 percent of corporate planners and 63 percent of association planners always select the destination before the hotel (*Successful Meetings* 1992). Factors determining the desirability of the destination included airport access, ground transportation, and number of meeting rooms and hotel rooms available (see figure 7-3).

Despite the fact that in recent years budgets have become tighter, the focus placed on price is less important than convenience. Sites that provide good overall services to groups are receiving first priority when doing site visitations.

Each sponsoring organization or corporation has its own personality. Some groups like the atmosphere of a big city that provides numerous opportunities to visit museums, theaters, and major tourism sites. Others prefer the quiet, peaceful atmosphere of a secluded resort or of a hotel in a smaller city or one located on the outskirts of a major metropolitan area. If the purpose of the meeting or convention is to provide intense training, perhaps the meeting planner would choose an airport hotel or facility that would provide easy access with very little opportunity for interruption. If the purpose was to combine business with pleasure, the meeting planner would be more likely to choose a site in a resort area that provided both excellent meeting facilities as well as plenty of opportunities for recreational activities. When choosing a city, those involved with the site selection process should review evaluations of past cities to determine what type of area their group seems to enjoy. Coupled with this information and the meeting agenda, objectives, and budget, the site selection process can be successfully accomplished. When selecting a host city, some of the questions that should be answered are:

1. Have you used the site before?
2. Is the site easily accessible for the majority of your participants?
3. Is the geographic area predetermined by a rotation cycle (i.e., every four years the meeting moves from the south, north, east, and west)?
4. Does the geographic area lend itself to pre- and post-meeting or conference excursions?
5. Is the ground transportation appropriate for the group?
6. What is the reputation of the site?
7. Is the climate acceptable to your participants?
8. Is there enough meeting space and sleeping rooms available to accommodate your group during the desired time period?

When choosing the actual meeting facility and the hotel, service sells the site. Service is the buzz word of the 1990s. Increasing

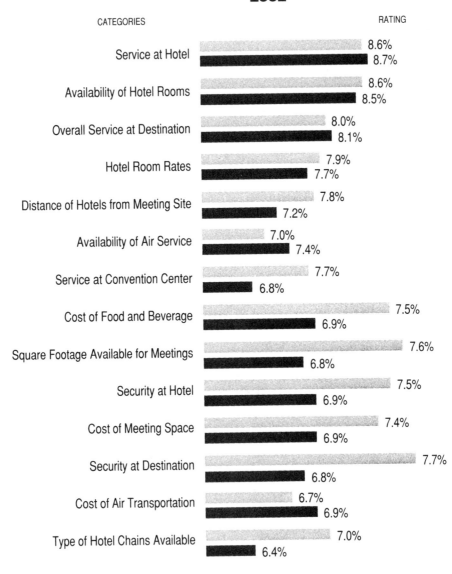

SITE SELECTION CRITERIA
(RATED ON A SCALE OF 1-10)
1991

CATEGORIES   RATING

Service at Hotel
8.6%
8.7%

Availability of Hotel Rooms
8.6%
8.5%

Overall Service at Destination
8.0%
8.1%

Hotel Room Rates
7.9%
7.7%

Distance of Hotels from Meeting Site
7.8%
7.2%

Availability of Air Service
7.0%
7.4%

Service at Convention Center
7.7%
6.8%

Cost of Food and Beverage
7.5%
6.9%

Square Footage Available for Meetings
7.6%
6.8%

Security at Hotel
7.5%
6.9%

Cost of Meeting Space
7.4%
6.9%

Security at Destination
7.7%
6.8%

Cost of Air Transportation
6.7%
6.9%

Type of Hotel Chains Available
7.0%
6.4%

Association Planners

Corporate Planners

Base: Association 182, Corporate 524

Figure 7-3   Picking the place—site selection criteria.

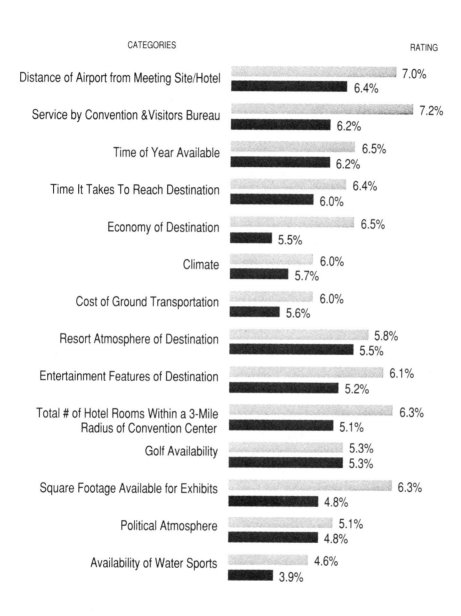

Figure 7-3   (continued)

competition in a saturated economy has forced the hospitality industry to reevaluate its attitude towards service. This coupled with the recession has affected all areas of the industry, but none more than those hotels, resorts, and convention and conference centers that gain a large percentage of their income from conferences and meetings. Associations and corporations that typically host meetings and conventions are faced with decreasing revenues; therefore, they are becoming very selective in the way they spend their income. For the hospitality industry this means that they must work harder to gain their portion of the pie. In the past this has meant offering newer rooms and more amenities, but the industry is also facing their own revenue shortage; thus the quality of service has become the point of distinction. Today's conference attendees are more selective in the number of meetings and conventions they are attending. Meeting planners and suppliers alike must focus on providing a level of service that leads the guest to feel at home, well cared for, and anxious to return (Callan 1990). In a recent study by Strick and Montgomery, members of the Professional Convention Management Association (PCMA) were surveyed to ascertain their perceptions regarding the importance of the service attitude of hotel staff in the site selection process. Of the respondents, 82 percent strongly agreed that, when considering a host property, the service attitude of the staff is important in the site selection decision-making process. (See chapter 4 for a complete discussion of service and the host property.)

Along with the service attitude of the staff, those planning meetings are also looking for a higher level of services for their special attendees. With the American with Disabilities Act being implemented in 1992, the needs of the disabled are coming into the forefront of major issues for the hospitality industry. Those associated with the meetings, conventions, and expositions industry are cognizant of the need to address the special needs of their meeting and convention attendees. The facilities, services, and amenities they feel are most important are handicapped accessibility (including ramps, big bathrooms, elevators, meeting rooms, and transportation), flexibility on the part of the staff in being willing and able to assist the needs of the physically disadvantaged, and the ability to accommodate special dietary needs.

Another important area to be considered for many associations and corporations is the host property's ability to meet the needs of their international attendees. The facilities, services, and amenities that need to be provided are multilingual staff, easy exchange of currency, interpreters, international codes and symbols on guest information and signage, and the ability to accommodate special dietary considerations. (For a more thorough discussion of international attendees and their needs, see chapter 10.) The types of facilities hosting meetings, conventions, and expositions range from airports to hotels to suburban hotels (see figure 7-4). (For a complete discussion of venues, please see chapter 4.)

When selecting the meeting facilities, some specific questions to be asked are:

1. Have you stayed in this facility before?
2. What have you heard from other groups regarding this facility?
3. Is the facility easily accessed from the airport?

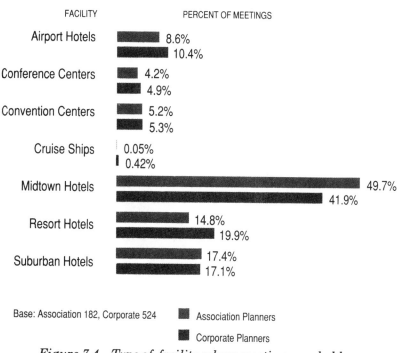

TYPE OF FACILITY
WHERE MEETINGS ARE HELD
1991

FACILITY	PERCENT OF MEETINGS
Airport Hotels	8.6% / 10.4%
Conference Centers	4.2% / 4.9%
Convention Centers	5.2% / 5.3%
Cruise Ships	0.05% / 0.42%
Midtown Hotels	49.7% / 41.9%
Resort Hotels	14.8% / 19.9%
Suburban Hotels	17.4% / 17.1%

Base: Association 182, Corporate 524　■ Association Planners
　　　　　　　　　　　　　　　　　　■ Corporate Planners

Figure 7-4　Type of facility where meetings are held.

4. Is the physical appearance appealing?
5. Is the facility kept in good repair?
6. What kind of first impression does the facility make?
7. Does the facility have the space available?
8. What is the number, size, and caliber of the meeting rooms and guest rooms?
9. Does the facility provide VIP accommodations?
10. Are nonsmoking rooms available?
11. Does the facility provide appropriate food and beverage services?
12. Does the facility provide appropriate recreational opportunities?
13. What time is check-in?
14. Can special arrangements be made for early check-in and late check-out?
15. Can special rates apply prior to the meeting and after the meeting in case the participants would like to arrive early or stay late?
16. What are check-in and check-out procedures?
17. Are staff members appropriately dressed, knowledgeable, and courteous?
18. Does the facility provide the support staff the group will need to successfully host the meeting, convention, or exposition?
19. Is the signage appropriate?
20. What is the proximity of the facility to shopping, restaurants, and entertainment?
21. Is the room rate appropriate for the group?
22. What sort of deposit is required?
23. What is the guarantee and cancellation policy?
24. What other groups will be on-site during your meeting?
25. What kind of a room block will they provide?
26. Are the safety and security features working and up to date?

The individual in charge of site selection should never sign a contract with a facility until after a site visit. It is suggested that the planner make two visits to the site—one announced and one unannounced. It is one thing for a planner to be chaperoned around a property with the convention service manager making the appropriate introductions; one should be guaranteed outstanding service during such a visit. If the service is questionable at this time, the site is not one that should be considered because, if they know the planner is coming to inspect the site and their best is not pleasing, imagine how the attendees will be treated. Once a scheduled trip has been successfully completed, the planner should visit the site unannounced, perhaps even using a different name. This visit will afford the planner a view of how guests are usually treated. If on this visit the treatment the planner receives varies greatly from the previous visit, the planner should question the quality of service the registrants will receive.

After successfully completing the two site visitations, the planner or representative from the sponsoring organization can negotiate and sign the contract. (Please see chapter 8 for a complete discussion of negotiations and contracts.)

Once the site has been selected, the actual meeting, conference, or exposition can be planned. A detailed agenda can be produced to include meeting rooms and recreational activities. A spousal program can also be designed. Upon completing this, the planner in conjunction with the sponsoring organization should implement their marketing strategy.

In the case of a corporate training meeting, the marketing may be no more than a flier or memo discussing the time, date, place, and agenda. If the event is a major convention, marketing starts a year prior to the event. Generally, the convention is marketed in the registration packet of the previous year's convention. The type of information that should be included in this marketing piece should be dates, place, and a general overview of the theme. As the dates for the meeting, convention, or exposition approach, the marketing material should become more specific. It is estimated that the average person does not assimilate information until it has been presented to them at least three times. Therefore, the very minimum number of marketing pieces sent to potential registrants should be three. Most sponsoring groups find that 6 to 8 pieces of mail yields the greatest return.

The planner should also develop the exhibitor correspondence and packet. The exhibitor correspondence should mirror the correspondence sent to the registrants, but should also include information specific to the exposition. The exhibitor packet may be developed by the meeting planner or by the exposition manager. (See chapter 6 for a thorough discussion of the exhibitor packet.)

The last thing the planner will be responsible for is developing the final blueprint for the actual meeting, convention, or exposition. This blueprint is often called the staging guide, staging book, planner's guide, planning book, or coordinator's book or guide. As the final set of blueprints for a building provide every detail regarding the construction of the building, so does the blueprint for the meeting, convention, or exposition. This book provides step-by-step detail as to everything required for the event. The book generally is in loose-leaf format and is housed in a three-ring binder, allowing for updates to be included and copies to be made without disrupting the flow of the document.

Each page of the planner's guide contains all of the specific information needed for each event. This guide enables planners easy access to all pertinent information during the event, thus allowing them to check all room setups, audiovisual needs, and so forth. Similar function sheets are also designed for all food and beverage functions (see figure 7-5).

On-site Activities

The execution of an event generally involves every waking moment of a meeting planner's day. Armed with an event guide, the meeting planner should arrive before any of the registrants or exhibitors do. In the case of a single meeting, this may be no more than an hour prior to the event, or in the case of a major convention or exposition the planner will need to arrive several days prior to the event to oversee the move-in activities. During the move-in process the planner will work closely with facility managers, event coordinators or convention service managers, service contractors, and suppliers, as well a number of individuals responsible for the successful execution the the event. The meeting planner acts as the director of the move-in process and coordinates the functions of these other key individuals.

When an event is sponsored by an association, the meeting planner will also be responsible for working with the executive staff as well as the association members who are working on volunteer committees. It is imperative that prior to move-in those individuals involved be trained in their respective roles and that during the event communication lines remain open between all key players.

Open communication is maintained through **preconvention meetings**. The pre-event briefing may include a number of the players, as is the case when the event is a conference or exposition, or it may include just the meeting planner, a representative of the sponsoring organization, and a representative from the host venue. Regardless of the size of the event, there should always be a pre-event briefing meeting to insure that all the bases are covered. Pre-event briefing meetings should include all responsible individuals on the venue's staff. This list of individuals could include, but is not limited to, the general manager, salesperson, convention service manager, catering manager, chef, front desk manager, and someone from the rooms division. The sponsoring organization should be represented by everyone who has management responsibilities.

If the sponsoring organization is an association, those attending the meeting could include, but are not limited to, the president, vice president, secretary, and treasurer of the association as well as the association's professional staff (executive director, meeting planners, etc.).

During the pre-event briefing the participants will brief one another on any changes that have taken place since the event guide was developed. The host property will go through each event function sheet to make sure that they are properly prepared. Each department head will also discuss the arrangements they have made to service the group.

Once the pre-event briefing is finished, the meeting planner and his or her staff will monitor all events to make sure that the attendees' needs are being met. They will also be responsible for managing all the people associated with the meeting, to make sure that the plan is properly executed.

The key to properly executing the plan is to have a thorough event guide and to keep open lines of communication between the sponsoring organization and the host venue. If the event lasts more than a day, there should be meetings at the start of each day, perhaps over an early morning breakfast, so as to enable the sponsoring organization's representative, the meeting planner, and the convention service coordinator to touch base and discuss any problems that may have arisen and review any changes made. No matter how thorough a planner has been, there will always be changes. The planner's ability to respond to those changes will determine the success of the event and ultimately the success of his or her career.

Another important function of the planner is to approve all invoices. It is generally the practice of host venues to present an invoice at the end of each major food and beverage function. It is

Sheraton Hotel & Conference Center

SHERATON HOTELS, INNS & RESORTS WORLDWIDE

2100 BUSH RIVER ROAD, COLUMBIA, SOUTH CAROLINA 29210 803/731-0300 FAX 803/731-2839

EVENT ORDER

	FILE :
	DAY:
POST AS	DATE:
COMPANY NAME	TELEPHONE-DAY
CONTACT	
LOCAL ADDRESS	TELEPHONE-EVENING
BILLING INSTRUCTIONS	FAX
NAME	
ADDRESS	TYPE OF FUNCTION

MEETINGS ROOM	EXPECTED ATTENDANCE	RENTAL	FUNCTION BEGINS	ENDS

SET UP INSTRUCTIONS:

STYLE: _____

_____

HEAD TABLE: _____

_____

REGISTRATION TABLE: _____

FLIP CHART/BLACKBOARD: _____

AUDIO VISUAL REQUIREMENTS: _____

_____

_____

_____

FLAGS & FLOWERS: _____

OTHER: _____

_____

_____

COFFEE SERVICE

AM TIME _____

LOCATION _____

AM TIME _____

LOCATION _____

PM TIME _____

LOCATION _____

To insure a successful function, carefully review this Banquet Event Order and return a signed copy within 7 days. Final guaranteed attendance must be submitted by noon 72 hours prior to your function. The Hotel reserves the right to charge for that guaranteed number if less are served. The Hotel will set up 10% over for groups up to 200 and 5% over for groups 200 or more. Please add 17% Service Charge and Local Sales Tax to all prices quoted.

DATE _____ SHERATON HOTEL _____

PER

ORGANIZATION REPRESENTATIVE SIGNATURE: _____

Figure 7-5   Food and beverage function sheets.

Sheraton Hotel & Conference Center

SHERATON HOTELS, INNS & RESORTS WORLDWIDE

2100 BUSH RIVER ROAD, COLUMBIA, SOUTH CAROLINA 29210 803/731-0300 FAX 803/731-2839

EVENT ORDER

	FILE :
	DAY:
POST AS	DATE:
COMPANY NAME	TELEPHONE-DAY
CONTACT	
LOCAL ADDRESS	TELEPHONE-EVENING
BILLING INSTRUCTIONS	FAX
NAME	
ADDRESS	TYPE OF FUNCTION

COCKTAILS

EXPECTED ATTENDANCE	GUARANTEE	RENTAL	FUNCTION BEGINS	ENDS

ROOM	BEVERAGE
SET-UP INSTRUCTIONS	Liquor Supplier:_____
	Cash Bar _____
	Host Bar _____
	Set-ups:
	Bartender Charge: _____
	No. of Bartenders _____
	No. of Cashiers _____

MEALS

EXPECTED ATTENDANCE	GUARANTEE	RENTAL	FUNCTION BEGINS	FOOD SERVED	ENDS

ROOM	MEAL PRICE PER PERSON	MENU
	$	

SET-UP INSTRUCTIONS:

Table Arrangements: _____
_____
_____
_____

Head Table: _____
_____

Registration: _____
_____

Audio Visual: _____
Dance Floor: _____
Stage: _____
Musical Arrangements: _____
Flags and Flowers: _____
_____

Coat Arrangements: _____
Other: _____
_____
_____
_____

To insure a successful function, carefully review this Banquet Event Order and return a signed copy within 7 days. Final guaranteed attendance must be submitted by noon 72 hours prior to your function. The Hotel reserves the right to charge for that guaranteed number if less are served. The Hotel will set up 10% over for groups up to 200 and 5% over for groups 200 or more. Please add 17% Service Charge and Local Sales Tax to all prices quoted.

DATE _____ SHERATON HOTEL_____

PER

ORGANIZATION REPRESENTATIVE SIGNATURE: _____

Figure 7-5 (continued)

the responsibility of the planner to check these invoices for accuracy and to make any changes necessary at that time. This is also the time to make the host venue aware of anything that the planner believes was unsatisfactory. Haggling over the bill may not be appropriate at this time, but if there is an item of contention it should be brought to the attention of the person presenting the invoice at this time. A detailed discussion should then take place at the debriefing.

Post-meeting
Debriefing
Evaluation
Thank-yous
Shipping
Plan for next year

Post-meeting Activities

Directly after the conclusion of the event, the planner should hold a **debriefing** session. This meeting should include all the individuals that were present at the pre-event briefing. The debriefing session is designed to bring closure to this event and to allow all those involved to discuss openly their perceptions of the meeting. At this time any items of contention will be discussed and resolved. This is also the appropriate time to discuss rebooking if that is an area of concern.

The meeting planner is also responsible for administering the evaluation. This can take place in a number of ways. The sponsoring organization may place evaluation information in each session so that they can evaluate the attendees' perceptions of each event. An overall evaluation form might also be placed in the attendees registration packet, and attendees should be encouraged to complete the evaluation form before they leave the site. Meeting planners may offer an incentive to the attendees, such as eligibility for a drawing for free registration to next year's conference, to entice them to complete the evaluation.

Evaluations may also be mailed to the attendees once they leave the meeting. A summary of the evaluations should be compiled and used in the planning phase of future events.

Conclusion

The job of planning a meeting has just recently begun to be recognized as a career. Until just a few short years ago it was generally believed that anyone could plan a meeting, that no special skills were required. However, as meetings have become more sophisticated, so have those individuals who plan them.

Today, there are a number of different people who may have the responsibility of planning a meeting. These individuals may work for an association, a corporation, the government, a travel agency, or themselves. Regardless of who they work for, the job of planning the meeting requires a great many pre-meeting activities (sometimes beginning more than a year before the scheduled event), on-site supervision and coordination during the meeting, and post-meeting follow-up and evaluation.

This chapter introduced the concept of managing a meeting. It also discussed who manages the meeting and the nuts and bolts of how meeting are managed.

References

Bastian, L. 1990. Going independent: nine common blunders to avoid. *The Meeting Manager,* (March 1990) pp. 30–34.

Callan, Roger J. 1990. Hotel award schemes as a measurement of service quality—an assessment by travel industry journalists as surrogate consumers. *International Journal of Hospitality Management.* 9(1):45–58.

Letich, Larry. 1991. Is this meeting necessary? *Meetings and Conventions,* (May) pp. 66–70.

The American Heritage Dictionary, 2nd Edition. 1982. Boston: Houghton Mifflin Company.

Professional Convention Management Association. 1992. PCMA's first annual meetings market survey. *Convene,* (March) .

State of the industry: 1992. 1992. *Successful Meetings,* (May) pp. 21–87.

Discussion Questions

1. How has the profession of meeting planning evolved?
2. How will the current trend of downsizing corporations affect corporate meeting planners?
3. Why is it important for meeting planners to understand both

the written and hidden agenda of a meeting? How will their understanding of the agenda effect their responsibilities?

4. Discuss the importance of establishing and adhering to a meeting budget.

5. One of the biggest challenges meeting planners face is attendance. How can a meeting planner help the sponsoring organization increase the attendance for their meeting, convention, or exposition?

6. Discuss the on-site activities a meeting planner is responsible for.

7. Why are post-meeting activities so very important?

Key Terms

meeting

meeting planner

association meeting planner

corporate meeting planner

independent meeting planner

government meeting planner

meeting agenda

meeting objectives

site selection

staging guide

8

Legal Issues

Learning Objectives

1. To understand the importance of legal and ethical issues in the meetings, conventions, and expositions industry.
2. To understand the negotiating process.
3. To describe the relationship between the host property and the sponsoring organization during the negotiation process.
4. To identify those items that are negotiable.
5. To define what a contract is.
6. To identify the various areas that should be covered in a contract.
7. To understand what ethics is.
8. To understand the importance of studying ethics.
9. To recognize the importance of developing one's own personal code of ethics.
10. To recognize the importance of organizations developing systems that allow their employees to act ethically.
11. To understand the reason that unethical behavior has such a negative impact on the entire hospitality industry.

Introduction

Today's society is ruled by legal issues. In the past a handshake and a man's word were all it took to seal a deal, but unfortunately those days are gone. Today, individuals associated with the meetings, conventions, and expositions industry must have keen insight into the legal and ethical issues surrounding meetings, conventions, and expositions. To be a successful business person, it is important to understand the complete scope of the legal and ethical implications surrounding your area of expertise. This chapter will provide a framework from which to study the legal issues that the meetings, conventions, and expositions industry must be concerned with as well as discuss ethics and the importance of making wise ethical decisions.

Negotiations

The art of negotiation and the ability to successfully write a contract that meets the needs of both the organization sponsoring a meeting, convention, or exposition and the host facility are two of the most important skills a meeting planner can possess. This chapter will discuss negotiation as it applies to the conference, meeting, and exposition segment of the industry. It will also address contracts and their key components.

Negotiating is defined as "bargaining or discussing with a view toward reaching an agreement" (Foster 1989). Negotiating is the time spent between parties preparing a contract that is reflective of arrangements agreed upon by both parties.

A **contract** is a legal document that binds two or more parties. In the case of meetings, conventions, and expositions, a contract binds an association or organization and the host facility. All meetings, regardless of their size, should have a contract. Since it is a legally binding document, careful consideration must be made to all details to ensure that all possible elements have been included. A contract protects both the association and the host, ensuring that all parties carry on with their business. The contract should include all arrangements, obligations, costs, and deadlines relevant to the meeting, convention, or conference.

While many host facilities have a standard contract they wish to use, experienced meeting planners actually view the contract as an outline of potential items to be negotiated. The old adage "everything is negotiable" is a perfect attitude for a successful meeting planner to possess.

Negotiations begin as soon as the meeting site has been chosen. In fact, some experts contend that negotiations begin as soon as a site has been visited. Either way, from that point on, many of the details necessary for a successful meeting, conference, or exposition have to be negotiated. "Negotiations can take the form of short, take-it-or-leave-it exchanges, or long, drawn out maneuvering. . . they can mean the difference between a mediocre meeting and a great one" (Wolfson 1988, p. 1).

Steps in Negotiation

The first step in negotiating a meeting is to know the group. What is important to them? What do you hope to accomplish through negotiation? The answer to these two questions will help the meeting planner in determining his or her objectives for the negotiations of the final contract. If, for example, the organization has a policy that it does not make advanced deposits to host properties, yet the host property's policy is to collect a 30 percent deposit when the contract is signed, this issue may need to be negotiated.

The second step in negotiating is information gathering. This is when the meeting planner and the facility manager find out as much as they can about one another and the organizations they represent. The organization sponsoring the meeting, conference, or exposition provides their information in the form of the group prospectus (see chapter 4 for a complete discussion of the group prospectus). The host facility likewise has a meeting planners guide that they provide to the sponsoring organization. This guide will outline all of their services and amenities. The information shared will provide some of the criteria necessary for determining how far you can go in negotiations (Foster 1989).

The third step is to discuss the specific items that are negotiable. The following is a partial list of negotiable items, suggested by Foster, when negotiating a convention center contract:

1. Exhibit hall rates.
2. Move-in costs: negotiate free time for moving in and moving out.

3. Number of days for move-in.
4. Meeting room rentals: If a group is renting a substantial amount of exhibit space, perhaps meeting room charges could be reduced or waived.
5. Deposit clauses: If the entire deposit can be waived, so much the better. If this is not possible, the percentage of deposit might be.
6. Utilities: while charges for these during a show may not be negotiable, charges for utilities during move-in and move-out may be waived.
7. VIP parking: Ask for free parking for staff and VIPs. Also, a percentage of parking lot revenues may in some cases be an issue worthy of negotiations.
8. Room setups or resets: theater-style setup is generally free, while other types of setups may cost anywhere from $1.50 to $2.50 per chair. Room setup charges may be negotiable. Often charging for room resets, convention centers may allow this issue to be negotiated out of the contract.
9. Material storage fees: while most convention centers will not let exhibitors store materials on the exhibit floor, free use of storage areas may be among the negotiable items.
(Foster 1989, pp. 33–35)

While this list is not meant to be all-inclusive, it gives the reader a good indication of the types of things that are negotiable, from a convention center's point of view.

Paula Auman-Butler, in her article "Where Can They Afford to Give?," explains negotiations as they relate to hotels and meeting planners. She suggests that hotels make money on the sale of guest rooms and that all other revenue centers within the hotel, such as restaurants, meeting rooms, lounges, recreational facilities, and so on, are the "icing on the cake," in that they generate a much smaller percentage of profit than rooms. Therefore, "before you (meeting planners) walk into a hotel to negotiate a piece of group business, it would be wise to learn a little bit about where the hotel makes its money and where it doesn't. You may then understand where you can negotiate and where you can't" (Auman-Butler 1986).

Remember, everything is negotiable. . . at least as far as meetings, conventions, and expositions are concerned. The key is to understand that negotiating is a give-and-take process. Successful negotiators must be willing to stand firm on those issues that are vitally important to the group they represent and to compromise on the others. As Stanley Wolfson explains in his book *The Meeting Planners' Complete Guide to Negotiating: You Can Get What You Want* (1988), successful negotiations result in both sides feeling a sense of accomplishment and reward. Although both sides may lose something during the negotiation, in the end each should leave with a good feeling about oneself and the other party.

Wolfson goes on to explain that a satisfaction approach helps alleviate the urge to "overnegotiate." Overnegotiation results when either party adopts the attitude of "out-to-get-you." This approach always upsets the other party and leaves behind a charged atmosphere that takes its toll at meeting time. When negotiations are successful, both parties leave with a sense of satisfaction (Wolfson 1988).

Once the negotiations have been concluded, it is imperative that everything be put in writing. For years, meeting planners and host facilities alike sealed their agreements with handshakes rather than documentation. This practice frequently left one or both parties in the lurch when things didn't go as planned. In an era of law suits, neither party can afford to be so informal. Today, if an agreement is not written down, then it doesn't exist.

The final step in the contracts and negotiations phase of planning a meeting, convention, or exposition is the signing of the legal document. Once both parties have had ample time to review the contract and their lawyers have done the same, the contract must be signed. However, it can only be signed by individuals who have the authority to do so. The contract is not binding, unless the signatures are valid. Therefore, it behooves both parties to take responsibility for making sure that only authorized persons sign the agreement.

The Uniform Commercial Code

The Uniform Commercial Code is a set of uniform rules designed to simplify, clarify, and modernize the law governing commercial transactions. The Uniform Commercial Code covers all contracts as they apply to meetings. This means that contracts involving meetings, conventions, and expositions must comply with all provisions under this code. It is not within the scope of this chapter to discuss the Uniform Commercial Codes, other than to mention their importance in defining some of the limitations of meetings' contracts. However, it is important to mention that it would behoove all meeting planners as well as host facility representatives to engage a lawyer whose specialty is contract law, to be sure that their contracts comply with all requirements.

According to the National Association of Exposition Managers Hotel/Client Agreement Guidelines and Information (NAEM 1985), there are many areas that need to be addressed in a contract that pertain to a meeting, convention, and/or conference. Depending on the type of functions being planned, these areas would include any or all of the following:

Room block
Complimentary accommodations
Walking guests
Function space
Food and beverage
Exhibit space rental
Agreements with unions
Cancellation clause
Arbitration
Indemnification clause
Insurance
Payment procedures

Room Block

Room block is the number of rooms held in reserve for a group (CLC, p. 18). These rooms specifically refer to sleeping accommodations (number of singles, doubles, suites, etc.) and include any specifications as to room location (such as Tower A) as well as function rooms.

The creation of a room block obligates both parties. The host facility agrees to hold a specified number of rooms, regardless of the arrival times of the guests. On the organization's side, they agree to pay for the rooms in the block, even if they remain empty.

Within this segment of the contract, move-in/move-out dates are specified. These are the dates set for the arrival and departure of the guests. In many contracts, it may be necessary to go one step further and specify beginning and ending hours to assure that guest functions start on time and that the host facility will be able to set up in plenty of time for the next group's functions.

Deposit requirements are spelled out under the room block portion of the contract. It is generally sufficient for attendees to make a deposit of one night's lodging. It may also be the policy of the host facility to require the organization or association to make a deposit, especially if the function is booked several years out. If this is the case, "planners should insist that the deposit be held in an escrow account and that any interest earned on the money be credited to the group's account" (Lieberman 1992).

Room rates are to be specified—broken down by type of accommodation (e.g., single rooms, double rooms, suites). If a range of rates is agreed to, these must be clearly delineated in the contract. If a flat rate is to be used, this rate must also be spelled out. Generally, a flat rate means that the same room rate is applied to each guest room, except for suites.

A cut-off date is designated when a group does not guarantee a room block and is the day by which the organization must release or add to the commitment for function rooms or sleeping rooms. After the cut-off date, the host facility is free to sell its rooms to any interested parties, and conferees who do not already have their rooms will be awarded rooms on a first-come/first-served basis.

Complimentary Accommodations

It is quite common to find a clause in the contract addressing the issue of complimentary and/or reduced rate rooms. A rule of thumb in this area is one complimentary guest room for every 50 to 100 guest rooms booked (Price 1989, p. 39). A hotel and meeting planner may further agree that a certain number of reduced rate rooms be included in the contract. These are usually rooms held for the organization or association's staff members, speakers, performers, and the meeting planner and are highly negotiable. The host facility may also include complimentary or reduced rate rooms that are going to be used for working space for such things as offices and press rooms. The exact terms should be specified in the contract.

Walking Guests

Walking guests addresses the question, "What does the host facility do if there are no rooms available for guests that have confirmed reservations?" Although all meeting planners hope that this doesn't happen to anyone in their group, the reality of the situation is that it may. Meeting planners want to know what the host facility's policy is on walking guests. This is a policy that should be written into the contract. Generally, the host facility locates another hotel of equal quality and agrees to transport the guest to that hotel. The host facility then pays for that night's lodging and for the return of the guest on the following day.

Function Space

This section of the contract outlines the dates, times, setup, and square footage requirements of each function room (Price 1989, p. 40). As with sleeping rooms, specific locations (e.g., the Alexandria Room) should be identified in the contract. This assures that the host facility will reserve the exact rooms desired for specific functions.

Function room charges are determined in many ways. In the case of the convention center, it is important to remember that the majority of its revenue comes from the sale of function space; therefore, meeting planners can expect that the rental fees will be significant. In the case of a hotel, function room charges are often determined by the number of sleeping rooms and the size and number of food and beverage functions booked by a group. This is done when hotels are in the business of selling sleeping rooms, and it is generally true that meeting rooms sell sleeping rooms. Therefore, if a group uses only a small percentage of a hotel's sleeping rooms but requires all of its meeting space, the function room charges will be higher.

In some cases there may be charges that are associated with setting up and tearing down function space. Most host facilities define how much setup and takedown is included with the price of the room rental; anything above and beyond that would mean that the sponsoring organization incur additional charges. It is not uncommon for host facilities to have separate rates for risers, head tables, seating, dance floors, draping, security, and so on. Additionally, fees for the rental of audiovisual equipment can get charged back to the organization or association requesting them.

Food and Beverage

In the area of food and beverage, the contract should address the issues of costs, taxes, gratuities, labor charges, and corkage fees. The contract should establish that on an agreed upon date the host facility will furnish specified food and beverage at guaranteed prices. It also specifies how much notice the host facility requires concerning exact attendance figures, with 48 hours being the most common guarantee time limit. Furthermore, the contract should specify the type of service required (e.g., French-style service, buffet service), the number of servers, and the number of bussers needed for each of the events. Additional details for each function, such as linen color, centerpieces, and other decorations, also need to be thoroughly spelled out in the contract. Each of these items comes with a price tag that needs to be written into the legal document.

Taxes

Taxes are charges that the host has no control over because they are imposed by the local governmental jurisdiction. Taxes are paid for by the organization or association holding the function and need to be included in the contract. Taxes may have a significant effect on the overall cost of the event. The exception to this is if an organization or association has tax-exempt status, as is the case with many nonprofit groups. In this case it is incumbent upon the meeting planner to notify the host facility of this status before the contract is written.

Gratuities

Host facilities have different policies concerning gratuities, and meeting planners need to determine how these fees are levied on the organization or association sponsoring the events. In some cases, the gratuity is included as part of the labor agreement. It is more likely, however, that gratuities will be added on to the food and beverage costs, either before or after taxes, depending on state regulations regarding this issue. Since gratuitous charges can have a significant impact on the overall cost of the event, a meeting planner should clearly understand the policies of the host facility before any contract is signed (NAEM 1985).

Labor Charges

Labor charges may be imposed under various conditions, as determined by the policies of the host facility. For example, it is quite common to charge for waiter service at a reception or add a bartender's fee for cash bars, particularly if attendance figures do not meet expectations. Additionally, there may be a labor charge applied to all food and beverage functions, if attendance does not meet a minimum level. "Also, these charges can be applied to restaurants or snack stands within an exposition if the dollar value on a daily basis falls below an established minimum" (NAEM 1985, p. 10). These labor charges and the formula by which they are imposed vary widely from one host facility to another and need to be thoroughly understood by both parties, so that no hidden costs appear at a later date. In many cases an astute negotiator can reduce if not eliminate a portion of these labor charges.

Corkage Fees

Finally, within the food and beverage portion of the contract, it is necessary to include a brief section on the host facility's policy toward bringing in food and beverages from outside, a practice known as corkage. Generally, a corkage fee is levied on these items because some amount of labor is required from the host facility. For example, this labor may be in the form of uncorking and serving wine or plating up and serving specialty food items.

Exhibit Space Rental

For those meetings, conventions, and conferences that include exhibits, the next portion of the contract would apply. Here, the contract must describe in detail booth number, size, and cost, booth signage, special service requirements, move-in/move-out dates, union requirements, and any rules and regulations imposed by both parties. The contract should clearly spell out the organization's need for space to set up exhibits as well as all costs involved with the use of the space.

Generally, charges for the rental of the host facility's exhibit space is based on net square footage needed. In the case of an exposition facility, this is generally a flat rate. Rental prices may or may not include "cleaning, lighting, ventilation, storage space, office space, electricity, gas, plumbing, water, necessary signage, telephone service, cost of hall cleaning, and specified level of security" (NAEM, p. 10). Host facilities should specify what furniture it will supply, such as chairs, tables, and so on, and which furniture items require a rental fee.

Move-in/move-out dates are a vital part of any contract that includes booths and/or exhibits. Move-in dates refer to the number of days before the actual exhibition that booth space can be set up. Some exhibits may take several days to build within the exhibit hall; therefore, move-in dates will need to be established several days before the opening of the convention. Other booths are relatively simple to construct and require only a couple of hours setup time before the doors open to attendees. The same situation occurs when the exhibition is over and it is time to move the booths out of the facility. The host facility and meeting planner need to work closely to assure enough time for exhibit setup (figure 8-1) and teardown, considering the fact that the host facility may be dealing with another group that is ready to start its move-in process. If the host facility's rules and regulations specify a penalty for violating move-in/move-out dates, these must be outlined. Also, if there are any additional charges specifically calculated for the move-in/move-out time period, these must be written into the contract.

Every host facility has some special limitations. These may include floor load limits, dock space, door sizes, truck marshaling, empty storage space, height and sign limitations, and trash removal (NAEM, p. 11). All of these limitations must be clearly communicated within the pages of the contract.

Every host facility also has a set of rules and regulations to which the associations and organizations must comply. While the list can be as varied as the host facilities themselves, these may include fire and safety codes, crowd control measures, exhibit hours, space sharing arrangements, union requirements, information about security service, and cancellation policies. Another regulation that may be imposed upon groups wishing to use a specific facility is known as exclusivity. This is a situation where a facility has signed a contract with a specific service contractor to

Figure 8-1   Move-in and move-out dates dictate when a booth can be set up and torn down. Most host facilities impose specific penalties for violating these dates. (Courtesy: Kitzing, Inc.)

be the sole agent to provide those services. An example of an exclusivity contract may involve an electrical contractor or a decorator. Groups using the facility must agree to adhere to any exclusivity contracts that apply. As with all of the other items discussed in this section, it is important that all rules and regulations be fully described in the contract.

Agreements with Unions

In cities where labor is unionized, information about specific union jurisdiction and regulations needs to be included. In some cities union workers are responsible for a significant amount of the labor involved with a meeting, convention, or exposition, and a meeting planner needs to know exactly what is and what is not within the jurisdiction of the union (figure 8-2). According to Hildreth (1990), a scenario in a union town may go something like this:

A union picks up your shipped material. Another union loads it on a truck. Another union drives the truck to the site. Another union unloads the truck on the dock and another union moves the equipment to its general location at the site. Equipment must then be unpacked and set up. You must deal with the electrical union for setup of electrical equipment, the plumbers' union, the gas workers' union, and, of course, the unions of the personnel and workers at the meeting site (Hildreth 1990, p. 119).

Figure 8-2   In cities with unionized labor, the meeting planner needs to know what is and what is not within the jurisdiction of the union, to assure that union regulations are not violated. (Courtesy: The Freeman Companies.)

While this may seem extreme, it is actually a very common scenario in many locations. There are also as many variations to this union setup as there are locations. For instance, in Atlanta, Georgia, meeting planners only have to deal with one union, the International Association of Theatrical Stage and Electrical Workers. Whatever the union jurisdiction may be, meeting planners must be made aware of the them. Union regulations, such as basic workday rates, workday hours, and overtime charges, should be written out in the contract. Additionally, some hotels require the hiring of union labor for such positions as ticket sellers, guards, and so on. All of this is very important information to an individual who is planning all the logistics of a meeting, convention, or exposition.

Cancellation Clause

The next item that must be addressed is the cancellation clause. Five or ten years ago planners and host facilities could rely on a simple exchange of letters to confirm a deal. Along with that informality, host facilities were often quite willing to forget a deal that a planner could no longer live up to. Today, the written contract includes a cancellation policy that binds both the meeting planner and the host facility. Generally, this cancellation policy states that the contract may be canceled by either party when written notice is issued by an agreed upon date (NAEM, p. 11).

Once the cancellation date has passed, penalty charges will be assessed. These may be determined in a couple of different ways. One way is for the host facility to try to sell the space to another party and the original party need only pay for any unrented space. The other way is called liquidated damages. The liquidated damages provision insists that the organization or association pay a fixed amount of money to the host facility upon cancellation. The penalty for cancellation is usually a percentage of the total profit to the facility. This percentage increases the closer that the cancellation date is to the actual dates booked.

There is a meeting planner's side to the cancellation issue. If the host facility agrees to renovate, improve, or add on services to its facility, this is placed in the agreement. In case the facility fails to complete the changes specified in the contract, Price recommends that a clause be included that

> specifies dates that a facility will be under renovation (or construction), areas of the facility affected, an agreement regarding stop-work during [the] event, and a non-recourse option to move the meeting if any of the above change, in addition to paying any costs that are incurred by your organization, plus a penalty for the inconvenience (Price 1989, p. 41).

There are occasions where cancellation is beyond either party's control. Acts of God, government regulations, emergency conditions, strikes, and so forth, all may cause meetings, conferences, and expositions to be canceled. Within the contract there may be a release clause stating that, should any of these occur, the contract will be rendered null and void.

Arbitration Clause

While everyone involved with the meeting, convention, or exposition hopes that everything will go smoothly and that none of the terms of the contract will be violated, this is not always the case. For this reason, it is wise to include an arbitration clause in the standard contract. An arbitration clause calls for an objective third party to be called in to settle any disputes. One such clause may look something like:

> Any controversy or claim arising out of or relating to this contract, or breach thereof, shall be settled by arbitration in accordance with the commercial arbitration rules of the American Arbitration Association and judgement upon the award rendered by the arbitrator(s) may be entered in any court having jurisdiction thereof (NAEM, p. 12).

A clause such as the one above is for the protection of all parties.

Indemnification Clause

No contract would be complete without an indemnification clause, also referred to as a hold harmless clause. A well-written reciprocal indemnification clause states that the host will "pay the legal fees and any judgements against the group if someone sues the group and the (host) for something that was the (host's) fault; conversely, the group will do the same if someone sues the (host) and the group for something that was the group's fault" (Lieberman, p. 70). For example, an attendee might sue the host facility as well as the association because of food poisoning contracted during a banquet. Under the reciprocal indemnification clause, the host facility assumes the burden of defending the association.

Insurance

Most host facilities now require that the group or organization sponsoring the meeting, convention, or exposition have insurance coverage. Likewise, it is vitally important for all concerned that the host facility be fully insured. Both parties must agree to carry adequate liability and other insurance to protect against any claims arising from activities conducted while the group was at the host facility. Insurance requirements are spelled out in the contract.

One example of the type of insurance coverage needed by those involved in the meetings, conventions, and expositions of today is liquor liability insurance. Any time alcoholic beverages are served to attendees, there is the potential for an alcohol-related accident. While the trend now is for planners to spell out in contracts that the host facility maintain control of the sale and service of alcohol (thus indemnifying and holding planners harmless), this may not relieve the meeting planner and/or the sponsoring organization of liability in the eyes of the courts. Therefore, it is vitally important that both the host facility as well as meeting planner and the group that he or she represents obtain adequate liquor liability insurance.

Another type of insurance that is vitally important to every meeting planner is called professional liability insurance. Essentially, professional liability insurance protects the meeting planner from any damages that may result from wrongful doing by the planner or any member of the staff (Hildreth, p. 137). The saying goes, if anything can go wrong at a meeting, it will. By assuring that all parties are adequately covered by insurance, a great deal of the potential financial burden is alleviated. For this reason, it is necessary that the insurance requirements for all parties be clearly outlined in the contract.

Payment Procedures

Finally, the establishment of a master account and its payment schedule must be thoroughly documented in the contract. The master account is a "form on which authorized charges incurred in a facility by a group are recorded" (CLC, p. 18). The meeting planner is responsible for furnishing a list of all individuals who are authorized to sign for charges that are to be placed on this master account. Furthermore, the meeting planner should review all charges at the end of each day, while they are still fresh in his or her mind and sign the master account before leaving the premises.

In regards to payment of bills charged to the master account, host facilities vary somewhat on their policies. Many require either no deposit or a minimum advanced deposit, but expect full payment within 30 days of the event's conclusion. These properties generally assess penalty charges for late payment (NAEM, p. 13). Other properties may require up to a 50 percent deposit on projected total charges. Still other host facilities' policies state that partial payment must be made prior to departure. Whatever the policy, it must be agreed to by all parties and clearly outlined in the contract.

While the above pages discuss many essential components of a contract between a host facility and an organization or association, it is essential to understand that to some extent contracts must be individualized. This means that the contract needs to reflect the actual events being planned and the specific services desired. For instance, some groups may contract with the host facility for shuttle service to and from the airport. This should be written into the contract. The general advice given to all those involved with contracts is that nothing should be left to memory. If it isn't written down, don't expect it to happen.

When planning a meeting, convention, or exposition, there are many other contracts that a meeting planner may be involved in. These may include decorators, florists, transportation companies, entertainment companies, security companies, and music copyrights. In a nutshell, whenever services are required from another party and payment will be rendered for those services, a contract should be written. This is the best assurance a meeting planner or contractor has that all parties will fulfill their commitments.

An example of an additional contract would be one that involves a speaker. According to Darcy L. Bouzeos, there are eight main points that should be covered in a speaker's contract. These are:

1. The nature of the meeting—is it to inform, entertain, or raise money?
2. Speaker's responsibilities—does the speaker just speak or also stay around for dinner or informal discussions?
3. Time and location.
4. The fee and terms of payment.
5. Travel and lodging— who pays?
6. Cancellation clauses.
7. Publicity and media—can the presentation be taped? Will media be covering the event? How will this event be advertised?
8. Security—while many politicians and entertainers travel with their own security, some do not (Bouzeos 1989).

This sort of a contract provides all the details necessary to ensure a clear understanding of what is expected by all parties involved.

International Contractual Considerations

With the rise in the number of international meetings being held, it is appropriate that the final portion of this section address contractual considerations of international meetings. Price advises that meetings that are held in foreign countries or meetings that are held in this country but include international visitors consider the following issues when drawing up a contract:

1. Contracts drawn up in one country may not be legal or binding in another country;
2. Contracts should state which country's laws will bind the parties;
3. Contract should be reviewed by legal counsel and an insurance agent familiar with the laws of both countries;
4. All terms should be defined and interpretation should be mutually acceptable by both parties;
5. Contracts should specify applicable local and national laws that may affect your meeting, such as taxes and collection procedures, energy regulations controlling the supply or hours of service, curfew, alcohol usage (Price, p. 441).

Ethics

The New Encyclopedia Britannica (1992) describes ethics or moral philosophy as "a discipline concerned with what is morally good and bad, right and wrong" (p. 578). The word ethics comes from the Greek root, ethos, which means character; guiding beliefs, standards, or ideals that permeate society (Sisk and Williams 1981). Ethics cannot be studied like one would study the subject of accounting, which has definite rights and wrongs and rules and regulations. Instead, the study of ethics is the viewing of ethical concerns and the possible consequences in light of one's own values (Keiser 1989).

The common notion of ethics as a treatise on moral life suggests that to live well morally, i.e., to lead a good human life, is both necessary and desirable. Any human being wishes to lead as happy a life as possible, and we have no hesitancy in associating a good moral life with a happy life, for this association is one that agrees with the facts of ordinary experience and is in conformity with the traditional approach to the study of ethics from the time of the ancient Greeks. To live well morally requires at least a minimum knowledge of what it is to live well as a human being. The purpose of ethics, therefore, from the standpoint of the science itself, and from the viewpoint of the knower, is a practical one: to live well as a human being.

Ethics—or good and bad, right and wrong—has been a topic of discussion and an area of study since the beginning of time, but the era deemed as the most important age of philosophy and ethics in the world occurred during the period of 469 B.C. to 322 B.C. (Hall 1992). This was the era of Socrates, Plato, and Aristotle, all of whom made a major impact on the modern day individual's understanding of ethics. The scholars of that time period centered their study around:

ESTHETICS (the study of ideal form, or beauty), *POLITICS* (the study of ideal form, or aristocracy, democracy, socialism, anarchism), *METAPHYSICS* (a study of matter [ontology], of the mind [psychology] and "matter" in the process of perception and knowledge [epistemology]), and finally *ETHICS* (the study of ideal conduct) (Hall 1991).

Ethics were also impacted by the teachings of Jesus Christ and Christianity, Islam and Mohammed, Buddhism and Buddha, and Mormonism and Joseph Smith. Throughout history, the religious order of the day has made its mark on the ethics of society.

Ethics and the study of ethics has become an increasingly important topic in society today. Business ethics is now being taught in various schools within the university system (Drucker 1991). One cannot attend a meeting or conference without having as one of the areas covered on the program the topic of ethics.

Ethical dilemmas plague society today. One cannot turn on the television nor read a newspaper without finding out about someone's unethical behavior. Government is haunted by the actions of past officials, corporations are reeling from recent allegations of misconduct, and individuals are daily faced with personal decisions about ethical behavior. James Keiser, in his book *Principles and Practices of Management in the Hospitality Industry,* states some reasons for the current interest in business ethics. These reasons are:

1. A drift toward materialism and greed, pushing people to acquire wealth or status beyond their real needs and to want more regardless of what it takes to get it.
2. The deregulation of some industries, intensifying competition and encouraging managers to cut corners.
3. The growing size of business enterprises, which dilutes and spreads personal responsibility for unethical acts.
4. A growing hedonism, leading people to be more concerned with their own happiness than with responsibility to others.
5. A lack of moral leadership among prominent people and abundant examples of people (even some religious figures) who prosper from moral laxity and greed.
6. The breakdown of the family and the sense of familial responsibility traditionally transmitted to children.
7. An increased reliance on government, which has decreased the individual's sense of responsibility for himself or others (Keiser 1989 p. 342).

The question is not whether there is a problem with society's ethics, but rather how can we correct the problems that are so prevalent in today's business world? "Man has aspirations toward the good, the beautiful, and the true," according to Harold Titus.

"Unless he can fulfill and express these functions, he falls short of self-realization and lasting happiness" (Titus, 1947 p. 233).

Unfortunately, the pressures of today place the individual in the position of making choices based on profit, promotion, or personal gain, thus throwing the individual into a stressful situation. Ethical strain results when short-term opportunities to maximize profit, promotion, or personal gain come at the expense of long-term quality concerns (Whitney 1992).

Based on the headlines of today's newspapers and the lead stories on the nightly news, it appears that many people have forgotten about ethics. Individuals today make their choices based on what appears to be logical or reasonable to them according to their own personal value system. This is called "ethical relativism" (Angelo and Vladimir 1991). In their book *Hospitality Today: An Introduction,* Angelo and Vladimir state that, "although we all have different personal values and morals, we should recognize that there are some universal principles that virtually all religions, cultures, and societies agree upon" (p. 390). It is upon these universal principles that one should build his or her own personal code of ethics.

Working Ethics according to Marvin T. Brown, author of *Working Ethics,* provides help to organizations and therefore individuals by:

1. Laying out the process of ethical reflection so that people can use it with their own issues;
2. Connecting ethical notions, such as rights and justice, to the management of systems of power so that people can manage these systems appropriately;
3. Showing how to analyze and evaluate the different components of the decision-making process so that people will have as many good resources available as possible; and
4. Offering methods of developing an organizational climate in which ethical reflection can be practiced and improved (Brown 1991, p. xxi).

Ethical practices stem from the organization's commitment to servicing their client in a fair and equitable manner. The structure of an organization dictates its ability to respond to situations in an ethical manner. Without structural support for an ethical decision-making process, it is impossible to expect individuals employed by the business to be able to make ethical decisions. Donald V. Seibert, CEO and chairman of the J.C. Penney company, was quoted as saying "During the four decades I have been in business, I have found that the corporate world is filled with businessmen who want to do what is right, not with Scrooges who delight in exploiting widows and orphans. The vast majority of today's executives are ethical and honest. Yet sometimes we can become so occupied with fretting over our mathematical models, sales projections and quarterly earnings statements that it is difficult to keep in mind one of the most basic truths of successful business—in the long run, the best business decision is that which is founded on the most ethical judgments" (Wright 1991).

In their book *It's Good Business,* Solomon and Hanson state that there are three reasons why ethics are practical. These are (Solomon and Hanson 1991):

1. Ethical errors end careers more quickly and more definitively than any other mistake in judgement or accounting.
2. Ethics provides the broader framework within which business life must be understood.
3. Nothing is more dangerous to a business—or to business in general—than a tarnished public image.

Ethics are a very personal component of one's psyche and therefore very difficult to change. They are ingrained at a very early age. Courses and books designed to address the issue of ethics do not for all intents and purposes change an individual's ethics, but they can cause an individual to review their ethical behavior in light of today's society. They can also force the individual to analyze their actions in view of ethics. This is a very important exercise, especially in light of the degrading ethical behavior of today. The quest for success and for the almighty dollar has led many individuals to act in ways that have caused personal and professional ruin. This greed has been the impetus for the lack of concern regarding ethical behavior in many organizations today. Society has become so concerned with what they view as a total lack of regard for right and wrong that it is demanding a more ethical approach to business.

Universities are responding by adding courses within their curricula on ethics. If they are not adding entire courses, they are adding sections on ethics within specific courses. Businesses are responding by implementing training programs designed to address ethics. Programs such as Corporate Values Program and Ethical Reasoning Program (Johnson 1990) are contrived to help businesses work towards a more ethical business behavior among their employees.

The Corporate Values Program is designed to be a workshop that places employees into small group situations where they examine their company's values. Once the group has a clear understanding of the company's values, they address the company's ethical responsibilities to its clients, stockholders, employees, and so on. They also discuss any barriers to ethical behavior. Many companies will use this workshop as the starting point for developing a "corporate values statement" (Johnson 1990).

The Ethical Reasoning Program (Johnson 1990) is the type of program being offered in most universities. It addresses the great readings on ethics and allows the students to contemplate and discuss these works. This type of class also allows the participants a chance to review their own personal codes of ethics as it relates to the broader scope of societal practices. Many professors use a case study approach to teach this course. Because there are a number of ethics courses being taught around the world in various business schools, many companies just pay for their employees to take these courses. Making use of preexisting courses avoids reinventing the wheel while still providing an excellent framework for addressing ethics.

"Business leaders realize that although they might not be able to change the values and morals of employees, they can change the behavior of employees on the job" (Johnson 1990, p. 167). In their book *The Power of Ethical Management,* Kenneth Blanchard and Norman Vincent Peale discuss the fact that ethical behavior on the part of the employee basically is related to one thing—how the employee perceives they are being treated by the organization and its management (1988). If employees believe that the company is not treating them fairly or that the company is only concerned about the bottom line and not about their employees or their customers, they are less likely to be concerned about their own ethical behavior. It is important to realize that, although society is focusing on major ethical issues, it is the day to day activities of a manager that transmits their beliefs and values to their workers. Therefore, a company's daily standard operating procedures are the best example of their ethical beliefs.

Blanchard and Peale state that the ethical behavior of a company must start at the top. They contend that at the root of ethical behavior there are "The Five Principles of Ethical Power for Organizations." These five principles are:

1. Purpose: The mission of an organization is communicated from the top. The organization is guided by the values, hopes, and vision that helps them to determine what is acceptable and unacceptable behavior.
2. Pride: They feel proud of themselves and their organization. They know that when they feel this way they can resist temptations to behave unethically.
3. Patience: They believe that holding to their ethical values will lead them to success in the long term. This involves maintaining a balance between obtaining results and caring how they achieve these results.
4. Persistence: They have a commitment to live by ethical principles. They are committed to their commitment. They make sure their actions are consistent with their purpose.
5. Perspective: Their managers and employees take time to pause and reflect, take stock of where they are, evaluate where they are going, and determine how they are going to get there. (Blanchard and Peale 1988, p. 128)

A company that adheres to the five principles of ethical power will be successful in meeting the needs of their employees and therefore will have an easier time of encouraging their employees to behave in an ethical manner.

The five principles of ethical power for organizations sets the framework for a company to develop a code of ethics that reflect their goals and objectives. It is important for a company to have its own code of ethics or corporate values statement. This statement must then be communicated to everyone in the organization. Many companies place a copy of their code of ethics in their employee handbook. Some companies require that their employees sign a statement saying that they agree to perform all duties in accordance with the company's code of ethics.

Employees will be more likely to respond in an ethical manner if they are familiar with the company's code of ethics and if they have had a chance to practice. Therefore, every training session, regardless of its subject matter, should have an ethical slant to it. There should be segments of the training program that ask the participants to react to certain situations based on the company's ethical beliefs and standards. A company might not be able to change their employees' ethical beliefs, but they can make every effort possible to train their employees to make decisions and to respond to important situations based on the company's ethical beliefs.

The commitment to ethical behavior must start at the top of an organization. If the leader of the organization does not understand the importance of acting in an ethical manner, those underneath have an up-hill battle to fight if they choose to adhere to their own personal code of ethics. However, if a company believes that ethics is good business, the administration must insure that the systems are put in place to encourage ethical behavior. Often, company policies dictate unethical behavior (remember the overbooking policy). If this is the case, then the company needs to reevaluate its policies and procedures in light of its own code of ethics.

Ethics in the Hospitality Industry

The hospitality industry is being faced with the demand for more and improved services. One cannot address the issue of service without addressing ethics.

> By nature, the hospitality industry is subject to ethical constraints and opportunities. Of all industries, it is the most intensely interactive: people serving people and providing comfort, sustenance, conviviality, transport, amusement, enlightenment, employment, and more. In this maelstrom of human behavior, concerns of right and wrong can be neither ignored nor hidden. For that reason, perhaps the most challenging of all hospitality industry problems is that of ethics. (Hall 1992, p. 7)

The hospitality industry, specifically the meetings, conventions and expositions segment of the industry, is constantly under siege in the ethical decision-making arena. The hospitality industry is ripe for deception and unethical behavior due to the very nature of the business. The pressure to make a profit often outweighs an individual's or company's code of ethics. A perfect example of this is the common practice of overbooking rooms. The supplier—in this case, the hotel—is guaranteeing a product that they know may very likely not be available to the customer. Although this conduct in and of itself could be interpreted as an unethical decision, failure to overbook may lead to a number of unsold rooms, resulting in a loss of profit. Decisions such as this occur daily in the hospitality industry.

The characteristics of the hospitality industry's working environment definitely influences the ethical choices made by individuals within the industry. Keiser states that there are four familiar occurrences centered around these facts (Keiser 1989):

1. Travelers are far from home.
2. Hospitality is a service, not a product.
3. The hospitality work force is vulnerable.
4. Alcoholic beverages often accompany the profession.

The fact that the hospitality industry deals with many individuals who are not in their normal surroundings means that it has a special responsibility to its clients. Individuals who are traveling and are unfamiliar with the area have a right to expect fair and equitable treatment from a lodging facility. Guests in a restaurant have a right to expect truth in the menu and to be served food that is wholesome and good to eat. In the case of the traveler, often times they will not remain in the area long enough to file a complaint with the management regarding wrongful treatment; therefore, it is incumbent upon the hospitality industry and the companies that service individuals to monitor their own behavior to avoid situations that place the entire industry in a bad light.

The fact that hospitality is a service and not a product is also an important issue when discussing ethical behavior. If an individual buys a faulty watch, he or she can take it back to the store from which it was bought and obtain a new watch or have the faulty one repaired. If an individual receives poor service or is treated inappropriately, it is more difficult to undo the damage.

The hospitality industry is also closely related to the service of alcoholic beverages. Alcoholic beverages and their effects on the customer open up an entirely different realm of questions regarding ethical behavior on the part of the hospitality industry. The consumption of alcoholic beverages by a customer may lead to impaired reasoning capabilities and therefore leave them open to mistreatment by an employee. For example, they may be too drunk to notice being overcharged or being treated poorly.

Figure 8-3 Service and ethics are closely related issues. The Ritz Carlton Hotel in Atlanta was the winner of the Malcolm Baldridge National Quality Award. (Courtesy: National Institute of Standards and Technology.)

Overconsumption of alcoholic beverages by customers also raises the important issues of liquor liability and ethical responsibility for the actions of the individual who has overconsumed. Laws are currently being tested in this area, but ethics are not necessarily dictated by law. Therefore, it is incumbent upon individual hospitality organizations to determine their own ethical responsibility to the customer and to the public.

The last area Keiser discusses is ethics as they relate to employees. Employees within the hospitality industry are oftentimes from lower economic backgrounds or are disadvantaged in some way and thus are susceptible to being taken advantage of by unscrupulous managers. Substandard wages and working conditions are not uncommon in many hospitality operations. "Ethics is not a set of absolute principles, divorced from and imposed on everyday life. Ethics is a way of life, a seemingly delicate but in fact very strong tissue of endless adjustments and compromises. It is the awareness that one is an intrinsic part of a social order, in which the interests of others and one's own interests are inevitably intertwined" (Solomon and Hanson 1985, p. 157). The ability to be ethical within the hospitality industry is not, as some would have us believe, an unattainable goal. As Kenneth Blanchard and Norman Vincent Peale say in their book *The Power of Ethical Management,* "There is no right way to do a wrong thing" (1988, p. 9). The key therefore is to develop business practices (see figure 8-4) that do not deviate from what is morally right and good.

Ethics in the Meetings, Convention, and Exposition Industry

If the hospitality industry in general is fertile ground for unethical practices, then the meetings, convention, and exposition industry is a gardener's dream. Here is a segment of the industry where business is built on relationships, where taking care of the personal needs of a customer is considered good business. Opportunities for unethical behavior abound. Certain practices within the meetings and conventions industry are more likely to lead to unethical behavior than others. A discussion of some of these follows.

Familiarization (FAM) trips, are designed to provide an opportunity for prospective buyers to review the facilities and services of a specific site. These trips generally provide royal treatment for all participants and therefore can be a very enjoyable experience. FAM trips are frequently abused by both planners and suppliers. Planners should only accept a FAM trip package if there is the potential for doing business with the supplier at some future date. Unfortunately, it has long been the practice of some planners to use these FAM trips as personal vacations, even though they have absolutely no intention of booking a meeting or convention with the particular property. It is incumbent upon meeting planners to refrain from going on FAM trips unless there is a strong likelihood that they will use the property in the future. It is also important that the properties qualify their guest list more carefully.

CODE OF ETHICS
HOSPITALITY SERVICE AND TOURISM INDUSTRY

1. We acknowledge ethics and morality as inseparable elements of doing business and will test every decision against the highest standards of honesty, legality, fairness, impunity and conscience.

2. We will conduct ourselves personally and collectively at all times so as to bring credit to the service and tourism industry at large.

3. We will concentrate our time, energy, and resources on the improvement of our own product and services and we will not denigrate our competition in the pursuit of our own success.

4. We will treat all guests equally regardless of race, religion, nationality, creed or sex.

5. We will deliver all standards of service and product with total consistency to every guest.

6. We will provide a totally safe and sanitary environment at all times for every guest and employee.

7. We will strive constantly, in words, actions, and deeds to develop and maintain the highest level of trust, honesty, and understanding among guests, clients, employees, employers, and the public at large.

8. We will provide every employee at every level all of the knowledge, training, equipment and motivation required to perform his or her tasks according to our published standards.

9. We will guarantee that every employee at every level will have the same opportunity to perform, advance, and will be evaluated against the same standards as all employees engaged in the same or similar tasks.

10. We will actively and consciously work to protect and preserve our environment and natural resources in all that we do.

11. We will seek a fair and honest profit, no more, no less.

Figure 8-4   Code of ethics for the hospitality and tourism industry. (Courtesy: IIQUEST.)

Incentive packages are another area of concern for the meetings and conventions industry. These packages are designed much like the frequent flier programs used by the airlines. The incentive packages offer gifts in return for certain levels of repeat bookings. These gifts are often personal in nature, such as expensive jewelry, personal vacations, or private car rentals for extended periods of time. If the meeting planner is planning the meeting or convention in a specific facility in an attempt to win one of these prizes instead of because the facility is the best suited for the meeting or convention, then the decision would appear to be unethical. If, however, the site would have been chosen regardless of the incentive package, there could still be a question as to whether or not the planner is responding in an unethical way by personally benefiting from the transaction.

Some meeting planners or association executives may also use their position to request personal favors. These personal favors take the shape of asking suppliers to provide discounted rooms (or requesting rooms in an otherwise heavy traffic period of time) or requesting discounted or free tickets for shows or other various forms of entertainment. With the industry facing tough economic times, these requests place the suppliers in an awkward position. If they honor the request, it may be costly and therefore affect the bottom line, but if they do not honor the request they may anger the client and risk losing any future business.

On the supplier side, there are individuals or corporations who routinely book business knowing that they physically cannot handle the demand. As stated in chapter 5, these are two unfortunate realities of a sales office:

1. Quotas are enforced on salespeople, frequently putting unrealistic pressures on the staff to book groups.
2. The average tenure of sales personnel is short enough that chances are good that the groups that an individual salesperson will book will arrive long after that salesperson has left the property. If a person knows that he or she probably will not be with the property by the time the group moves in, they may be more inclined to book the business to meet quotas, regardless of whether or not the facility can adequately service the group.

These are just a few examples of how the meetings, conventions, and expositions segment of the hospitality industry is open to ethical dilemmas. Individually, it may be argued that these practices hurt no one, but collectively these practices convey a sense of unethical behavior that will ultimately blacken the eye of the entire industry.

There have been movements within the industry to develop an industrywide code of ethics. Professional associations related to the meetings, conventions, and expositions industry have developed codes of ethics for their memberships to adhere to. An example is PCMA's code of ethics, shown in figure 8-5. There is no question that ethics are vitally important to the success of any given industry, but especially to the hospitality industry and specifically for the meetings, conventions, and expositions segment of the industry. But, as stated earlier, ethics is an important and integral part of an individual's psyche and therefore cannot be dictated by anyone but the person themselves.

Hunter Lewis, in his book *A Question of Values,* states that there are six ways an individual develops his or her own personal code of ethics. The six ways are (adapted from Hunter Lewis's book *A Question of Values* 1990, pp. 10–11.) :

1. **Authority**—Individuals base their own personal beliefs on what they have been told. Formal religion often serves as the authority in this case.
2. **Deductive logic**—In this scenario individuals deduce their own personal code of ethics from what appears to be logical from past experiences.
3. **Sense experience**—Individuals base their own personal code of ethics on what they have learned through their five senses. They believe something because they have seen it themselves, heard it themselves, and so on.
4. **Emotion**—Often times emotions play an extremely important role in an individual's perception of what is right and wrong. They "feel" a certain way about something, and this feeling dictates whether or not something is right or wrong.
5. **Intuition**—Often referred to as the "gut feeling." People use their unconscious or intuitive mind to arrive at what they believe is good or bad.
6. **Science**—This is the collection of facts, the development of a hypothesis, the conduction of an experiment, and the arrival at the "truth," from which an individual will then derive a personal code of ethics.

Regardless of the constraints placed on people by outside forces, such as the organizations they work for, the governments they live under, or the professional organizations they belong to, it is important for individuals to develop their own personal code of ethics. They must at sometime determine what exactly they believe in and what truths govern their lives. Based upon these truths, they can develop their own personal code of ethics. They must

The Professional Convention Management Association *represents the highest levels of ethical behavior and authoritative resourcefulness in the convention planning industry. It is therefore appropriate that this association has adopted these* **PRINCIPLES OF PROFESSIONAL CONDUCT** *and that its members use them as standards of honorable behavior by which they may evaluate their relationships with organizations, suppliers and colleagues.*

I will:

I.   *Approach all meetings in accordance with the highest ethical standards of professionalism and personal conduct.*

II.   *Negotiate all agreements in good faith respecting the rights of all parties involved.*

III. *Respect the policies and regulations of those organizations with whom I deal.*

IV.   *Participate and encourage others to participate in continuing education endeavors/opportunities related to my chosen profession.*

V.   *Refrain from activities that will cause damage or discredit to myself, my organization or my profession.*

VI.   *Seek opportunities to increase public understanding and awareness of the convention management industry.*

VII. *Not use my position for personal gain or benefit to the detriment or disadvantage of my organization and, I will advise my organization of any circumstances that may have the appearance of a conflict of interest.*

VIII. *Further the stated purpose of the Professional Convention Management Association.*

Figure 8-5   PCMA's Code of Ethics.

then judge all actions based on this code. Solomon and Hanson, in their book *It's Good Business,* suggest "Ten Critical Steps" to assist in ethical decisions and dilemmas. These steps are (from *It's Good Business* by Robert C. Solomon and Kristine Hanson.):

1. What really is the problem?
2. How did the problem arise? What is the history and structure of the organization? Anyone at fault?
3. What is the antagonist's position? (Be sympathetic; play devil's advocate with yourself.)
4. Whom are you serving? Where is your loyalty?
5. Whom does your action injure? How? How badly?
6. Can you negotiate? Is there a compromise? (There almost always is.) With whom should you speak?
7. Will this decision seem like the right one a year from now? 5 years from now? In a book on the history of the company/association/institution 15 years from now?
8. Could you describe your actions and intentions to your supervisor, your CEO, the stockholders, the board of directors, the trustees? Would you have to distort or seriously edit your description? If so, what is wrong?
9. Could you tell your family about your action? Could your children use your action as a model? Could you describe it without qualms to the media?
10. What self-interested motives guide your action? What altruistic motives are guiding or could guide the same actions? How could your motives be misinterpreted or misunderstood? What symbolic value (bolstered bottom line, improved company reputation, reduced regulation, social justice, etc.) could result when your action is properly described?

Summary

This chapter has reviewed the importance of contracts for those involved with the meetings, conventions, and expositions industry. All the players must be cognizant of the factors involved in the negotiation phase as well as be able to knowledgeably review a contract.

This chapter also reviewed the overall concept of ethics. Ethics has been an area of concern since the beginning of time. Great works have been written about the importance of ethical behavior and social responsibility. Although ethical dilemmas appear to be receiving a lot of press lately, unethical behavior has always been a source of contention within the business community. In no other segment of the business world is ethics more important than in the hospitality industry.

Ethics is an important area of concern for the meetings, conventions, and expositions industry. This industry cannot ignore the need to reevaluate its ethical standards. For a transformation of the overall ethical behavior of an industry, changes must take place on a personal level. These changes cannot not be wrought by any other means than to closely review one's own personal code of ethics in view of today's standards and practices.

References

Angelo, R.M., and A.M. Vladimir. 1991. *Hospitality Today: An Introduction.* East Lansing, Mich.: Educational Institute of the American Hotel & Motel Association.

Astroff, M.T., and J.R. Abbey. 1988. *Convention Sales and Services,* second edition. Cranbury, N.J.: Waterbury Press.

Auman-Butler, Paula. 1986. Where can they afford to give? *Corporate Meetings and Incentives,* pp. 13–21.

Blanchard, K., and N.V. Peale. 1988. *The Power of Ethical Management.* New York: Fawcett Crest, p. 8.

Bouzeos, Darcy. 1989. Inking the deal. *Successful Meetings,* (October) pp. 63–66.

Brown, M.T. 1991. *Working Ethics.* San Francisco: Jossey-Bass, p. xii.

Butler, Charles. 1991. The party's over. *Successful Meetings,* (November) pp. 32–36.

Convention Liaison Council Glossary. 1986.

Crystal, Susan. 1991. Twists on liquor liability. *Meetings and Conventions,* (January) pp. 42–55.

Del Prete, Dom. 1990. Despite unions, Javits finds willing exhibitors. Meetings and Conventions, (April) p. 22

Drucker, P.F. 1991. Morality, what's in it for me? *Ethical Chic,* pp. 47–48.

Dubois, D. A. 1990. Ethics in the meeting industry. *Convene Magazine,* pp. 15, 18– 19.

Encyclopedia Britannica. 1992. Ethics, Vol. 4, Chicago: Encyclopedia Britannica Inc. pp. 578–579.

Foster, John. 1989. Armed for the deal. *Association Meetings,* (December) pp. 32–35.

Hall, S. J. 1991. *Ethics in Hospitality Curriculum.* East Lansing, Mich.: IQUEST.

Hall, S. J. 1992. *Ethics in Hospitality Management,* p. 7. East Lansing, Mich.: Educational Institute.

Hildreth, Richard A. 1990. *The Essentials of Meeting Management.* Englewood Cliffs, N.J.: Prentice Hall.

Johnson, V. 1990. Business ethics. *Successful Meetings,* (June) p. 103.

Keiser, J.R. 1989. *Principles and Practices of Management in the Hospitality Industry,* second edition. New York: Van Nostrand Reinhold. p. 342.

Lieberman, Gregg. 1992. Think before you ink. *Meetings and Conventions,* (January) pp. 58–70.

Meyerowitz, Steven A. 1989. Mayhem at meetings. *Business Marketing,* (September) p. 81.

National Association of Exposition Managers. 1985. Hotel/Client Agreement Guidelines and Information.

Price, Catherine. 1985. *The AMA Guide for Meeting and Event Planners.* American Management Association.

Osterle, John A. 1957. *Ethics, the Introduction to Moral Science.* Englewood Cliffs, N. J.: Prentice Hall.

Sisk, H.L., and J.C. Williams. *Management & Organization,* fourth edition. Cincinnati: South-Western Publishing Co.

Solomon, R.C., and K. Hanson. 1985. *It's Good Business,* p. 5–7. New York: Antheum.

Titus, H.H. 1954. *Ethics for Today, 2nd ed.,* p. 233. New York: American Book Co.

Wright, J.H. (1991) " Ethics in the Meetings and Convention Industry," Remarks at Convention/Expo Summit II. Las Vegas, Nevada.

Wolfson, Stanley. 1988. *The Meeting Planners' Complete Guide to Negotiating: You Can Get What you Institute Want.* Institute for Meeting and Conference Management.

Discussion Questions

1. Discuss the importance of maintaining a strong personal code of ethics.
2. How can participants in negotiations strive for a "win-win" settlement?
3. What items are negotiable and why?
4. Develop your own personal code of ethics.
5. How can systems within the hospitality industry be designed to enable its employees to follow sound ethical behavior?
6. How can poor ethical judgements impact one's career? Use specific examples.

Key Terms

negotiations

contracts

uniform commercial code

arbitration

cancellation clause

gratuities

labor charges

corkage

indemnification clause

ethics

9

Meeting Technology

Learning Objectives

1. To provide an introduction to technology and its impact on the meetings, conventions, and expositions industry.
2. To inventory the types of technology available to the meetings, conventions, and expositions industry.
3. To provide basic knowledge about how various types of technology are used within the industry.

Introduction

The subject of technology as it pertains to meetings encompasses many different areas. First, there is the issue of technology as it is used to enhance meeting presentations. Here the topics range from overhead projectors to telecommunications, three-dimensional image projection, and computerized meetings. The second area where technology strongly influences meetings is in the planning stages of the meetings themselves. Meeting planners and host properties alike have found such technological advances as the fax machine and desktop publishing capabilities to be invaluable. The third area is in relationship to the attendees themselves. Subjects addressed include check-in, check-out, and business centers within the host facility.

The purpose of this chapter is to present an overview of the technological advances as they relate to the meetings, conventions, and expositions industry. It is also important to discuss the various formats that host facilities use for providing audiovisual and other media equipment services to the client and how that equipment is maintained.

The Meeting

"This is the height of the Information Age, the era of telephone bank transfers, fax machines, and voice mail. Inundated with information, spoiled by the electronic media and computers, today's attendees are nothing like the meeting-goers of ten, or even five years ago" (Crystal 1992, p. 73).

Crystal, in her article "Plugged In" (*Meetings and Conventions* 1992), suggests that the onset of the information age has truly changed expectations of meeting attendees. Consider the influence of television. The average attendee's attention span is 20 minutes—the same amount of time between television commercials. Furthermore, if the attendees' interest is not maintained, they will use their mental remote control to tune out the program. Just as on TV, people today want their information quick and easy, and they expect to be entertained while they learn.

Peter McGugan advises meeting planners to "plan your meetings with the mind-set of a television producer or a media specialist, because meetings today are show business" (Crystal, p. 79). This means incorporating several different mediums into the sessions. Using flashes of color, rapid pacing, humor, imagination, and storytelling, rather than lecturing, are all techniques that incorporate variety into a presentation. All of these expectations are a result of the information age. Meeting planners and speakers who acknowledge and incorporate advanced technology in their presentations will have greater success in the implementation of their meetings.

Meeting Technology Implementation

While the amount of new technology to be applied to meetings seems endless, it is necessary to acknowledge that many meetings, conventions, and expositions need only incorporate traditional audiovisual equipment into their presentations. In this section we will address traditional as well as new innovations in meeting technology. The advantages and disadvantages of these mediums will also be discussed briefly.

When choosing the best medium to be used, the importance of a visual presentation must be emphasized. Catherine Price in her AMA guide for meeting and event planners acknowledges that retention is doubled when a person both sees and hears information. The options for visual presentations are expanding considerably. Traditional visual equipment includes projection media, such as overhead projectors, slide projectors, 16mm movies, and videocassettes, as well as non-projection media, such as chalkboards, white boards, flip charts, and easels. New technologies include electronic writing boards, teleconferencing, and closed-circuit television.

Overhead projectors operate "on the principle of passing an intense light through a transparent slide. The image is then passed through a mirrored lens and reflected on the screen"(Forrest, p. 136). Transparent slides are made of plastic, cellophane, or acetate. The slides are easily made by photocopying printed materials onto the plastic, cellophane, or acetate slide. Color slides are possible as long as the original is in color, and color photocopying capabilities are available.

There are many advantages to using overhead projectors.

1. Most host facilities keep overhead projectors on their standard list of audiovisual equipment, making them easily accessible in most situations.

2. The slides are easy to transport.
3. The speaker can face the audience while using overhead slides.
4. The room does not have to be completely darkened for overhead transparencies to be effective.
5. The equipment is user friendly.

Overhead projectors require a projection screen to be set up in the front of the room. Visibility may be limited due to room obstructions or distance to the back of the room. It is therefore recommended that overhead projectors be used in groups that include no more than 60 participants.

The most recent technological development concerning overhead projection has been the introduction of an LCD projection panel. This is a special attachment that sits on top of a standard overhead projector and is attached to a personal computer. The LCD panel projects whatever is on the computer monitor, making it large enough for easy audience viewing. The introduction of this computer attachment has been an invaluable tool in many training seminars.

Another very common visual medium is 35mm slide projectors. These projectors accommodate transparent pictures mounted in 2-by-2-inch cardboard frames. The image is projected onto a screen by passing a strong light through the transparent picture. There are many advantages to using 35mm slides and projectors:

1. Slides are compact and convenient to transport.
2. Slides project clear, detailed images (if the photography is of high quality).
3. Additional or replacement slides are easily accommodated in the slide carousel.
4. Fully automated slide projectors change slides at a predetermined rate.
5. Slide projectors are simple to use and require minimum training.
6. Most slide projectors can be connected to an audio-sync tape recorder to provide music and/or a narrative accompaniment.
7. Slide projectors can accommodate a wireless remote control system to allow the presenter freedom of movement.

When using 35mm slides, presenters need to remember that a single slide should be exposed for a minimum of 5 seconds to give the viewer time to absorb the information and not longer than 90 seconds to avoid boredom (Forrest, p. 135).

An endangered species of the audiovisual world is the film projector. Not many years ago, films (motion pictures) were a popular method by which to create variety in the dissemination of information. But there were many problems with using them. Film projectors were difficult to operate and were always breaking. The film itself was continuously breaking or coming off the reel, and the quality of both audio and visual were less than ideal. Today's meeting planners will rarely if ever have to accommodate a film projector. However, they should know where to find one, should the occasion arise.

Today, film projectors have been replaced by more user friendly videotape recorders. Video tape recorders, as with their motion picture predecessors, "display events or a sequence of events with movement as compared to still photographs, overhead transparencies, 35mm slides. . ." (Forrest, p. 137).

There are many advantages to incorporating video recordings into meetings, conventions, or expositions:

1. Videos can be substituted for live demonstrations, especially when expensive equipment or long periods of time may be needed to do the complete demonstration.
2. Videos can be substituted for expert speakers, when the speaker is either unavailable for the specific dates requested or is prohibitively expensive. For example, fees for professional speakers start at about $2,500 and can go well over $10,000 (not including traveling expenses), while the cost of a speaker tape will be at most $500 (Alonzo 1991).
3. Videos are excellent substitutions for either demonstrations or speakers when the subject matter needs to be repeated during several different sessions.
4. Video recorders have instant replay capabilities.
5. Video recordings are easily transported, and a minimum amount of training is required to use the playback equipment.

The major drawback to the use of video is cost. Professional quality production costs about $1,000 to $4,000 per minute (Forrest, p. 138). Therefore, having a video recording made for a specific need may be cost prohibitive.

Non-projection media, such as chalkboards, white boards, and flip charts, are certainly at the low end of the technology spectrum. However, they are often vitally important to the overall success of a meeting, convention, or exposition.

White boards are the newest version of the old-fashioned chalkboards. Since white boards use dry-erase markers instead of messy chalk, they are the more favorable choice. White boards wipe clean with a simple eraser, leaving no chalk dust behind. Clearly, white boards are cleaner and more convenient, and thus more desirable, than their predecessors.

Flip charts have been a staple in the meetings, conventions, and expositions industry for many years. A flip chart consists of a pad of paper (generally 27 by 34 inches) mounted on an easel. This medium is frequently used to record thoughts and ideas from the audience or key points as they are developed by a speaker or trainer. The presenter fills one page with as many thoughts as desired and then simply flips to the next page to record additional thoughts. By using a flip chart, the hard copy remains for use as a reference at some future point.

As the demand for these technological advances evolves, so do their systems of delivery. In the past, demands were fairly simple, and host properties felt confident that they could own, maintain, and operate the types of equipment requested. However, as equipment became more sophisticated, the skills needed to operate and maintain the equipment became more specialized. As a result, host properties have found it prohibitively expensive to support a complete audiovisual department within the confines of their facilities.

One solution that many host properties have turned to is the independent audiovisual supplier. This is a company that can provide all the services needed to successfully execute a meeting convention or exposition. "Typically the outside contractor is based near the property and has its own technicians available to operate and service the equipment. The supplier owns equipment—which saves the hotel the expense—and replaces it when it either breaks down or becomes outmoded" (Serlen 1990, p. 58).

Essentially, this puts the host property in the role of an intermediary, referring the planner to the AV supplier the same way they would make referrals for decorators, florists, or any other outsourced service. Generally, the supplier bills the host property and the host bills the meeting, convention, or exposition as part of the master account.

For some properties the use of an outside AV supplier is too restrictive. In these cases the recent trends have been to literally move the outside supplier inside, giving them independent on-premise status. In this arrangement the AV equipment is owned by the supplier, but is stored on the host property. Also, the technicians have an office on property, although they are employees of the AV supplier, not the host facility. The advantages to this arrangement are that the technicians are intimately familiar with the host property and its capabilities, technicians are responsible for the maintenance of the equipment, the host property does not need to invest in expensive AV equipment that maybe outdated in the near future, and an AV expert is constantly on-site.

Videoconferencing

When it comes to technology, there are many new developments that can be used to enhance meeting presentations. Certainly, one of the more familiar technological advances and one that warrants some discussion here is the videoconference.

Videoconferencing (as illustrated in figure 9-1) is defined by the International Teleconferencing Association as a telecommunication system that combines audio and video media that pro-

Figure 9-1   Videoconferencing allows individuals to meet face-to-face with their counterparts around the world. (Courtesy: AT&T.)

vides both voice communication and motion video images. It includes transmissions with one-way video and two-way audio (also known as business television) as well as two-way video and two-way audio transmissions (Johnson, p. 114).

When videoconferencing was first introduced, it was expected to cause the demise of hotels and conference centers. Meetings in the traditional sense were predicted to disappear and be replaced by videoconferencing. It was thought that videoconferences, especially at the corporate level, would eliminate the need for air travel, food, and lodging expenses. Thus, hotels and conferences would not be needed for their meeting space or for their guestrooms.

In an effort to be proactive, some hotels and conference centers made the decision to create video telecommunication centers in their facilities. Their reasoning was that, if closed-circuit meetings reduced the need for travel and meeting space, they could get into the business of attracting video conferees (Levin 1988).

Since the equipment needed for video teleconferencing is extremely expensive to install and maintain, many properties (especially smaller ones) found it prohibitive. Fortunately for the meeting's industry, videoconferencing has never been utilized to the extent predicted. The primary reason that videoconferencing has never replaced face-to-face meetings is due to corporations' and associations' belief that there is no substitution for the human interaction side of meetings. This concept is reflected in John Nesbitt's high-tech, high-touch theory. This theory suggests that, although people love high-tech efficiency, there is also a craving for intimacy—the more technologically advanced we become, the more we will need to get back to the basics of sharing and relating with other people. "Nothing will ever take the place of looking into the eyes of the person across the table, because it is only there that you develop a rapport and trust" (Levin, p. 26).

Despite the fact that videoconferencing has not caused the revolution that was prophesied, it certainly is regarded as a crucial communication link in many industries. The real appeal of this technology lies in the ability to electronically link people who ordinarily could not otherwise gather (Levin 1988). One example is universities. Recently, Marriott Corporation held a broadcast designed to be heard by all hospitality students across the country. This was a give-and-take session conducted by Marriott's top executives and dealing with many current hospitality-related issues. The broadcast was received by hundreds of students across the country who would not otherwise have had the chance to benefit from such expertise. Another example of the value of videoconferencing involves the medical profession. "Doctors at the Mayo Clinic consult with colleagues at branches in Arizona and Florida over a three-way 'telemedicine' network. The American Speech/Language/Hearing Association and the Medical Group Management Association run 'video conference' seminars for their members" (Levin, p. 26).

Another innovation in meeting technology is the computer. Although computers have been around for many years, their role in meetings, conventions, and conferences has been limited primarily to the planning stage of a meeting, an aspect of computer utilization that will be discussed later in this chapter. In this section the discussion is confined to computers as they influence meeting implementation. As mentioned above, the use of computers in conjunction with LCD projection panels has created exciting possibilities in meeting implementation because it allows presenters to share with the audience whatever is on the computer screen. Another use for computers in meeting technology is to create more of an interactive environment. One example is IBM's recently released program called Team Focus. "This program involves a group of up to two dozen people working out a problem, brainstorming a topic or formulating a plan—through the anonymous medium of personal computers" (Grimaldi, p.101). Meetings that use such techniques as TeamFocus require a meeting room with one personal computer for each participant and a facilitator who schedules the meeting, organizes the agenda, and keeps the session on track.

There are many advantages to conducting meetings that use interactive computer programs. They cut the time of the average business meeting by 60 percent, and they encourage true brain-storming by allowing participants to input their thoughts anonymously.

Finally, what does the crystal ball in meeting implementation technology look like? According to Gregg Lieberman, the future of meeting technology looks interesting. He speculates that within the next 15 years intangible attendees might begin to show up at meetings.

Researchers right now are busy perfecting technology that will broadcast holographic projections, or three-dimensional images, of walking, talking humans. . . . they can be people who were unable to make it to the meeting but want to have a 'presence' there, or a speaker unable or unwilling to fly in for the day. This 3-D technology could give a sense of reality to a projected image that flat-screen technology cannot (Lieberman, p. 103).

Remember *The Jetsons?* It doesn't seem that far out anymore.

Technology In The Planning Phase

When people think of meeting technology, they generally think about the types of things mentioned above—technology as it has influenced meeting implementation. However, technology perhaps has had an even more profound effect on meeting planners and convention service managers and how they do their jobs. This section will discuss some of the influences that technology has had on the planning phase of meetings, conventions, and expositions.

Ten years ago, the idea of software designed specifically for meeting planners was no more than a glimmer in the eye of a few forward thinking individuals. The meeting planner tech mavericks did their work by begging and borrowing time on the company's mainframe computer or fiddling with a database in the accounting department to store some names and addresses for mailing lists.

. . . Today, there are about six dozen software packages useful for the meeting planner. There are products for general registration, room setup, association membership coordination, desktop publishing, budgeting, exhibit services, research and evaluation, logistics management, nametags, marketing, and—with a few keystrokes—selecting a site that fits detailed specifications. (Waldrop 1991, p. 76)

By utilizing these types of software packages, meeting planners and the corporations or associations they represent experience the benefits of increased efficiency, greater control, and cost savings. Here are some examples of how software technology is proving invaluable to those who plan and oversee the management of meetings, conventions, and expositions:

On-site registration—With the aid of current software, only one assistant is needed to register attendees, where traditionally seven or eight were needed (see figure 9-2).

Logistics—Computers have revolutionized the nuts-and-bolts of meeting planning, by allowing the planner to print name badges, signs, and even tickets in-house. More than 600 name badges can be printed in less than 20 minutes. These badges are of typeset quality, and save the association or corporation $1 to $2 per badge... There is also technology that allows the planner to make 2-foot-by-3-foot signs from what's on an $8\frac{1}{2}$-inch-by-11-inch sheet of paper (Waldrop, p. 79–80).

Site selection—Selecting the hotel or resort where a meeting will be held can be greatly simplified on the computer. Using the

Figure 9-2   Computers have had a profound effect on meeting planners and convention service managers and how they do their jobs. (Courtesy: The Breakers.)

planner's criteria, a database consisting of hundreds of properties can be accessed to provide a comprehensive list of the properties that will meet the needs of the group (Waldrop 1990).

Room layouts—Technology now exists that gives meeting planners the ability to "design a room layout that incorporates actual features of the room; pillars, podium, stage, or registration area, for instance. . . The planner can adjust the number of inches allowed between tables or rows, and plug in limitless styles of food-and-beverage setups" (Waldrop, p. 80).

Meeting evaluation and analysis—With decreasing funds being spent on attending meetings, conventions, and expositions, more emphasis is being placed on understanding exactly what will meet the needs of the targeted audience. This can be accomplished through the use of evaluation tools, made all the more accessible by the improvement in technology. Today's meeting planners can, with the help of someone familiar with survey techniques and the software necessary to provide basic analytic data, design their own evaluation tools to be administered any time they deem necessary. Associations have developed comprehensive needs assessment surveys for their memberships to ascertain whether or not they are providing all of the services desired by those they serve (see figure 9-3). Conference evaluation surveys have been designed to enable the conference sponsors to determine what criteria their attendees use to decide whether or not they will attend the annual convention. Surveys such as these provide invaluable feedback to the associations, thus allowing them to better serve their constituents.

Desktop publishing is another area where computers have significantly changed how meeting planners do their jobs. "With desktop publishing, sophisticated communications materials, from meetings brochures to full-sized association magazines, can be produced in-house on a computer screen" (Muraskin, p. 61). Corporations and associations are saving thousands of dollars each year by bringing these capabilities in-house rather than having them typeset through an outside agency.

Of course, the more choices, the more confusion. Meeting planners who choose to streamline their activities through the use of computer assistance should educate themselves before purchasing anything. Many associations and corporations have found that

CONFIDENTIAL SURVEY

Member Perceptions of the Annual CHRIE Conference

**PLEASE COMPLETE ALL FOUR (4) PARTS OF THE SURVEY.
ALL RESPONSES WILL BE HELD IN CONFIDENCE.**

Principal Investigators:

Rhonda J. Montgomery, Ph.D.
Assistant Professor
Hotel, Restaurant & Tourism
  Administration
(803) 777-6665
FAX (803) 777-6427

Sandy Strick, Ph.D.
Assistant Professor
Hotel, Restaurant & Tourism
  Administration
(803) 777-6665
FAX (803) 777-6427

University of South Carolina

Figure 9-3 Member perceptions of the annual CHRIE conference.

PART I
RESPONDENT INFORMATION

1. What is your present age?

    ( )   Under 25 years
    ( )   25 - 34 years
    ( )   35 - 44 years
    ( )   45 - 54 years
    ( )   over 55 years

2. What is your gender?

    ( )   Male
    ( )   Female

3. What is your status?

    ( )   Part-time faculty
    ( )   Full-time faculty
    ( )   Graduate student

4. Are you currently tenured?

    ( )   Yes
    ( )   No

5. What is your rank?

    ( )   Graduate Student
    ( )   Instructor
    ( )   Assistant Professor
    ( )   Associate Professor
    ( )   Full Professor
    ( )   Other (*Please specify*)_____

6. What CHRIE membership do you hold?

    ( )   Educator at an institution granting baccalaureate and graduate degrees
    ( )   Educator at an institution granting associate degrees, certificates and diplomas
    ( )   Educator at secondary school
    ( )   Retired educator
    ( )   Graduate student
    ( )   Industry professional
    ( )   Association/Business/Government executive
    ( )   Institution granting baccalaureate and graduate degrees
    ( )   Institution granting associate degrees, certificates and diplomas
    ( )   Allied association
    ( )   Basic corporate/organization membership
    ( )   Standard corporate/organization membership
    ( )   CHRIE supporter
    ( )   CHRIE partner

7. What regional chapter do you belong to?

( )	HEMAR	( )	OHIO	( )	BRITISH COLUMBIA
( )	FLORIDA/CARIBBEAN	( )	MAHE	( )	ILLINOIS CHRIE
( )	SOUTHEAST	( )	CANADA	( )	EUROPEAN CHRIE
( )	PAC CHRIE	( )	MICHIGAN	( )	NER CHRIE
( )	TEXAS CHRIE	( )	HEAR CHRIE	( )	KOMA CHRIE
( )	ONTARIO CHRIE				

Figure 9-3 (Continued)

240

8. Are you currently pursuing a degree?

    ( )   Yes (*Please specify degree:*_____)
    ( )   No

9. Is the program you are currently associated with: (*Check all that apply*)

    ( )   Associate degree, diplomas and certificates granting program
    ( )   Baccalaureate degree granting program
    ( )   Graduate degree granting program

PART II

10. To what other professional association(s) do you belong?
    (*Please give full names*)
    1.   _____
    2.   _____
    3.   _____

11. How many years have you been a member of CHRIE?

    ( )   New member
    ( )   1-3   years
    ( )   4-6   years
    ( )   7   years or more

12. Have you ever held a position as a Board Member/Regional Officer/Committee Member of CHRIE?

    ( )   Yes   ( )   No

13. Are you active in your regional CHRIE Chapter?

    ( )   Yes   ( )   No
    If no, why_____

PART III

14. What annual CHRIE conferences have you attended? (*Check all that apply*)

    ( )   None
    ( )   1981 Montreal, Quebec   ( )   1987 Atlanta, GA
    ( )   1982 Phoenix, AZ   ( )   1988 Toronto, ON
    ( )   1983 Orlando, FL   ( )   1989 Las Vegas, NV
    ( )   1984 Denver, CO   ( )   1990 Washington, DC
    ( )   1985 Seattle, WA   ( )   1991 Houston, TX
    ( )   1986 Boston, MA   ( )   1992 Orlando, FL

Figure 9-3 (Continued)

15. If you have not attended an annual conference in the last two years (either one or both), check the most <u>important</u> reason for not attending (*Check one only*)
    - ( ) Time of the year
    - ( ) Prior professional commitments
    - ( ) Location of conference city
    - ( ) Budget not sanctioned/approved
    - ( ) Travel too expensive
    - ( ) Registration too expensive
    - ( ) Hotel too expensive
    - ( ) Length of conference too long
    - ( ) Lack of interest in topics offered at conference
    - ( ) Dissatisfaction with the quality of speakers/presenters
    - ( ) Prior personal commitments
    - ( ) Other_____

16. Who makes the decision as to whether you will attend the annual conference of CHRIE?

    - ( ) I make the decision
    - ( ) My supervisor
    - ( ) Other *(please specify)* _____

17. Who pays your conference registration fee?
    - _____ You
    - _____ Your Employer
        - _____ Contingent on Making a Presentation
        - _____ Not Contingent on Making a Presentation
    - _____ Other

18. What services can be provided/upgraded that would encourage you to attend the CHRIE National Conference?
    - Priority #1 _____
    - Priority #2 _____
    - Priority #3 _____
    - Priority #4 _____
    - Priority #5 _____

19. What other conferences do you attend? *(Please give full names)*
    1. _____
    2. _____
    3. _____

20. At how many CHRIE Conferences, have you served as a presenter or speaker?
    - _____ None
    - _____ One
    - _____ Two to Four
    - _____ Five to Seven
    - _____ More than Seven

21. As a presenter, how important is it for you to have an abstract or summary published in a Conference Proceedings?
    - _____ Very important
    - _____ Important
    - _____ Not very important
    - _____ Unimportant
    - _____ Never Use

Figure 9-3 (Continued)

22. In your opinion, do you have enough information about the conference services provided by CHRIE?

( ) Yes   ( ) No

23. If CHRIE had two conferences, one that focused on professional service and one that focused on scholarly research (paper presentation), would you attend:

_____ professional
_____ scholarly research
_____ both
_____ neither - why_____

24. If CHRIE were to hold its annual conference outside the United States, would you attend?

_____ yes   _____ no

If yes, please check the geographic region you would most like to visit: (*check only one*)

____	United Kingdom	____	Mediterranean
____	Far East	____	South America
____	European Continent	____	Canada

PART IV
CONFERENCE ATTITUDES

Instructions: The following statements are ones that people might make about attending the CHRIE conference. Some of these statements may represent your feelings, while others may not. Please indicate the extent to which you agree or disagree with each statement by circling the appropriate number.

	Strongly Disagree	Disagree	Neither Agree nor Disagree	Agree	Strongly Agree
25. I attend the CHRIE conference because it is important to my career.	1	2	3	4	5
26. I attend the CHRIE conference because it provides an avenue for professional development for me.	1	2	3	4	5
27. It is important that the CHRIE conference offer as many opportunities as possible for me to present my research.	1	2	3	4	5
28. It is important that the CHRIE conference offer workshops to help me improve my teaching skills.	1	2	3	4	5
29. The CHRIE conference provides excellent opportunities for me to network with other hospitality educators.	1	2	3	4	5
30. The CHRIE conference provides excellent opportunities to network with industry experts.	1	2	3	4	5
31. I would recommend that my colleagues attend the annual CHRIE conference.	1	2	3	4	5
32. My dean and/or department chair are supportive of my attending the CHRIE conference.	1	2	3	4	5
33. My university/college recognizes CHRIE as the primary association in hospitality education.	1	2	3	4	5
34. The location is a very important factor in my decision to attend the annual CHRIE conference.	1	2	3	4	5
35. Whether or not I am on the program directly influences my decision to attend.	1	2	3	4	5
36. The keynote speaker influences my decision to attend the Annual CHRIE Conference.	1	2	3	4	5

Figure 9-3 (Continued)

	Strongly Disagree	Disagree	Neither Agree nor Disagree	Agree	Strongly Agree
37. Attending paper presentations is a very important aspect of the Annual CHRIE Conference.	1	2	3	4	5
38. Attending special interest sessions (i.e. poster sessions, round table discussions, or panel discussions) is a very important aspect of the Annual CHRIE Conference.	1	2	3	4	5
39. The conference proceedings are very beneficial to me.	1	2	3	4	5
40. The social activities (meals, receptions, special events, etc.) are beneficial to me.	1	2	3	4	5

Figure 9-3 (Continued)

hiring an outside consultant to perform a needs analysis is a good investment. This consultant can objectively review the tasks performed by the meeting planner and analyze whether or not a computer could assist in the performance of those tasks. They can also suggest the type of computer and software that will best meet their needs (see figure 9-4).

There is no doubt that technology has made the job of the meeting planner easier. Aside from the capabilities of the computer, there are other technological advances that are beginning to have significant influence on how meeting planners spend their time. Promotional videotapes, fax machines, and electronic mail have become invaluable aids for planning successful meetings. Promotional videotapes are now available from many host properties to assist the planner in selecting the site. These videotapes are designed to present an overview of all that the host property has to offer. While promotional videotapes are not meant to be a sub-

Figure 9-4   Desktop publishing programs allow meeting planners to create sophisticated communication materials in-house, rather than having them typeset. (Courtesy: IBM.)

stitute for a site inspection, they do help the meeting planner narrow down the choices, which in turn saves them both time and money.

The facsimile (FAX) machine has made communication easier and more effective than ever before.

> The FAX machine is used to transmit documents. The sending device scans a document and converts graphic images to electronic signals using a process called digitized. Digitized electronic signals are compressed and sent through normal voice telephone lines to a receiving FAX machine. The receiving FAX converts the incoming electronic signals into printer commands. The printer produces an exact replica (facsimile) to the original document. The process normally takes less than 30 seconds per page (Kasavana, p. 60).

In an industry where much of the communication takes place over long distances, the FAX machine has essentially eliminated the miles. Contracts and seating charts can be received instantly. "Planners have used the machine to clear up problems months in advance, bridge the gap between domestic and overseas businesses, and improve the quality of their everyday correspondence" (Midgal, p. 41).

"Electronic mail (E-mail) provides another step in the 'get it there faster and better race.' E-mail works just as the name implies, using computer technology as a postman to send messages (from a simple letter or memo to a detailed budget, or a newsletter with extensive graphics) between computers electronically" (Waldrop 1990, p. 122). For example, in the next few years E-mail will play a major role in registration communication. Attendees can register electronically and pay via credit card. They will receive their confirmation instantly, along with lodging information, the conference program, and any other pertinent information.

Technology for the Meeting Attendee

A chapter on meeting technology would not be complete without addressing the influence of high tech on the attendees. In this day and age, attendees, as is the case with all business travelers, are becoming quite sophisticated in their needs and expectations. Business centers, telecommunication technology, and computerized check-in/check-out are the most frequently sought after technologies. They allow the attendee to conduct essential business while still attending the meeting, convention, or exposition. Often, those attending rely on much of this technology to complete business transactions that may have been initiated during the meeting or conference.

Business centers, once considered a luxury, are now an essential element of the host property. These centers "come in all shapes and sizes. And the centers, whether in a separate space or in effect, in the guestroom, are becoming more and more common in—and necessary to—a hotel, particularly one geared toward the business traveler" (Wolff 1990, p. 44). As figure 9-5 suggests, "the business

Figure 9-5 For business travelers, business centers have become the nerve center of the hotel, allowing busy executives to use state-of-the-art telecommunications at any time of the day or night. (Courtesy: Stouffer Concourse Hotel, St. Louis International Airport.)

center is a nerve center, allowing busy executives to use state-of-the-art telecommunication whenever necessary" (Wolff 1991, p. 58).

Services most frequently requested are FAX, photocopying, secretarial, and the use of computers, especially laptops. Many other services may be provided from a fully staffed business center. These may include Federal Express, portable phone rental, translation services, and airline reservation services.

Host facilities find that the attendee never stops being a business traveler. This means that incoming message systems may be relied upon very heavily. Voice mail is a fairly recent piece of technology that allows guests to handle their own messages. The guest receives messages in the caller's own voice: this not only provides better communication, but also allows for more thorough messaging. "Research indicates that 25 percent of hotel guests already expect it, and at least half of the 800 new hotels being built each year are requesting voice mail services from the moment they open their doors" (Freeman 1991, p. 36).

Technology is catching up with host properties in terms of alleviating check-in/check-out bottlenecks. Attendees frequently encounter long lines at the front desk, as they attempt to check in or check out. The credit card–activated system lets the guest check in or out without encountering the front desk. The guest simply inserts a credit card into a freestanding kiosk-type device and within seconds gets not only a printed out registration form, but the room key as well (Selwitz 1991, p. 30).

Conclusion

As has been discussed in this chapter, technology has had an incredible impact on the meetings, conventions, and expositions industry. All aspects of this industry have been impacted by the implementation of new technology. The industry has weathered the fear of being replaced by technology and is now in the infancy stages of allowing improved technology to enhance and enrich the business.

References

Alonzo, Vincent. 1991. Speaker tapes—the next best thing to being there. *Meetings and Conventions,* (December) pp. 33–39.

Crystal, Susan. 1992. Plugged in. *Meetings and Conventions,* (May) pp. 73–95.

Forrest, Lewis C. 1990. *Training for the Hospitality Industry,* second edition. East Lansing, Mich.: Educational Institute AH&MA.

Freeman, Susan. 1991. Hotels profit with new telecom technologies. *Lodging,* (September) pp. 35–36.

Grimaldi, Lisa. Meetings anonymous: IBM does it with computers. *Meetings and Conventions,* (January) pp. 101–102

Hoyle, L. H., Dorf, D. C., and T. S. A. Jones. 1989. *Managing Conventions and Group Business.* East Lansing, Mich.: Educational Institute AH&MA.

Johnson, Virginia. 1991. Videoconferencing. *Successful Meetings,* (April) pp. 114–116.

Kasavana, Michael. 1990. The FAX food revolution. *Restaurant Business,* (March) p. 60.

Levin, Jay. 1988. Videoconferencing. *Meetings and Conventions,* (September) pp. 26–29.

Lieberman, Gregg. 1991. You ain't seen nothing yet! *Meetings and Conventions,* (August) pp. 103–104

Migdal, Dave. 1990. The FAX factor. *Meetings and Conventions,* (March) pp. 41–46.

Muraskin, Ellen. 1990. Automation magic. *Meetings and Conventions,* (February) pp. 61–66.

Price, Catherine. 1989. *The AMA Guide for Meeting and Event Planners.* American Management Association.

Selwitz, Robert. 1991. Credit cards: multiple uses hring new level of guest service. *Hotel and Motel Management,* (January) pp. 29–30.

Serlen, Bruce. 1990. Make the most of AV resources. *Hotel and Resort Industry,* (September) pp. 56–60.

Serlen, Bruce. 1989. Promotional videotapes supplement—not replace—site inspections. *Corporate and Incentive Travel,* (August) pp. 40–41.

Waldrop, Heidi. 1990. Paperless meeting planning. *Successful Meetings,* (February) pp. 122–124.

Waldrop, Heidi. 1991. Software odyssey. *Successful Meetings,* (February) pp. 76–81.

Wolff, Carlo. 1991. An essential amenity. Lodging Hospitality, (February) pp. 57–58.

Wolff, Carlo. 1990. Travelers deem business centers essential. *Hotel and Motel Management.* (March 12) pp. 44–46.

Discussion Questions

1. Discuss the role technology plays in providing outstanding service to participants in meetings, conventions, and expositions.

2. How has new technology changed meetings, conventions, - and expositions?
3. Speculate about the role technology will play in the future of meetings, conventions, and expositions.
4. What are the positive and negative side effects of videoconferencing?

Key Terms

three-dimensional imagery
LCD panel
audio-visual

videoconferencing
business centers

10

Changes Affecting the Meetings and Conventions Industry

Learning Objectives

1. To understand the importance of adult education in the meetings, conventions, and expositions industry.
2. To understand the changes affecting convention cities.
3. To understand the impact that the global economy is having on the meetings, conventions, and expositions market and how meetings, conventions and expositions must adapt to their international clients.

Introduction

This chapter will provide the reader with a crystal ball overview of what the meetings, conventions, and expositions industry will be facing through the beginning of the next millennium. Currently the industry is in the height of the Information Age. Attendees work daily with fax machines, voice mail, and telephone bank transfers. Instead of technology enabling people to slow down and have more personal time, technology has just enabled individuals to accomplish more work in the same amount of time. People are used to the fax machine spitting out reams of documents that need to be dealt with immediately, and cellular phones have turned every car, boat, train, or plane into a workplace. Attendees are inundated with various forms of media and are tied into their computers more closely than any other generation. They work in a fast-paced world that doesn't allow for "time-wasting" activities. They expect that the meetings they attend will be productive for them in a number of ways.

In the future, attendees will be looking at three specific areas for determining whether or not they will be attending a meeting, convention, or exposition. First they will want to have a clear understanding of what the payback for their time and money will be. The conspicuous consumption trend of the 1980s is a thing of the past, and budgets no longer include money to spend on events just to put in "face time." Individuals, companies, and associations expect the event to be productive. How will this meeting, convention, or exposition benefit their business? Will it provide adequate return on their investment? If the answer to these questions is positive, then the event is worth attending.

Secondly they will expect the meeting to enable them to grow personally or to provide an arena for them to indulge themselves just a little bit. In the future attendees will expect to attend events that will allow them to do serious business and yet to take care of themselves as well. Agendas will be designed to provide time for physical activities, such as aerobics or beach walks, as well as providing workshops on personal development. The sites chosen for these meetings will play an important role in the attendees' personal decision as to whether or not to attend the event. Attendees will expect the event to provide opportunities for them to see new and interesting sites or to provide them opportunities for relaxation and self-reflection. The quality of the experience will be vitally important. They may not expect a lot of time to indulge themselves, but what time they do take will be spent on quality activities.

The third area the attendees will be carefully reviewing will be the area of service. Service will be evaluated from two viewpoints:

1. What services and amenities will be provided during the event.
2. What is the perceived quality of service they will receive?

As suggested in figure 10-1, attendees are savvy consumers of meetings, conventions, and expositions, and they will no longer accept programs that do not provide a high level of service. Suppliers are already understanding that service is the point of distinc-

Figure 10-1   Attendees are savvy consumers and will no longer accept programs that do not provide a high level of service. (Courtesy: Stouffer Concourse Hotel, St. Louis-Lambert International Airport.)

tion, and they are spending more time and money on training their employees in the fine art of providing hospitable service. Those associated with the planning of meetings, conventions, and expositions must follow in their footsteps and pay careful attention to the importance that service plays in their relationship with their clients. They must service their clients as they never have before, because competition will be fierce and those individuals who will become successful or remain successful into the next millennium will be those who understand the importance of providing hospitable service to their clients.

As stated earlier in this book, the future for meetings, conventions, and expositions is a bright one. There is not a question as to whether or not this segment of the industry will grow, but rather how it will grow and change.

People meet for various reasons, but primarily for the purposes of educating themselves and networking. This chapter will look at the role of professional education in the future. It will also address the importance of the globalization of our world and its impact on meetings, conventions, and expositions. Finally, this chapter will address the impact that meetings, conventions, and expositions will have in the future on the cities who host them.

Changes Affecting Host Cities

Meetings, conventions, and expositions mean big money for the cities that host them. Because of this, many cities previously not associated with group business have gotten on the meetings, conventions, and expositions bandwagon and are soliciting group business. At a time when recessionary woes have struck most of the communities in this country, communities are looking for new ways to generate revenue. As smaller communities realize the impact that meetings, conventions, and expositions have on larger municipalities, they are choosing to invest in products and services that will enhance their image in this market. Many smaller locations are looking to the meetings industry to provide new revenue. To solicit this business means many changes for some cities. These changes often involve large expenditures of money to upgrade existing facilities or to create new ones. Cities need to consider the state of their public transportation and airport access and then implement the necessary changes that will make their communities easily accessible to group business. They also need to look at intercity transportation systems to make sure that groups can move easily in and about the city. Existing tourist attractions need to be promoted and other tourist attractions developed to make the city more appealing to group business. A perfect example of a city that is doing this is Charlotte, North Carolina. Not only has the city invested in building outstanding convention facilities (see figure 10-2) but they have also committed to the development of professional sports. This move has revitalized the community and brought national recognition to Charlotte. Other cities who have taken this proactive stance and developed convention facilities have seen tremendous returns on their investments.

Larger cities are plagued with the reputation of being crime centers and too expensive for many of the associations or corpora-

Figure 10-2   The New Charlotte Convention Center will be open by 1995, and the city is getting itself ready to handle large numbers that will undoubtedly be arriving. Airport and highway expansion efforts, hotel construction, shopping malls, and so on, are all in the works. (Courtesy: Charlotte Convention Center.)

tions to do business in. No longer are Chicago, New York, Dallas, and Los Angeles the only places groups are choosing to do business. Smaller groups are beginning to plan more of their meetings in smaller second-tier cities, where they will be the "big fish in a small pond" instead of a "little fish in a big pond." There are only a handful of conventions or expositions that are limited to the larger cities due to space requirements; therefore, cities who are committed to soliciting and servicing group business are very successful.

Professional Education Into the Next Millennium

From the birth of professional or trade associations, the education of its members has been the cornerstone of their existence. Members of professional organizations have learned through serving apprenticeships with master craftsmen, attending professional meetings, reading professional publications, and participating in professional certification programs. Professional education has played an important role in the past and stands to play an even more important role in the future. It is estimated that over $30 billion dollars is spent annually to provide or attend professional education opportunities.

Every organized profession has its own professional association. These associations strive to improve the professionalism of their members through providing continuing education opportunities. Lifelong learning is no longer a luxury but a necessity for those individuals wishing to excel in their profession. Many professions have developed certification courses designed to maintain certain levels of excellence among its members. These certification programs are based on criteria derived from the standards set forth by the professional organization. The associations then design programs to provide continuing education to their members. These programs ensure that high standards are maintained and that the profession is continuously improving itself.

More individuals are being educated by corporations and associations on any given day than by all of the institutions of higher learning in the entire world. The corporate world in conjunction with professional associations are leading the way in educating the workforce. They are educating the workforce through the use of meetings, conventions, and expositions.

Professionals in the meetings, conventions, and expositions industry must remain on the cutting edge of technological and educational changes in order to facilitate the ever-changing world of continuing education. Planners, facilities managers, and other suppliers must understand the impact that continuing education will have on their own area of expertise and do everything they can to provide the services needed to enhance adult education. Not only will the educational systems themselves be changed, but those participating in continuing education will change dramatically as well.

As the world grows older and there are fewer young people entering the workforce, professions will no longer be able to count on a fresh new supply of workers joining their industry every ten years. The workforce will be compelled to rely on older workers for its productivity. This group of older workers is proving to be healthier and more committed than their counterparts and are demonstrating a great propensity for motivating their younger coworkers (Partlow and Strick 1993). Older workers are increasingly more educated and more affluent than their predecessors and want to continue making a contribution in whatever way possible. The average retirement age continues to be lowered, but instead of growing old and becoming unproductive, these younger retirees are striking out on new career paths and they need retraining.

The retraining centers of tomorrow will have to be in part centered around the older worker. The implications for designing programs for this group of adult learners are far reaching. First of all, the traditional educational system is designed to have older individuals teaching the young, whereas in this new system many of the instructors trained to teach may be much younger than their students and therefore lacking in the experience and understanding of the older students' perceptions of the topic.

This challenge can be met in a couple of ways. First, the educational system can develop a cadre of older people who are trained to provide the education for their colleagues. Second, the system can provide training designed to educate the existing teachers on how to teach and relate to the older student.

Either way, the workforce of the future depends on the educational system, whether it be the traditional educational system or one designed by associations or corporations. A key factor in the success of this educational system will be the ability to identify potential students and then develop programs that will motivate them to continue their education and training for new careers.

Not only will there be a shortage of younger workers entering the workforce, but due to improvements and advancements in technology, the worker of tomorrow will have to be highly trained. In a report published by the U.S. Departments of Education and Labor (1988), it was estimated that by the 21st century a majority of jobs will require some postsecondary education. This education may be provided by institutions of higher learning, or it may be provided by corporate training programs or association educational programs. It is still not clear who will take a leadership role in providing this education, but there is no doubt that it will have to be provided.

The leaders of the future will have to have a thorough understanding of how adults learn. Adult learners need a comfortable environment in which to learn. Often times the traditional method of lecturing does not yield the desired results, requiring other, more innovative methods of teaching.

The participation of the learner in the training session is vital to the success of the educational process. The entire program revolves around the learner.

Adult learners must also see a strong correlation between what they are learning and why it is important; the instructors need to take a realistic approach to teaching so that learners have something concrete to take home with them. Adult learners need to have specific motivation for learning, and they must be able to interact freely with both peers and instructor (see figure 10-3). Also, the majority of adult learners learn best with a hands-on approach to training.

There are many who believe that associations are perfect vehicles for providing this education. Associations are putting more and more of their dollars into educational opportunities for their members. They are also designed to educate large groups of people and are familiar with adult education. Corporations are looking to associations to provide their workers with the kinds of continuing education necessary to keep their employees abreast of the changes in their field. Unfortunately, institutions of higher education have been too slow in responding to the needs of industry and are therefore missing a tremendous opportunity for growth. For associations who are tracking events and changing with the times, higher education's loss will be their gain.

Figure 10-3 Adult learning is a fairly new concept. As the workforce continuously changes, training and retraining of adults is a must. Meetings are a perfect forum for this type of education. (Courtesy: Radisson Hotels.)

Globalization of the Meetings, Conventions, and Expositions Market

In the future, global communications and expanding travel will continue to change the makeup of meetings, conventions, and expositions. Our global society opens an entirely new worldwide market for meetings, conventions, and expositions. The shrinking globe enables us to participate freely in work projects, meetings, and information sharing with colleagues all over the world. Multinational companies dictate the need for those involved with this industry to be able to deal with several different cultures in the same meeting environment. The mixture of cultures in meetings, conventions, and expositions dictates having to review learning styles, travel agendas, and needs that may be entirely different from past attendees. It will be important for the leaders of this industry to understand how to process the information about various cultures and be able to set a climate for shared communication between multicultural participants.

Although meetings are meetings the world over and the secret of success for a meeting is centered around the attention given to the small details, no two countries are the same and therefore the details change drastically from country to country or from culture to culture.

Marjina M. Kaplan, president of Marjina Communications Associates, suggests that company or association executives discuss three key factors before they make the decision to go international with their meeting, convention, or exposition. First of all, they must review the profile of the participants. Any successful meeting planner knows that the success of an event rests on their ability to understand the needs and desires of their participants. A complete demographic profile of the membership should be reviewed. Questions to be answered when analyzing the demographic profile are (adapted from *Going International: Yes or No?* by Marjina M. Kaplan, 1987):

1. What are the ages and physical conditions of the members? Are they able to travel alone, or do they need to travel in groups?
2. What is the ethnic or religious background of the members? Does their background prevent them from traveling to any specific parts of the world?
3. Where is the majority of the membership located? Are they all in one country, on one continent, or internationally scattered?
4. Are they risk takers? Do they perceive the world as a safe place in which to travel?
5. Do they enjoy new experiences?
6. Are they willing to invest time and money attending international meetings?
7. What are the unique opportunities offered to the attendees at international meetings?

Secondly, the executives planning the meeting, exposition, or convention need to carefully review the objectives of the event.

Are they conducive to an international setting? Can they best be achieved in the international arena? If the answers to these questions are unclear, then perhaps those planning the meeting need to reconsider their decision to go international.

Finally, the decision makers need to carefully review the benefits with the participants who attend the international meeting. "Members can: learn how the industry or profession operates in a different culture or location; assimilate new methods or technologies that pertain to the industry or profession; study changes in the workplace and workforce; share different value systems and share knowledge" (Kaplan 1991). If, after reviewing these three areas, those planning the event determine that an international meeting is appropriate for their group, they need to look at the logistical aspects of planning the meeting.

The Logistics of Planning an International Meeting

A meeting is a meeting is a meeting; although the meeting may be taking place on foreign soil, there are many logistical details that will remain the same. However, many things do change when meetings go international, and you must know who to ask to get the right answers. Whether the group is a company planning an international meeting to assemble all of the components of its international corporation or an international association who wants to conduct a meeting, convention, or exposition in the city of one of its regional groups, it is necessary to have a local host or host association responsible for many of the organizational details. Communication with the in-country host is vitally important, and careful attention must be given to deciding what the responsibilities of the various players are, to insure that nothing falls through the cracks.

Groups planning international functions should first contact the tourist board of the country in which they are planning to meet. The tourist board functions similarly to a convention and visitors bureau in the United States, except that they represent an entire country instead of just one city or community. One of its major functions is to serve as a link between American planners and the suppliers in their country. Initially, the tourist board can help the planner design a site inspection. They can help in the air transportation arrangements, set up appointments with various suppliers, and provide interpreters and tour guides. Their job is to help the group decide to choose their country as the group's next destination.

Once a country has been selected, tourist boards should be able to direct the planner to destination management companies, hotels, attractions, service contractors, and audiovisual firms. International meetings, conventions, and expositions require longer lead time than national or regional meetings, due to the added time in transferring information from one country to another.

All information circulated regarding the meeting, convention, or exposition should be printed in the primary languages of the majority of the participants. Although many countries have English as their second language and members of international associations or businesses generally have a fairly good understanding of English, planners would be wise to make sure that all written material is accurately translated into the predominant languages of the group. Properly communicating information will enhance the probability of a large turnout. In the future, the FAX machine will improve international communication and allow for a shorter turnaround time regarding meeting information.

Mailing costs may become significantly greater and therefore should be carefully budgeted for. Shipping mailing pieces to the country and then having a representative there mail them to the participants reduces mailing expenses, but this requires extensive cooperation and communication between the planner and the host country's representative.

Registration is also another major area of concern for international meetings. Decentralized registration offices can be set up in various countries as long as the planner is able to ensure open lines of communication between the various registration offices. Local registration offices enable the participants to register in local currency and provides a network for groups of people traveling from the same country to an international meeting.

Planners must also work closely with banks in the countries in which the events will be hosted. Local banks will need to set up currency exchange systems that are convenient for the participants. The planner will also need to keep the participants informed as to the exchange rates and the system by which they can exchange currency.

The tourist board should also be able to provide valuable advice on all of these areas as well as provide the group with guidelines for proper protocol.

. . . meeting planners new to international events often approach the matter of protocol with trepidation or, worse yet, leave it for others to worry about. Protocol is the lubricant that permits people of disparate cultural backgrounds to interact in an atmosphere of understanding and mutual respect. It is not an arcane ritual, and as a professional, the planner has an obligation to inform both themselves and their groups of the proper procedures (Wright 1992).

If the participants speak different languages, it is imperative that the planner provide for translation and interpretive services. To do this the planner must work closely with a representative providing the interpreters services so as to become familiar with the requirements and logistics necessary to provide all attendees with an accurate translation or interpretation of the proceedings. Simultaneous interpretation has become a standard service provided at international meetings, but the cost of providing such a service must be carefully considered when planning interpretation services.

Security is also another major issue to be considered by those planning international meetings, conventions, and expositions. International meetings bring more attention to the event and therefore require careful scrutiny of security procedures. Terrorists look to international conferences, particularly those frequented by Americans, to gain attention on an international basis. Therefore, planners should work closely with international security firms to ensure the safety of all of their participants.

Planners must also be prepared to meet the needs of their international guest on the home front. International time differences and jet lag of attendees need to be considered when planning an agenda. Many cultures also observe holidays other than the traditional holidays celebrated in the United States, and these practices may affect the meeting schedule. Many of the same areas that we have spoken about in this chapter apply to international groups holding their meeting in the United States. If the planner does not have a history with the group, they need to survey the group to ascertain the special needs of their international clients. Once they know their needs, they must make every effort to be hospitable. This means educating employees and the host venue regarding the customs of the international clients, as well as ensuring that signage is in languages internationally understood. The food and beverage department should be apprised of the special needs of the international attendees, both from a dietary standpoint as well as a timing standpoint (in many foreign countries, people eat large lunches and late dinners). Interpreters may be needed, and any written communication should be provided in the participants' native language. International attendees may need transportation assistance once they've arrived in the host city. "An important element of a successful international meeting is building the culture of the host country into the event as much as possible. To overlook that unique resource is to waste one of the most pleasurable and unique opportunities an international meeting provides" (Price 1989, p. 435). Taking the time to meet the needs of *all* the participants is the sign of a true professional.

Summary

Into the next millennium, this industry is pegged for tremendous growth. The changes we will see are as numerous as the people involved. In this chapter we have chosen to look at only three changes we believe will be very signficant. Cities and municipalities who look to the future for their revenue must act now if they want this revenue to come from the meetings, conventions, and expositions industry.

The impact of education and its role in the meetings, conventions, and expositions industry is only now beginning to play a serious role. This role will continue to dominate this segment of the industry into the next millineum. We live in a technology-centered world; therefore, people will have to be continuously trained and their skills upgraded. This upgrading should be a focus for the professional and trade associations of the future.

The globalization of our world also will seriously impact the meetings, conventions, and expositions industry. We are no longer operating on a national level and therefore must make the changes necessary to enable us to compete in an international arena.

References

Partlow, C., and S. Strick. 1993. Intergenerational contact in the workplace. *The Journal of Hospitality and Tourism Research,* 4(1).

Price, C. 1989. *The AMA Guide for Meeting and Event Planners.* New York: Ameri can Management Association.

Popcorn, F. 1991. *The Popcorn Report.* New York: Bantam Doubleday Dell Publishing Group, Inc.

U.S. Department of Education and U.S. Department of Labor. 1988. *The Bottom Line: Basic Skills in the Workplace.* Washington, D.C.: U.S. Department of Education and U.S. Department of Labor.

Wiswell, J. 1990. Ask tourist boards for the world. *Corporate Meetings and Incentives,* (November).

Wright, R. 1992. Adhere to protocol at international meetings. *Meeting News.* 16(11):26.

Discussion Questions

1. Currently the meetings, conventions, and exposition industry are in the height of the Information Age. How does this impact the industry?
2. Into the next millennium, service will continue to be one of the most important challenges faced. How can industry professionals prepare themselves for the future?
3. What changes in host cities are expected? How will these changes impact meetings, conventions, and expositions?
4. Discuss the importance of professional education.
5. Discuss the changes that will take place in meetings, conventions, and expositions due to the globalization of the world.

Key Terms

professional education
re-training centers
adult learners

globalization
international meetings

11

Career and Resource Information

Learning Objectives

1. To describe the various career opportunities for the hospitality student in the area of meetings, conventions, and expositions.
2. To provide a framework from which the student can develop a network within this segment of the hospitality industry.
3. To familiarize the student with all of the associations connected with meetings, conventions, and expositions.

Introduction

We hope that, as you have read this book and studied the various aspects of the meetings, conventions, and expositions industry, you have been inspired to look beyond the introductory level. There are many exciting and new opportunities in this relatively young segment of the hospitality industry.

To help you in your pursuit, this chapter contains information about some of the careers associated with the meetings, conventions, and expositions industry. The job descriptions provided are to be considered as a sampling of the types of responsibilities and opportunities that might be afforded an individual in one of these positions (see figures 11-2 through 11-12). Many seemingly relevant job descriptions are not included here. This is not to say that these jobs are any less important, but rather to indicate that this industry is so new that many job descriptions have not yet been developed.

Figure 11-1   Convention services manager. (Courtesy: Hyatt Hotels and Resorts.)

Management Profile: DIRECTOR OF CONVENTION SERVICES

Hotel Size: AA   **Salary Grade:**   50B

Previous position requirements:

- o   Director of Catering at convention or resort hotel, or
- o   Grade 47 Convention Services Manager, or
- o   Director of Corporate Sales at A hotel, or
- o   Two-time Marriott management positions, one of which must be a Convention Servic... lanager, or
- o   7 years hospitality sales management or convention experience with appropriate technical skills training to be completed within the first 4 weeks in the position

Technical Skill Requirements:

- -   Working knowledge of Convention Service documents and diary
- -   Able to develop a budget and manage it

Managerial Skill Requirements:

- -   Actively supports the development, training, mentoring of associates
- -   Knows how and when to impose deadlines and delegate tasks
- -   Adheres to Marriott EEO and AA policies
- -   Manages the Quality process in areas of customer service and associate satisfaction
- -   Demonstrates leadership by example
- -   Motivates and provides a work environment in which associates are productive
- -   Demonstrates self-confidence, energy and enthusiasm
- -   Has effective public speaking and presentation skills
- -   Presents ideas, expectations and information in a concise, well-organized way
- -   Uses effective listening skills
- -   Identifies positive public relations and teamwork opportunities
- -   Manages group or interpersonal conflict situations effectively
- -   Understands how to manage in a culturally diverse work environment
- -   Establish, measure, monitor, and evaluate processes, policies and procedures
- -   Uses problem solving methodology for decision making and follow up
- -   Understands how to develop business plan and evaluate business trends to modify strategies
- -   Interprets analyzes and manages budget to meet business objectives
- -   Has personal integrity, manages time well, highly visible in areas of responsibility
- -   Provides constructive coaching and counseling to associates

Academic Requirements:

- -   High School Diploma or equivalent
- -   College degree preferred

Training courses taken:
(The following training courses are required for internal career progression. Outside hires require equivalent training.)

- -   TQM

Figure 11-2   Director of Convention Services. (Courtesy: Marriott, San Francisco.)

Management Profile: CONVENTION SERVICES MANAGER

Hotel Size: A, AA   **Salary Grade:**   43/44

Previous position requirements:

- o   Convention Service Manager ID, or
- o   Convention Service Manager, or
- o   Marriott management experience with appropriate technical skills training to be completed within the first 4 weeks in the position, or
- o   1 year management experience in a related hospitality field

Technical Skill Requirements:

- -   General knowledge of all departments within the hotel
- -   Able to schedule employees while remaining within budget/provide quality customer service
- -   Maintenance of meeting room area sanitation and set up via daily, weekly, and monthly inspections
- -   Complete operating knowledge of all audio-visual equipment
- -   Communicate group needs to various departments within the hotel

Managerial Skill Requirements:

- -   Provides constructive coaching and counseling to associates
- -   Actively supports the development, training, mentoring of associates
- -   Knows how and when to impose deadlines and delegate tasks
- -   Adheres to Marriott EEO and AA policies
- -   Manages the Quality process in areas of customer service and associate satisfaction
- -   Motivates and provides a work environment in which associates are productive
- -   Demonstrates self-confidence, energy and enthusiasm
- -   Presents ideas, expectations and information in a concise, well-organized way
- -   Uses effective listening skills
- -   Manages group or interpersonal conflict situations effectively
- -   Understands how to manage in a culturally diverse work environment
- -   Uses problem solving methodology for decision making and follow up
- -   Has personal integrity, manages time well, highly visible in areas of responsibility

Academic Requirements:

- -   High School diploma or equivalent
- -   College degree preferred and/or

Training courses taken:
(The following training courses are required for internal career progression. Outside hires require equivalent training.)

- -   TQM

Figure 11-3   Convention Services Manager. (Courtesy: Marriott, San Francisco.)

This chapter will also provide a current listing of relevant associations and organizations related to the meetings, conventions, and expositions industry. Several of these groups have been discussed within the context of the preceding ten chapters, and many more have been included as a means of enabling the student to gain more insight into the industry.

Management Profile: SENIOR CONVENTION SERVICES MANAGER

Hotel Size: A, AA   **Salary Grade:**   47B

Previous position requirements:

- o   Grade 45 or 46 Convention Service Manager or Catering Manager, or
- o   Grade 45 Sales Manager with previous convention service experience, or
- o   18 months Marriott management experience with appropriate technical skills training to be completed within the first 4 months in the position

Technical Skill Requirements:

- Working knowledge of Convention Service documents and diary

Managerial Skill Requirements:

- Provides constructive coaching and counseling to associates
- Actively supports the development, training, mentoring of associates
- Knows how and when to impose deadlines and delegate tasks
- Adheres to Marriott EEO and AA policies
- Manages the Quality process in areas of customer service and associate satisfaction
- Motivates and provides a work environment in which associates are productive
- Demonstrates self-confidence, energy and enthusiasm
- Presents ideas, expectations and information in a concise, well-organized way
- Uses effective listening skills
- Manages group or interpersonal conflict situations effectively
- Understands how to manage in a culturally diverse work environment
- Uses problem solving methodology for decision making and follow up
- Has personal integrity, manages time well, highly visible in areas of responsibility

Academic Requirements:

- High School diploma or equivalent
- College degree preferred and/or

Training courses taken:
(The following training courses are required for internal career progression. Outside hires require equivalent training.)

- TQM

Figure 11-4   Senior Convention Services Manager. (Courtesy: Marriott, San Francisco.)

Employment Forecast for Occupations in Meetings, Conventions, and Expositions

According to the federal government and industry trends, positions in the hospitality industry should continue to grow at a faster rate than most other occupations. The meetings, conventions, and expositions industries growth will mirror this. Every segment of the industry—associations, host venues, suppliers (such as exhibit

Management Profile: DIRECTOR OF NATIONAL ACCOUNTS

Hotel Size: A/AA   **Salary Grade:**   49/50

Previous position requirements:

- o   Senior Sales Manager, or
- o   Director of National Accounts, or
- o   Director of Reservation Sales, or
- o   Director of Group Sales, or
- o   Director of Catering, or
- o   7 years hospitality sales management experience with appropriate technical skills training to be completed within the first 4 weeks in the position

Technical Skill Requirements:

- Able to achieve sales goals
- Able to conduct effective sales programs
- Able to develop and implement effective marketing plan
- Knowledge of accounting functions: budgeting process, P&L statements and forecasting
- Familiar with legality of contractual agreements
- Recruiting
- Good public speaking/communication skills

Managerial Skill Requirements:

- Actively supports the development, training, mentoring of associates
- Knows how and when to impose deadlines and delegate tasks
- Adheres to Marriott EEO and AA policies
- Manages the Quality process in areas of customer service and associate satisfaction
- Demonstrates leadership by example
- Motivates and provides a work environment in which associates are productive
- Demonstrates self-confidence, energy and enthusiasm
- Has effective public speaking and presentation skills
- Presents ideas, expectations and information in a concise, well-organized way
- Uses effective listening skills
- Identifies positive public relations and teamwork opportunities
- Manages group or interpersonal conflict situations effectively
- Understands how to manage in a culturally diverse work environment
- Establish, measure, monitor, and evaluate processes, policies and procedures
- Uses problem solving methodology for decision making and follow up
- Understands how to develop business plan and evaluate business trends to modify strategies
- Interprets analyzes and manages budget to meet business objectives
- Has personal integrity, manages time well, highly visible in areas of responsibility
- Provides constructive coaching and counseling to associates

Academic Requirements:

- High School diploma or equivalent
- College degree preferred

Training courses required:
(The following training courses are required for internal career progression. Outside hires require equivalent training.)

- Successful Selling Courses I, II and III
- TQM

Figure 11-5   Director of National Accounts. (Courtesy: Marriott, San Francisco.)

Management Profile: DIRECTOR OF GROUP SALES

Hotel Size: AA   **Salary Grade:**   50

Previous position requirements:

- o   Senior Sales Manager, or
- o   Director of National Accounts, or
- o   Director of Reservation Sales, or
- o   Director of Group Sales, or
- o   Director of Catering, or
- o   Two-time Marriott Sales management positions, one of which must be a Sales Manager, or
- o   7 years hospitality sales management experience with appropriate technical skills training to be completed within the first 4 weeks in the position

Technical Skill Requirements:

- Excellent selling skills
- Strategizing skills to maximize group sales revenue
- Able to develop a budget and manage it
- Knowledge of safety standards
- Familiar with legality of contractual agreements
- Communication of group sales to sales team and other departments in the hotel
- Ability to analyze marketing information through ASAP and/or SAM

Managerial Skill Requirements:

- Actively supports the development, training, mentoring of associates
- Knows how and when to impose deadlines and delegate tasks
- Adheres to Marriott EEO and AA policies
- Manages the Quality process in areas of customer service and associate satisfaction
- Demonstrates leadership by example
- Motivates and provides a work environment in which associates are productive
- Demonstrates self-confidence, energy and enthusiasm
- Has effective public speaking and presentation skills
- Presents ideas, expectations and information in a concise, well-organized way
- Uses effective listening skills
- Identifies positive public relations and teamwork opportunities
- Manages group or interpersonal conflict situations effectively
- Understands how to manage in a culturally diverse work environment
- Establish, measure, monitor, and evaluate processes, policies and procedures
- Uses problem solving methodology for decision making and follow up
- Understands how to develop business plan and evaluate business trends to modify strategies
- Interprets analyzes and manages budget to meet business objectives
- Has personal integrity, manages time well, highly visible in areas of responsibility
- Provides constructive coaching and counseling to associates

Academic Requirements:

- High School diploma or equivalent
- College degree preferred

Training courses required:
(The following training courses are required for internal career progression. Outside hires require equivalent training.)

- Successful Selling
- Director of Sales Course
- TQM

Figure 11-6   Director of Group Sales. (Courtesy: Marriott, San Francisco.)

273

Management Profile: DIRECTOR OF FOOD AND BEVERAGE

Hotel Size: AA   **Salary Grade:**   53/B, 54/B

Previous position requirements:

o   Director of Food and Beverage in a B or larger property

Technical Skills Requirements:
- Extensive knowledge of all food and beverage operations
- Extensive knowledge of P&L budgeting
- Working knowledge of hotel mission
- Thorough knowledge of SOPs

Managerial Skill Requirements:
- Actively supports the development, training, mentoring of associates
- Knows how and when to impose deadlines and delegate tasks
- Adheres to Marriott EEO and AA policies
- Manages the Quality process in areas of customer service and associate satisfaction
- Demonstrates leadership by example
- Motivates and provides a work environment in which associates are productive
- Demonstrates self-confidence, energy and enthusiasm
- Has effective public speaking and presentation skills
- Presents ideas, expectations and information in a concise, well-organized way
- Uses effective listening skills
- Identifies positive public relations and teamwork opportunities
- Manages group or interpersonal conflict situations effectively
- Understands how to manage in a culturally diverse work environment
- Establish, measure, monitor, and evaluate processes, policies and procedures
- Uses problem solving methodology for decision making and follow up
- Understands how to develop business plan and evaluate business trends to modify strategies
- Interprets analyzes and manages budget to meet business objectives
- Has personal integrity, manages time well, highly visible in areas of responsibility
- Provides constructive coaching and counseling to associates

Academic requirements:
- High School Diploma or equivalent
- 4-year college degree or 2-year culinary degree

Training courses required:
(The following training courses are required for internal career progression. Outside hires require equivalent training.)
- Related discipline course enhancement (i.e., Restaurant Manager Seminar, Catering Successful Selling Seminar, Beverage Seminar, Food Management Class, etc.)
- Related business seminar coursework
- Should have completed all training seminars that direct report managers are responsible for attending
- TQM

Figure 11-7   Director of Food and Beverage. (Courtesy: Marriott, San Francisco.)

MANAGEMENT PROFILE: DIRECTOR OF CATERING OPERATIONS/SALES

Salary Grade: 49 - Hotel Classification: I

Previous position requirements:

- o   Director of Catering Operations/Sales, or
- o   Director of Catering, or
- o   Senior Catering Manager, or
- o   18 months as a Marriott department head with appropriate technical skills training to be completed within the first four weeks in the position, or
- o   5 years management experience in a food or beverage operation with sales in excess of $4,500,000 annually, with appropriate technical skills training to be completed within the first four weeks in the position.

A.   Technical Skill Requirements:
- -   Knowledge of service standards, SOPs, scheduling and beverage control standards
- -   Knowledge of P&L, budget line items, lead tracking and follow-up
- -   Marketing and sales knowledge (how to drive sales, create profits)
- -   Knowledge of food and wine

B.   Managerial Skill Requirements:
- -   Actively supports the development, training, mentoring of associates
- -   Knows how and when to impose deadlines and delegate tasks
- -   Adheres to Marriott EEO and AA policies
- -   Manages the Quality process in areas of customer service and associate satisfaction
- -   Demonstrates leadership by example
- -   Motivates and provides a work environment in which associates are productive
- -   Demonstrates self-confidence, energy and enthusiasm
- -   Has effective public speaking and presentation skills
- -   Presents ideas, expectations and information in a concise, well-organized way
- -   Uses effective listening skills
- -   Identifies positive public relations and teamwork opportunities
- -   Manages group or interpersonal conflict situations effectively
- -   Understands how to manage in a culturally diverse work environment
- -   Establish, measure, monitor, and evaluate processes, policies and procedures
- -   Uses problem solving methodology for decision making and follow up
- -   Understands how to develop business plan and evaluate business trends to modify strategies
- -   Interprets analyzes and manages budget to meet business objectives
- -   Has personal integrity, manages time well, highly visible in areas of responsibility
- -   Provides constructive coaching and counseling to associates

Academic requirements:
- -   High School Diploma or equivalent
- -   College degree preferred

Training courses required:
(The following training courses are required for internal career progression. Outside hires require equivalent training.)
- -   Catering Successful Selling
- -   TQM
- -   Food Sanitation Certification
- -   OPTS
- -   Service Standards Seminar/Maitre d' School
- -   Food Knowledge and Menu Composition Workshop
- -   House Wine Training Program

Figure 11-8   Director of Catering Operations/Sales. (Courtesy: Marriott, San Francisco.)

Management Profile: DIRECTOR OF MARKETING

Hotel Size: AA   **Salary Grade:**   53

Previous position requirements:

- o   Director of Marketing at B/A/AA hotel, or
- o   Director of Group Sales A/AA hotel

Technical Skill Requirements:

- Excellent selling skills
- Able to develop and implement an effective marketing plan
- Able to develop and manage a budget
- Able to manage budget/exceed room revenue goals
- Knowledge of accounting services
- Knowledge of advertising and public relations
- Knowledge of safety standards
- Familiar with legality of contractual agreements
- Able to develop a sales plan
- Understanding of MARSHA/yield applicants
- Ability to analyze marketing information through SAM and/or ASAP

Managerial Skill Requirements:

- Actively supports the development, training, mentoring of associates
- Knows how and when to impose deadlines and delegate tasks
- Adheres to Marriott EEO and AA policies
- Manages the Quality process in areas of customer service and associate satisfaction
- Demonstrates leadership by example
- Motivates and provides a work environment in which associates are productive
- Demonstrates self-confidence, energy and enthusiasm
- Has effective public speaking and presentation skills
- Presents ideas, expectations and information in a concise, well-organized way
- Uses effective listening skills
- Identifies positive public relations and teamwork opportunities
- Manages group or interpersonal conflict situations effectively
- Understands how to manage in a culturally diverse work environment
- Establish, measure, monitor, and evaluate processes, policies and procedures
- Uses problem solving methodology for decision making and follow up
- Understands how to develop business plan and evaluate business trends to modify strategies
- Interprets analyzes and manages budget to meet business objectives
- Has personal integrity, manages time well, highly visible in areas of responsibility
- Provides constructive coaching and counseling to associates

Academic Requirements:

- High School diploma or equivalent
- 4 year College degree

Training courses required:
(The following training courses are required for internal career progression. Outside hires require equivalent training.)

- Successful Selling
- Director of Sales Course
- Director of Marketing Course
- TQM

Figure 11-9   Director of Marketing. (Courtesy: Marriott, San Francisco.)

Management Profile: HOSPITALITY COORDINATOR (Room Service)

Sales Volume: ≥ $2.1 million dollars   **Salary Grade:**   Hourly
                                                     Hotel Class: I or II

Previous position requirements:

     o   Marriott hourly or management associate, or
     o   Outside hire with Sales or PR experience

Technical Skill Requirements:
- Hospitality skills
- Marketing and sales knowledge (how to drive sales, create profit)
- Creative skills

Managerial Skill Requirements:
- Provides constructive coaching and counseling to associates
- Actively supports the development, training, mentoring of associates
- Knows how and when to impose deadlines and delegate tasks
- Adheres to Marriott EEO and AA policies
- Manages the Quality process in areas of customer service and associate satisfaction
- Motivates and provides a work environment in which associates are productive
- Demonstrates self-confidence, energy and enthusiasm
- Presents ideas, expectations and information in a concise, well-organized way
- Uses effective listening skills
- Manages group or interpersonal conflict situations effectively
- Understands how to manage in a culturally diverse work environment
- Uses problem solving methodology for decision making and follow up
- Has personal integrity, manages time well, highly visible in areas of responsibility

Academic requirements:

- High School diploma or equivalent
- College degree preferred

Training courses to be attended:

- Successful Selling I
- Q.C.T.
- TQM
- OPTS

Figure 11-10   Hospitality Coordinator. (Courtesy: Marriott, San Francisco.)

managers, decorators, and so on)—projects growth through the next millennium. Associations, corporations, and other groups are meeting at an even faster rate than was predicted five years ago. Recessionary economics has not severely impacted this segment of the industry and because of its growth other segments of the industry are joining in on the efforts to make this segment grow at an even greater pace. In the 1980s the scare of teleconferencing putting face-to-face meetings out of business was just that—a

Management Profile: DIRECTOR OF HUMAN RESOURCES   **Hotel Size:** AA

Salary Grade: 52B

Previous position requirements:

- o   Director of Human Resources, or
- o   Marriott Executive Committee position with appropriate technical skills training within the first 4 weeks in the position, or
- o   Corporate or Regional staff position with at least 2 positions in a Human Resources management position with appropriate technical skills training within the first 4 weeks in the positi

Technical Skill Requirements:
- Able to develop and implement recruiting marketing plan
- Knowledge of affirmative action, EEO and Guarantee of Fair Treatment
- Able to develop and deliver training programs
- Accounting knowledge: P&L statements, budgeting process, and forecasting
- Able to analyze and improve turnover through retention programs
- Computer literacy
- In depth personnel skills as outlined in Management Development Model
- Able to train in all areas of Human Resources Manager skills

Managerial Skill Requirements:
- Actively supports the development, training, mentoring of associates
- Knows how and when to impose deadlines and delegate tasks
- Adheres to Marriott EEO and AA policies
- Manages the Quality process in areas of customer service and associate satisfaction
- Demonstrates leadership by example
- Motivates and provides a work environment in which associates are productive
- Demonstrates self-confidence, energy and enthusiasm
- Has effective public speaking and presentation skills
- Presents ideas, expectations and information in a concise, well-organized way
- Uses effective listening skills
- Identifies positive public relations and teamwork opportunities
- Manages group or interpersonal conflict situations effectively
- Understands how to manage in a culturally diverse work environment
- Establish, measure, monitor, and evaluate processes, policies and procedures
- Uses problem solving methodology for decision making and follow up
- Understands how to develop business plan and evaluate business trends to modify strategies
- Interprets analyzes and manages budget to meet business objectives
- Has personal integrity, manages time well, highly visible in areas of responsibility
- Provides constructive coaching and counseling to associates

Academic requirements:
- High School diploma or equivalent
- 4-year college degree

Training courses required:
(The following training courses are required for internal career progression. Outside hires require equivalent training.)
- Human Resources Skills Training Workshop
- Human Resources Training Program
- OPTS
- TQM

Figure 11-11   Director of Human Resources. (Courtesy: Marriott, San Francisco.)

Management Profile: RESIDENT MANAGER

Hotel Size: AA   Salary Grade: 53/B

Previous position requirements:

- o   Two previous positions as Marriott Resident Manager, or
- o   Three previous Marriott Executive Committee positions, or
- o   Corporate* or Regional Staff position, grade 54 or above with appropriate technical skills training to be completed within the first 4 weeks in the position

Technical Skill Requirements:
- Extensive P&L/budgeting knowledge
- Working knowledge of hotel mission
- Guest service champion/TQM
- Thorough knowledge of SOPs
- Claims management
- Thorough knowledge of rooms areas

Managerial Skill Requirements:
- Actively supports the development, training, mentoring of associates
- Knows how and when to impose deadlines and delegate tasks
- Adheres to Marriott EEO and AA policies
- Manages the Quality process in areas of customer service and associate satisfaction
- Demonstrates leadership by example
- Motivates and provides a work environment in which associates are productive
- Demonstrates self-confidence, energy and enthusiasm
- Has effective public speaking and presentation skills
- Presents ideas, expectations and information in a concise, well-organized way
- Uses effective listening skills
- Identifies positive public relations and teamwork opportunities
- Manages group or interpersonal conflict situations effectively
- Understands how to manage in a culturally diverse work environment
- Establish, measure, monitor, and evaluate processes, policies and procedures
- Uses problem solving methodology for decision making and follow up
- Understands how to develop business plan and evaluate business trends to modify strategies
- Interprets analyzes and manages budget to meet business objectives
- Has personal integrity, manages time well, highly visible in areas of responsibility
- Provides constructive coaching and counseling to associates

Academic requirements:
- High School diploma or equivalent
- College degree preferred

Training courses required:
(The following training courses are required for internal career progression. Outside hires require equivalent training.)
- Related business seminar course work
- Should have completed all training seminars that direct report managers are responsible for attending
- TQM

*Corporate to include other divisions

Figure 11-12   Resident Manager. (Courtesy: Marriott, San Francisco.)

scare. By the 1990s people understood that it is the very nature of the face-to-face encounter that enables individuals to work together. The fear of becoming technology hermits was replaced with an even greater yearning for personal contact through meetings, conventions, and expositions. It is now understood that these events will be enhanced by technology, not replaced by it.

As travel trends changed in the 1990s, from the lone businessperson traveling to businesspeople combining business with pleasure and bringing their family along with them, so did the focus of meetings, conventions, and expositions. Spousal programs became an intricate part of most programs, and facilities started catering to the needs of the participants' families. Child care and children's programs sprung up overnight.

This trend will continue to grow, thus making meetings, conventions, and expositions even more desirable because they meet the needs of both the individual (interacting in the business community as well as spending quality time with their family) and the businesses they represent, whose need for a good return on their investment in continuing education and networking with other professionals continues to increase.

Combine the projected growth in the number of meetings, conventions, and expositions with the projected decline in the number of people entering the workforce and an environment ripe for the enterprising individual to become a success is created. The person who properly prepares themselves through a combination of education and practical experience will have no trouble finding a job in the meetings, conventions, and expositions industry.

Salary Compensation and Working Conditions

Salary compensation and working conditions are as varied as the types of associations, host venues, and suppliers. Compensation and conditions will vary depending on the size of the property or group, the location of business, and the level of responsibility associated with the position. People associated with the meetings, conventions, and expositions industry range from the secretary who pulls together a meeting for his or her boss a couple of times a year to the executive director of an association with 100,000 members or to a general manager of a 5 star, 5 diamond resort. Entry-level positions for a college graduate depend upon the amount of relevant industry experience they have and their plan of study. Obviously, those who have dedicated a portion of their education and practical experience to the meetings, conventions, and expositions industry will enter the field at a higher-level position than a college graduate with no relevant industry experience or education. Therefore, entry into this segment of the industry could be as a bellperson making $4.35 an hour to an assistant department manager making between $18,000 and $25,000 per year. On the other end of the spectrum, the sky is the limit regarding compensation, with many of the industry's successful busnesspeople making six figures.

Working conditions are not for the faint of heart. This is a fast-paced, highly demanding segment of the hospitality industry. Individuals working in this segment must be capable of performing under pressure and working well within deadlines. They must also have a strong sense of organization. Working hours are sporadic and there are no set days off; individuals work on an as-needed basis. If a convention is booked over the weekend, then they will most definitely be working the weekend. It's the same if you're in the association side of the business. Except for crunch times around major deadlines, it might be conceivable to have a "9 to 5" existence for some of the work year. Benefits are becoming increasingly more competitive, and people entering this segment of the industry could expect medical coverage, life insurance, vacation, and sick pay.

Resource Information

As is the case in all careers, networking within the meetings, conventions, and expositions industry is an integral component to any professional's career. Being a member of the professional associations affiliated with your career is a wise choice; in fact it is the opinion of most professionals that students should become active in professional associations while still in school. To enable this to happen, many professional associations have special membership categories for students. This special membership category generally provides students with access to all educational and business meetings as well as allowing them to receive any publications provided through the association. The student member usually pays a reduced membership fee and is not allowed to hold office or vote. Following is a list of associations related with meetings, conventions, and expositions and their addresses and phone numbers.

Industry Associations

Air Transport Association of America (ATAA)
1301 Pennsylvania Ave., N.W.
Suite #1100
Washington, DC 20004
(202) 626-4000

American Hotel & Motel Association (AH&MA)
1201 New York Ave., N.W.
Washington, DC 20005-3917
(202) 289-3114

American Society for Training & Development
(ASTD)
1640 King St., P.O. Box 1443
Alexandria, VA 22313
(703) 683-8100

American Society of Association Executives (ASAE)
1575 Eye St., N.W.
Washington, DC 20005
(202) 626-ASAE

American Society of Travel Agents, Inc. (ASTA)
1101 King St.
Alexandria, VA 22314
(703) 739-2782

Association for Convention
Operations Management (ACOM)
1819 Peachtree St., N.E.
Suite 712
Atlanta, GA 30309
(404) 351-3220

Association of Conference and Events
Directors—International (ACED)
Colorado State University
Rockwell Hall
Fort Collins, CO 80523

Association of Corporate Travel Executives
P.O. Box 5394
Parsippany, NJ 07054
(800) ACTE-NOW

Association of Independent Meeting Planners
(AIMP)
5103 Wigville Rd.
Thurmont, MD 21788
(301) 271-3872

Convention Liaison Council
1575 Eye St., N.W.
Suite 1200
Washington, D.C. 20005

Council of Engineering and Scientific Society
Executives (CESSE)
2000 Florida Ave., N.W.
Washington, DC 20009

Cruise Lines International Association
500 5th Ave.
Suite 1407
New York, NY 10110
(212) 921-0066

Exhibit Designers and Producers Association
(EDPA)
611 E. Wells St.
4th Floor
Milwaukee, WI 53202
(414) 276-3372

Exposition Service Contractors Association (ESCA)
400 S. Houston St.
Suite 210
Dallas, TX 75202

Foundation for International Meetings
2111 Wilson Blvd.
Suite 1100
Arlington, VA 22203
(703) 243-3288

Health Care Exhibitors Association
5755 Peachtree-Dunwoody Rd.
Suite 500-G
Atlanta, GA 30342
(404) 252-3663

Hotel Sales and Marketing Association
International (HSMAI)
1300 "L" St., N.W.
Suite 800
Washington, DC 20005
(202) 789-0089

Institute of Association Management Companies
104 Wilmot Rd.
Suite 201
Deerfield, IL 60015
(708) 940-4646

International Association of Auditorium Managers
(IAAM)
4425 West Airport Frwy.
Suite 590
Irving, TX 75062
(214) 255-8020

International Association of Conference Centers
(IACC)
243 N. Lindbergh
Suite 315
St. Louis, MO 63141
(314) 993-8575

International Association of Convention and
Visitors Bureaus (IACVB)
P.O. Box 758
Champaign, IL 61824-0758
(217) 359-8881

International Association of Fairs & Expositions
(IAFE)
P.O. Box 985
Springfield, MO 65801
(417) 862-5771

International Communications Industries
Association (ICIA)
3150 Spring St.
Fairfax, VA 22031-2399
(703) 273-7200

International Exhibitors Association
5501 Backlick Rd.
Suite 200
Springfield, VA 22151

International Federation of Women's Travel
Organizations
4545 N. 36th St.
Suite 126
Phoenix, AZ 85018
(602) 956-7175

Life Insurance Marketing & Research
Association (LIMRA)
8 Farm Springs Rd.
Farmington, NM 06032
(203) 677-0033

Meeting Planners International (MPI)
1950 Stemmons Freeway
Suite 5018
Dallas, TX 75207
(214) 746-5222

National Association of Exposition
Managers (NAEM)
One College Park
Suite 630
8910 Purdue Rd.
Indianapolis, IN 46268
(317) 871-7272

National Coalition of Black Meeting
Planners
1 Commerce Center
Suite 1106
Columbia, MD 21044
(202) 628-3952

National Association of Reunion
Planners
P.O. Box 540836
Orlando, FL 32854
(407) 291-2941

National Speakers Association (NSA)
3877 N. 7th St.
Suite 350
Phoenix, AZ 85014
(602) 265-1001

National Business Travel Association
King St.
Suite 301
Alexandria, VA 22314
(703) 684-0836

New England Innkeepers Association
P.O. Box 1089
North Hampton, NH 03862
(6030 964-6689

New England USA
76 Summer St.
Boston, MA 02110
(617) 423-6967

Pacific Asia Travel Association (PATA)
1 Montgomery St.
Suite 1750
San Francisco, CA 94104
(415) 986-4646

Professional Convention Management
Association (PCMA)
100 Vestavia Office Park
Suite 220
Birmingham, AL 35216
(205) 823-7262

Religious Conference Management
Association
One Hoosier Dome
Suite 120
Indianapolis, IN 46225
(317) 632-1888

Society of Company Meeting Professionals
2600 Garden Rd.
Suite 208

Monterey, CA 93940
(408) 649-6544

Society of Corporate Meeting Professionals
2600 Garden Rd.
Suite 208
Monterey, CA 93940
(408) 649-6544

Society of Government Meeting Planners
1133 15th St., N.W.
Suite 620
Washington, DC 20036

Society of Incentive Travel Executives (SITE)
21 W. 38th St.
10th Floor
New York, NY 10018
(212) 575-0910

Trade Show Bureau
1660 Lincoln St.
Suite 2080
Denver, CO 80264
(303) 860-7626

Travel Industry Association of America
Two Lafayette Center
1133 21st St., N.W.
Washington, DC 20036
(202) 293-1433

Western Fairs Association
1329 Howe Ave.
Suite 202
Sacramento, CA
(916) 927-3100

Industry Publications

Association Management (ASAE monthly magazine)
1575 Eye St., N.W.
Washington, DC 20005-1168

Meeting News (monthly)
 1515 Broadway
 New York, NY 10036

Successful Meetings (monthly)
 633 Third Ave.
 New York, NY 10017

Meetings & Conventions (monthly)
 500 Plaza Dr.
 Secaucus, NJ 07096

Association Trends (weekly newspaper)
 4948 St. Elmo Ave.
 Bethesda, MD 20814

USAE (weekly newspaper)
 4341 Montgomery Ave.
 Bethesda, MD 20814

Directory of Conventions Exhibits Schedule: Annual Directory of Trade and Industrial Shows (annual)

Successful Meetings Magazine
 633 Third Ave.
 New York, NY 10017

Trade Show Week Databook/Tradeshow Week
 (annual)
 12233 West Olympic Blvd.
 Suite 236
 Los Angeles, CA 90064

The Encyclopedia of Associations
 Gale Research Company
 835 Penobscot Building
 Detroit, MI 48226

National Trade & Professional Associations of the United States and Canada

Columbia Books, Inc.
 777 14th St., N.W.
 Washington, DC 20005

Who's Who In Association Management/Allied Societies Directory

ASAE
1575 Eye St., N.W.
Washington, DC 20005-1168

Key Terms

travel trends   salary compensation
employment forecasts

Appendix 1

International Association of Conference Centers Criteria for Membership

Common Primary Criteria Applicable To All Conference Centers Regardless Of Category Are:

1. A minimum percentage of net facility space devoted to meeting space is dedicated, single-purpose conference space;

2. A minimum percentage of occupied room nights, or sales volume in the case of non-residential centers, generated by conferences;

3. Conference room design incorporating the following:

   * A majority if conference setups using upholstered armchairs with the minimum comfort rating of six hours;
   * A majority of conference setups using tables designed for meetings, providing a hard writing surface;
   * Appropriate light (30-50 foot candles at tabletop, adjustable);
   * Climate controlled conference rooms;
   * Wall surfaces suitable for tacking or other mounting of flipchart-type sheets;
   * Appropriate accoustics for conference communication;
   * Adequate electrical, audio-visual and telephone outlets;

4. Conference rooms available to clients on a 24-hour basis for storage of materials, and other preparations;

5. An average group size of 45 people or less;

6. Location where surroundings do not distract from the learning process.

Appendix 2

Sample Menus*

---

*Courtesy: Sheraton Hotel and Conference Center, Columbia, SC.

Buffet Breakfast
(50 Person Minimum)

BREAKFAST BUFFETS

Sheraton Breakfast
A Selection of Chilled Juices
Assorted Cold Cereals
Freshly Sliced Fruit Platter
Scrambled Eggs
Bacon Strips
Sausage Links
Hot Buttered Grits
Breakfast Potatoes
Assorted Breakfast Breads
Coffee, Hot Tea, Decaffeinated Coffee
$7.95 Per Person

Brunch Buffet
Fresh Fruit Juices
Assorted Yogurt
Assorted Breakfast Breads
Freshly Sliced Fruit Platter
Andrew's Quiche
Scrambled Eggs
Crisp Bacon and Sausage Links
Hot Buttered Grits
Lyonnaise Potatoes
Broiled Chicken Breast
Sliced Ham and Roast Beef
Stir-Fried Vegetable Medley
Assorted Cakes and Layer Pies
Coffee, Hot Tea, and Decaffeinated Coffee
$11.95 Per Person

Rise N Shine Buffet
Cold Cereals
Assorted Chilled Juices
Assorted Breakfast Breads
Fresh Fruit Platter
Scrambled Eggs
Crisp Bacon
Sausage Links
French Toast and Syrup
Quiche
Hot Buttered Grits
Hash Browns
Coffee, Hot Tea and Decaffeinated Coffee
$9.95 Per Person

Prices shown are subject to 17% service charge and applicable state sales tax.

Breakfast
Entrees

Bacon and Eggs
Scrambled Eggs
Crisp Bacon Strips or Sausage Links
Breakfast Potatoes or Hot Buttered Grits
Fresh Homemade Biscuits and Muffins
$6.95 Per Person

Eggs Francais
Freshly Baked French Croissant
Stuffed with Scrambled Eggs and Cheese
Mixed with your choice of Bacon,
Ham, or Sausage
Breakfast Potatoes and Slices of Fresh Fruit
$6.95 Per Person

Andrew's Quiche
Diced Ham, Bell Pepper, Mushrooms and Onion
Scrambled with Eggs and Topped with Cheese
Breakfast Potatoes and Fresh Fruit
Assorted Homemade Muffins
$8.50 Per Person

Crepes A La Reine
Sauteed Chicken Strips in a Reine Wine Sauce
with Diced Celery and Onions
Wrapped in Freshly made Crepes
Fresh Homemade Biscuits and Muffins
Freshly Sliced Fruit
$8.95 Per Person

Filet and Eggs
Scrambled Eggs Served with a 4 oz. Filet Mignon
Breakfast Potatoes or Hot Buttered Grits
Fresh Homemade Biscuits and Muffins
$10.95 Per Person

Omelettes
Three Egg Omelettes
Choice of any Three Ingredients
Breakfast Potatoes or Hot Buttered Grits
Fresh Seasonal Fruit
Fresh Homemade Biscuits and Muffins
$9.50 Per Person - Maximum 100 People

Texas Style French Toast
Lightly Browned Texas Style Bread Topped
with Nutmeg
and Served with Hot Maple Syrup
Crisp Bacon Strips or Sausage Links
Fresh Homemade Biscuits and Muffins
$6.95 Per Person

Silver Dollar Pancakes
Fluffy Butter Milk Pancakes
Served with Scrambled Eggs
Crisp Bacon Strips or Sausage Links
Fresh Homemade Biscuits and Muffins
$7.50 Per Person

Eggs Benedict
Poached Eggs and Canadian Bacon
on English Muffins
Breakfast Potatoes
Fresh Seasonal Fruit
Fresh Homemade Biscuits and Muffins
$9.25 Per Person - Maximum 150 People

** All Breakfast Entrees Served with Jellies, Butter, Coffee, Tea, Sanka, or Milk and your Choice of any Juice.
Prices Shown are subject to 17% service charge and applicable state sales tax.

MORNING COFFEE BREAKS AND SPECIALTIES

Express Continental Breakfast
Choice of Chilled Juices
Assorted Breakfast Breads
(Croissants, Fruit Danish, Biscuits and Muffins)
Coffee, Tea, Decaffeinated Coffee
$3.75 per person

Deluxe Continental Breakfast
Choice of Chilled Juices
Fresh Sliced Seasonal Fruits
Granola Bars and Assorted Yogurt
Assorted Breakfast Breads
(Croissants, Fruit Danish, Biscuits and Muffins)
Coffee, Hot Tea, Decaffeinated Coffee
$5.50 Per Person

Tea Time Break
Assortment of Imported Herbal Teas
Fresh Baked Muffins, Breads and Coffee Cakes
Coffee and Decaffeinated Coffee
$4.00 Per Person

Individual Items Available Upon Request

Cracker Barrel Break
Pecan Cheese Ball with an Assortment of
Cubed Cheeses and Crackers
Whole and Sliced Fruits
Individual Sausages
Flavored Mineral Waters
Assorted Soft Drinks
$4.75 Per Person

Prices shown are subject to 17% service charge and applicable state sales tax.

AFTERNOON COFFEE BREAKS AND SPECIALTIES

Half Time / 7th Inning Stretch
Large Hot Soft Pretzels with Assorted Mustards
Popcorn, Roasted or Boiled S.C. Peanuts
Non-Alcoholic Beer
Assorted Soft Drinks
Iced Tea or Lemonade
$4.50 Per Person

Chocaholic Break
Homemade Brownies and Chocolate Chip Cookies
M&M's and Snickers Bars
Yoo Hoo Chocolate Drinks
Diet and Regular Soft Drinks
$4.25 Per Person

Ice Cream Special
Create your own sundae with a selection
of 10 assorted Toppings
A Variety of Ice Cream Bars
Assorted Diet and Regular Soft Drinks
$4.75 Per Person

Healthy Choice
Lemonade, Iced Tea
Freshly Sliced Fruit
Assorted Yogurt
Granola Bars
Assorted Mineral Waters
$4.50 Per Person

LUNCHES

LUNCHES FROM

OUR LIGHTER FARE

SANDWICH CROISSANT

Your Choice of Sliced Roast Beef and Monterey Jack Cheese, Shaved Ham and Swiss, or Shaved Turkey with Provolone Cheese all served with Lettuce and Tomato.

$8.50

OLD FASHION CHEF SALAD

Iceberg Lettuce, Cheese, Turkey, Ham, Pepperoni, Eggs, Tomatoes and Choice of Dressings.

$8.50

FRESH FRUIT AND SALAD PLATE

Your Choice of Shrimp and Crab Salad, Turkey Salad or Tuna Salad Stuffed in two tomato halves, Surrounded by a Rainbow of Fresh Fruit.
$8.95

GRILLED CHICKEN BREAST SANDWICH

A Boneless Chicken Breast, Grilled to perfection served on a Kaiser Roll with Lettuce, Tomato and Sliced Onion.

$8.95

HUMONGOUS HOAGIES

Six inch French Bread loaded with Ham, Turkey, Roast Beef and Pepperoni, dressed with Oil, Vinegar and Herbs, and accompanied by Shredded Lettuce, Tomato and Onion.
$8.95

CAROLINA SANDWICH

Roast Beef, Crisp Bacon and Provolone Cheese on Rye Bread with Tomato and Lettuce
$8.95

Sandwiches include Pickle and Potato Salad or Chips. Salads include breads, crackers and dressings. All Light Fare Entrees include dessert, coffee, tea, or milk.

Prices shown are subject to 17% service charge and applicable state sales tax.

LUNCHEON BUFFET

LUNCHEON BUFFET

LUNCHEON BUFFETS INCLUDE

A "Salad Bar" including a Garden Green Salad, three Cold Salads du Jour
accompanied by five Assorted Salad Toppings and two Assorted Dressings

ENTREES*

MEAT SELECTIONS

Oven Roasted Pork and Gravy
Roast Beef and Gravy
Ham with Pineapple Sauce
Beef Stroganoff
Beef Stir Fry
BBQ Pork with Buns

SEAFOOD SELECTIONS

Shrimp Stir Fry
Seafood Newburg
Shrimp Creole
Fried Catfish Filets
Seafood Fettuccine
Fresh Baked Fish

POULTRY SELECTIONS

Chicken Cacciatore
Baked, Fried or BBQ Chicken
Roast Turkey with Dressing
and Gravy
Honey Pecan Chicken
Chicken Stir Fry

BUFFET DESSERTS
(Choose One)

Hot Fruit Cobbler (Apple, Peach or Cherry)
Homemade Banana Pudding and Chocolate Mousse
Assorted Layer Cakes and Pies

* Lunch Buffet #1 Choice of Two Entrees and Three Vegetables of the Day $10.95
* Lunch Buffet #2 Choice of Three Entrees and Four Vegetables of the Day......................$11.95

50 Person Minimum on all Buffets
* All Hot Luncheon Buffets include our Deluxe Salad Bar
Entree Section, Fresh Baked Dinner Rolls, Butter, Coffee or Tea.

DELI CUT BUFFET - $9.95

Garden Salad and Dressings
with an array of Condiments,
Sliced Roast Beef, Ham & Turkey Baked
Potato Bar with Assorted Toppings,
Sliced Cheeses, Cole Slaw, Potato Salad,
an Assortment of Breads and Condiments
and a selection from the Buffet Desserts.

PASTA BUFFET - $10.95

Garden Salad and Dressings
with an array of Condiments,
Antipasto, Pasta Salad, Marinated
Vegetables, Pasta Pinwheels, Fettuccine,
Pasta Shells, Ziti, Alfredo Sauce,
Marinara Sauce, White Clam Sauce,
Garlic Bread, Grated Parmesan Cheese
and Amaretto Mousse.

SEAFOOD BUFFET $13.95

Garden Salad and Dressings
with an array of Condiments, Seafood
Chowder, Shrimp and
Crab Salad, Peel and Eat Shrimp,
Seafood Fettuccine, Shrimp Creole, Fried
Shrimp, Fried or Baked Catch of the
Day, Hushpuppies, Rice, Chef's
Vegetables of the Day and a selection
from the Buffet Desserts.

Prices Shown are subject to 17% service charge and applicable state sales tax.

LUNCHEON MENUS

MEAT ENTREES

PRIME RIB SANDWICH
Slowly Roasted Prime Rib Topped with Sauteed Mushrooms and Melted Cheddar Cheese on French Bread
$10.95

BROILED RIB EYE STEAK
7 Ounce Broiled Rib Eye Steak with Au Jus.
$11.95

ROAST SIRLOIN OF BEEF
Juicy Slices of Beef Medallions topped with a Mushroom Sauce.
$10.95

BREADED PORK CHOPS
Lean Trimmed Pork, Breaded and Cooked to Perfection. Served with Baked Apple.
$9.95

SOUTHERN STYLE STEAK
Batter fried Steak with Country Gravy.
$9.95

PRIME RIB LUNCH
7 Ounces of carefully trimmed choice Prime Rib with Baked Potato and Vegetables.
$11.95

CHICKEN ENTREES

HONEY PECAN CHICKEN
This Unique Chicken is Sweet, Crunchy, and Rich. Served Piping Hot. Drizzled with Sweet Pecan Sauce.
$9.95

RASPBERRY CHICKEN
Sauteed Boneless Chicken Breast Finished with a light Raspberry Sauce.
$9.95

CHICKEN MONTEREY
Boneless Chicken Breast layered with Canadian Bacon and Monterey Jack Cheese. Served with a White Wine Sauce.
$9.95

GRILLED MARINATED CHICKEN BREAST
Served on a Bed of Fresh Sauteed Vegetables.
$9.95

SEAFOOD ENTREES

CAROLINA PLATTER
Sliced Tenderloin, Marinated Scallops, Boiled Shrimp and Grilled Chicken served on Boston Lettuce with Basil Sauce, Cocktail Sauce, Green Beans, Potato Salad and Fresh Croissant.

$14.95

GRILLED SWORDFISH
Premium Fish Filet grilled with fresh Parsley and Lemon.
$11.50

CALIFORNIA PLATTER
Grilled Filet Mignon, Chicken Breast and Shrimp with Steamed Vegetables over rice.
$13.95

STUFFED FILET OF FLOUNDER
Filet of Flounder Stuffed with Shrimp and Crabmeat topped with Chardonnay Sauce.
$10.95

SHRIMP ANTHONY
Fresh Gulf Shrimp Served on a bed of rice, Finished with Walnuts, Snowpeas, and Water Chestnuts in a Cream Sauce.

$12.95

French Onion Soup (1.00/pp), Soup du Jour (1.00/pp), Bay Shrimp Salad (1.00/pp) She Crab Soup (1.50/pp) Exotic Greens Salad (1.00/pp), Fruit Salad with Poppy Seed Dressing (1.00/pp)

All Luncheon Selections include *Fresh Baked Bread and Butter, Chefs selection of Garden Fresh Vegetables, your choice of either Tossed Salad, Caesar Salad or Spinach Salad, Dessert and Coffee, Tea, or Milk

Prices shown are subject to 17% service charge and applicable state sales tax.

DINNER BUFFETS

DINNER BUFFET

(Minimum 50 People)
DINNER BUFFETS INCLUDE

A "Salad Bar" including Garden Green Salad, three Cold Salads du
Jour accompanied by five Assorted Salad Toppings and two Dressings

ENTREES*

Tortellini Pasta with Chicken
Prime Rib *($1.50 extra)*
Roast Turkey Breast
Whole Boneless Ham
Steamship Round of Beef
Beef Pepper Steak
Braised Beef with Noodles

Seafood Newburg
Fried Shrimp
Baked Chicken with Lemon, Lime and
Orange
Fried or BBQ Chicken
Honey Pecan Chicken
Smothered Pork Chops with Onions

Roast Pork and Raisin Dressing
Crab Cakes
Fried Catfish
Shrimp Creole
Baked Fish with Brandied Shrimp
and Almonds
Baked Potato Bar with 5 toppings
(.95 extra) (free with prime Rib)

BUFFET DESSERTS

(choose one)
Hot Fruit Cobbler (Apple, Peach or Cherry)
Homemade Banana Pudding and Chocolate Mousse
Assorted Layer Cakes and Pies

* Dinner Buffet #1 Choice of Two Entrees and Three Vegetables of the Day $15.95
* Dinner Buffet #2 Choice of Three Entrees and Four Vegetables of the Day.....................$16.95
50 Person Minimum On All Buffets.

FLAMING DESSERT TABLE

*Flambe` Chef will prepare Bananas Foster, Cherries Jubilee, Fresh Fruit Fantasy, or Strawberries Au Kirsh
Served over Ice Cream. Choice of Two.*

$4.50 / person

*Dinner Buffets include Fresh Baked Dinner Rolls, Butter, Choice of Coffee or Tea.
Carvers Fee - $35.00*

Prices Shown are subject to 17% service charge and applicable state sales tax.

DINNER SELECTIONS

SALADS

YOUR CHOICE OF:
Garden Salad, Caesar Salad, Spinach Salad,
Fruit Salad (.50), Bay Shrimp Salad (1.50)

APPETIZERS & SOUPS

Fruit Compote (.50), Soup du Jour (1.50), Piccata Chicken Strips
(3.00), Shrimp Cocktail (5.00),
Crabmeat Cocktail (5.00).

MEAT ENTREES

PRIME RIB
Slowly Roasted Prime Rib Served with Au Jus.
Managers Cut...$16.95 Executive Cut...$17.95

BROILED RIBEYE STEAK
A 10 oz. Ribeye Steak, Trimmed, Seasoned &
Topped with Herb Butter
$17.95

CLASSIC FILET MIGNON
Broiled 8 oz. Filet Mignon Served with a Rich Mushroom
Bordelaise Sauce.
$19.95

ROAST SIRLOIN OF BEEF
Perfectly Trimmed Lean Tasty Medallions of Beef
Served with Brown Sauce.
$15.95

VEAL GULF COAST
Veal Medallions with Large Shrimp and Mushrooms, with melted
Monterey Jack Cheese in Special Sauce.
$16.95

VEAL MADERIA
Sauteed Veal Medallions with a Rich Maderia Wine Sauce

$15.95

PREMIUM DESSERTS

Chocolate Mousse ($.75 extra)
Hot Pecan Pie a la Mode ($1.00 extra)
Apple Pie a la Mode ($1.00 extra)
Strawberry Shortcake ($2.00 extra)
Cheese Cake ($2.00 extra)
Dave's Killer Pie ($2.95 extra)

CHICKEN ENTREES

RASPBERRY CHICKEN
Sauteed Boneless Chicken Breast finished with a Light
Raspberry Cream Sauce
$13.50

CHICKEN TERIYAKI
Tender Boneless Chicken Breast broiled and then baked with a
Teriyaki glaze.
$13.95

CHICKEN MONTEREY
Boneless Chicken Breast Layered with Canadian Bacon and Monterey
Jack Cheese Served with a Champagne Sauce.
$13.95

HONEY PECAN CHICKEN
This Unique Fried Chicken Dish is Sweet, Crunchy & Rich. Served
Piping Hot & Drizzled with Sweet Pecan Sauce.
$13.95

CHICKEN WITH MUSHROOMS
Boneless Breast of Chicken braised with Scallions, and Mushrooms
with a hint of Lemon.
$13.95

COMBINATION PLATTERS

CALIFORNIA PLATTER
Grilled Filet Mignon, Chicken Breast
and Shrimp with Steamed Vegetables
over Rice.
$19.95

PRIME RIB & CAJUN SHRIMP
Roasted Prime Rib accompanied
by 4 Grilled Shrimp in a Cajun
Butter.
$19.95

LOBSTER & FILET
Broiled Lobster Tail served with a
4 oz. Grilled Filet Mignon
Market

PRIME RIB & CHICKEN
Roasted Prime Rib accompanied
by a Boneless Chicken Breast
$18.95

FILET & CRAB CAKE
6 oz. Filet Mignon with Crabcake
in Lemon Butter
$21.95

FILET & SWORDFISH
4 oz. Filet Mignon served with a
Grilled 4 oz. Swordfish Filet
$20.95

*All Dinner Selections include Choice of Salad, Chef's Selection of garden Fresh Vegetables, Fresh Baked Dinner Rolls, Butter &
Choice of Coffee or Tea. Dessert of The Day with Dinner.*

Prices shown are subject to 17% service charge and applicable state sales tax.

THEME BUFFETS

THEME BUFFETS

CHINA TOWN BUFFET

Salad Bar
Chicken Chow Mein
Beef Pepper Steak
Sweet & Sour Shrimp
Egg Rolls
Fried Rice
Stir Fried Vegetables
Fortune Cookies
Rolls & Butter
Assorted Cakes and Pies

$16.00 Per Person

MEXICAN FIESTA

Taco Bar with Seasoned Meat, Cheese,
Sauces, Tomatoes, Lettuce, Hard and Soft
Shells, Taco Salad Shells, Beans and Rice,
Salad Bar, Guacamole with Chips, Latin
Lasagna, Chicken or Shrimp Fajitas
Assorted Cakes and Pies

$15.00 Per Person

COUNTRY BARBECUE

Salad Bar, BBQ Beef Ribs, Fried Chicken,
Roast Beef, Pork BBQ, Succotash, Rice,
Baked Beans, Corn on the Cob, Cole Slaw,
Rolls & Butter, Corn Bread,
Fruit Cobbler, Assorted Cakes and Pies

$16.50 Per Person
For Chef carved Beef, add $35.00 per hour Carver Fee.

CLAM BAKE

Salad Bar with Assorted Dressings,
New England Clam Chowder, Vegetable Tray, Cole
Slaw, Pasta Salad, Oysters on the Half Shell,
Steamed Clams,
Peel & Eat Shrimp, Fish of the Day, New Potatoes,
Corn on the Cob, Green Beans, Rolls & Butter

$19.00 Per Person

HAWAIIAN LUAU

Ambrosia, Relish Tray, Carrot Raisin Salad, Salad Bar,
Hawaiian Chicken, Steamed Ginger Shrimp, Chicken
Sesame, BBQ Pork Spareribs, Fried Rice, Stir Fry
Vegetables, Salad Bar, Bread & Butter
Assorted Cakes and Pies

$19.00 Per Person

PICNIC BUFFET

Hamburgers, Hotdogs with Chili,
BBQ, Baked Beans, French Fries, Hot
Vegetables, Potato Salad, Cole Slaw,
Watermelon, Assorted Buns & Condiments,
Chips & Dips
Assorted Cakes and Pies

$12.00 Per Person

*Prices shown are subject to 17% service charge and applicable state sales tax.
All theme buffets are for a minimum of 50 people.*

HORS D'OEUVRES

HORS D'OEUVRES

All Hot and Cold Selections are priced per 100 pieces

COLD SELECTIONS

$75.00 PER ORDER

Celery Sticks with Cream Cheese, Stuffed Deviled Eggs, Salami-Cream Cheese Horns, Vegetarian Canapes, Ham and Chicken Bouchees, Pecan Cheese Ball with Crackers, Chef's Crab Cocktail, Vegetable Platter.

$110.00 PER ORDER

Asparagus wrapped in Crepes, Smoked Salmon Canapes, Cucumber with Salmon Mousse Canapes, Smoked Salmon Pinwheels, Shrimp Mousse, Fresh Fruit Tray, Assorted Cheese and Cracker Platter, Mini Coldcut Sandwiches, Meat Salad Sandwiches.

HOT SELECTIONS

$110.00 PER ORDER

Fried Chicken Tenders, Mini Quiche Lorraine, Egg Rolls, Bacon wrapped Water Chestnuts, Ham Biscuits, Swedish or BBQ Meatballs, Fried Chicken Drummettes, Mushrooms Stuffed with Crabmeat, Mushrooms Stuffed with Sausage and Cheese, Baked Brie, Pastry Franks, Buffalo Hot Wings, Mini Smoked Sausages, Chicken Fajitas, Fried Potato Skins with Toppings, Beef Brochette, BBQ Baby Back Ribs, Red Cabbage Meatballs.

$175.00 PER ORDER

Oysters Rockefeller, Fried Scallops, Fresh Jumbo Shrimp, Fried Oysters, Oysters on the Half Shell, Crab-Shrimp Rangoons, Angels on Horseback, Bacon Wrapped Scallops, Crab Cakes, Coconut Shrimp.

DIPS

$25.00 EACH

Cold Spinach Dip	Hot Chocolate Fondue
Black Bean and Chili Dip	Crab Dip/Crackers
Hot Artichoke Dip	Blue Cheese Dip/Crackers,
Hot Nacho Cheese/Chips	Chips, or Celery

SHOW STOPPERS

Whole Roasted Pig with Carver (Sauces, Cole Slaw & Breads Included) ....$450 each
Decorated Poached Whole Salmon ....$110.00 each
Strawberry Trees ....Market Price

FINISHING TOUCHES

Meat and Cheese Platter ....$3.50 / pp
Mixed Nuts...$15.00 / lb
Cocktail Peanuts..$9.00 / lb
Chip and Dip Tray ....$25.00 / Tray
Mints ....$6.00 / lb
Ice Carvings ....starting at $150.00
Fruit Punch ....$15.00 / gal
Champagne Punch ....$30.00 / gal
Petit Fours...$15.00 / doz
Cookies ....$8.00 / doz
Chocolate Covered Strawberries ....$15.00 / doz

SPECIALITIES

Whole Roast Tenderloin ....each $110.00
Steamship Round of Beef.............................per lb. $9.75
Roasted Boneless Turket Breast......................per lb. 9.75
Glazed Boneless Smoked Ham ....per lb. $9.75
Six Foot Sub Sandwich $80.00

Carver - $35.00 per hour
Prices Shown are subject to 17% service charge and applicable state sales tax.

SPIRITS

HOST RECEPTION

The complete bar package catered by the hotel including Liquor, Beer, Wine, Mixers, and Bar set-ups is priced per drink and is charged to the Master Account. Bartender Charge will be $12.00/hour. Host Reception will be subject to 17% Service Charge and tax. Bartender fees will be totally waived if $500.00 in bar sales is reached.

HOUSE WINES

Chardonnay	$2.25 Glass	$10.00 Bottle
Red	$2.25 Glass	$10.00 Bottle
White Zinfandel	$2.25 Glass	$10.00 Bottle

CORKAGE BAR

This package gives you the option of furnishing your own Alcohol of any kind and is inclusive of mixers, ice, glasses, bar fruit, set-ups and all bartender fees. Prices subject to a 17% service charge and tax.

First Hour 3.50++/pp
Second Hour 1.25++/pp
Each Additional Hour 1.00++/pp

SPARKLING WINES

Totts	$10.00 Bottle
Freixenet	$15.00 Bottle
Mumms	$24.00 Bottle
Moet & Chandon, White Star	$45.00 Bottle
Moet & Chandon, Dom Perignon	$115.00 Bottle

CASH BAR

Highballs, Cocktails, Beer and Wine to be served and charged on an individual basis. Requirement for Cash Bars 20 to 100 people - $100.00 Minimum Sales.
Over 100 people - $1.00 per person Minimum Sales. Does not include Bartender charges of $12.00 per hour.

PREMIUM WINES

Chardonnay	$2.50 Glass	$18.00 Bottle
Cabernet Sauvignon	$2.75 Glass	$20.00 Bottle
White Zinfandel	$2.50 Glass	$18.00 Bottle

Please see our wine list for additional selections.

LABOR CHARGES

For Host and Cash Bars
Bartender charge is $12.00 per hour.
Bar Back charge is $12.00 per hour.
Minimum Staffing Levels
1 Bartender per 100
1 Barback per 300

Glossary

Accommodation   a rented place to sleep, including hotels, motels, conference centers, inns, bed and breakfasts, resort condominiums, youth hostels, and health spas

ACOM   Association for Convention Operations Management

ADA   Americans with Disabilities Act

Agenda   subjects to be discussed at a meeting

AH&MA   American Hotel and Motel Association

Amenities   complimentary items in sleeping rooms, such as shower caps, shampoo, and shoe shine mitt provided by facility for guests

Arbitration   an objective third party called in to settle a contractual dispute

ASAE   American Society for Association Executives

Association   organized body that exhibits some variety of volunteer leadership structure, which may employ a staff and which serves a group of people that share some common interest, activity, or purpose

Attendee   an individual attending the meeting session

Banquet   formal, often ceremonial dinner for a select group of people

Booth   specific area assigned by management for exhibitor, under contractual agreement

Break-even attendance   a minimum number of paying attendees the event must have in order not to lose money

Breaks   periods between sessions, where refreshments are frequently served

Buffet   assortment of foods offered on a table, self-served

Cancellation clause   statement that the contract may be canceled by either party in writing by an agreed upon date

Check-in   procedure for guest arrivals and registration at hotels or meetings

Check-out   procedure for guest departure from hotels

CLC   Convention Liaison Council

Conference   participatory meeting designed for discussion, fact finding, problem solving, and consultation

Continental breakfast   light morning meal generally consisting of pastries, juices, and hot beverages

Contract   a legal document defining responsibilities for all parties concerned

Convention   assemblage of delegates, members of an organization, and so on for a common purpose

Convention and visitors bureau   not-for-profit umbrella organization that represents a city or urban area in the solicitation and servicing of types of travelers to that area or city, whether for business or pleasure

Convention center   a public assembly facility designed to host meetings and exhibits and is without sleeping rooms

Convention service manager   individual employed by a convention hotel whose primary job is to service group business

Corkage fee   service charge on food and/or beverage brought into the establishment by the group, but served by the host property; fee generally determined by the amount of labor involved in the service of the product.

Corporate meeting planner   an individual who works for one corporation whose sole or primary responsibility is to plan meetings for that company

CSM   convention service manager

Decorator   general contractor or service contractor usually hired to set up an exhibition

Destination management company   a company that provides on-site coordination of hospitality programs and other special events

DMC   destination management company

Director of marketing   individual whose primary responsibilities include administration, coordination, and supervision of the group sales department

Drayage   transfer of exhibit properties from point of arrival to exhibit site

EC   European Community

Ecotourism   environmentally oriented tourism in which natural resources are preserved

EDPA   Exhibit Designers and Producers Association

ESCA   Exposition Service Contractors Association

Exclusive contractor   contractor appointed by show or building management as the sole agent to provide services

Exhibit manager   1. person in charge of individual exhibit booth; 2. show management staff in charge of entire exhibit area

Exhibition   European term for exposition

Exhibitor   company or organization sponsoring exhibit booth

Exhibitor appointed contractor (EAC)

Exhibitor manual   packet containing the rules and regulations of the exposition, contracts, promotional pieces, and information about official service contractor

Exposition   an event designed to bring together purveyors of products, equipment, and services in an environment in which they can demonstrate their products and services to a group of attendees at a convention or trade show. Also called exhibition, trade show, or industrial show

Exposition manager   *see* trade show manager

Exposition service contractor   *see* general exposition contractor

FAM trip   *see* familiarization trip

Familiarization trip   a hosted trip to allow meeting planners and association or corporate executives to assess facilities, location, and/or services

Fixed expenses   costs that remain the same regardless of the number of attendees

Float   an exhibitor booth deposit

General exposition contractor   multitalented individual or company that is equipped to serve all exhibit requirements

Ground service operator   a company or person in the destination city handling local transportation and other local travel needs; also known as a ground service handler

Guarantee   the number to be paid for, whether or not actually utilized

Head count   actual number of people attending a function

Hospitality suite   room or suite of rooms used to entertain guests

Host property   any facility used to house a meeting, convention, or exposition

Hotel room tax   tax levied to visitor hotel bills based on a percentage of the room rate paid

HSMAI   Hotel Sales and Marketing Association International

IACC   International Association of Conference Centers

Indemnification clause   a hold harmless clause whereby, if both parties in the contract are sued, the party not at fault will not be required to pay legal damages

IACVB   International Association of Convention and Visitors Bureaus

IEA   International Exhibitors Association

Incentive travel   travel offered as a prize to stimulate productivity

Independent audiovisual supplier   an audiovisual rental company

Independent meeting planner   a meeting planner who is also a private entrepreneur

Marketing plan   written blueprint of an organization's activities with respect to a particular meeting, convention, or exposition

Master account   form on which authorized charges incurred in a facility by a group are recorded

Meeting   an assembly or gathering of people, as for a business, social, or religious purpose

Meeting planner   the individual in an organization whose duties consist in whole or in part of planning the details attendant to meetings of various types and sizes

MPI   Meeting Planners International

NAEM   National Association of Exposition Managers

Negotiations   bargaining or discussing with a view toward reaching an agreement

NRA   National Restaurant Association

Overhead projector   equipment that projects an image on a screen by passing light through a transparent slide or other transparency

Panel   discussion with a moderator and two or more participants

PCMA   Professional Convention Management Association

Pipe and drape   tubing draped with fabric to create separate exhibit booths

Post-con   *see* post convention meeting

Post-convention meeting   meeting held between planner and key hotel staff after the event is over for the purpose of critiquing all activities

Precon meeting   *see* preconvention meeting

Preconvention meeting   meeting with planner, key hotel staff, and key suppliers to review purpose and details of upcoming event

Professional association   not-for-profit organization designed to assist individuals in their pursuit of common goals and interests

Prospectus   site selection data and meeting specifications submitted to prospective facilities

Reception   stand-up social function with food and beverage

Room block   number of rooms held for a group for a specified period of time

Site inspection   personal, careful investigation of a property, area, or facility

Service contractor   *see* general exposition contractor

Spouse programs   educational and/or social events planned for spouses and guests of meeting participants

Subcontractor   company retained by general contractor to provide services

Theme party   party at which food, decorations, and entertainment all relate to one theme

TSB   Trade Show Bureau

Trade show   *see* exposition

Trade show manager   individual responsible for managing all aspects of the trade show or exhibition; also known as a show organizer or show producer

Tour operator   a person or company that creates and/or markets inclusive tours and/or subcontracts their performance

Trade association   not-for-profit organization designed to address needs of for-profit businesses

Tourist   one who spends more than one night but less than one year away from home for pleasure or business, except diplomats, military personnel, and enrolled students

Variable expenses   costs that fluctuate depending on the number of attendees

Videoconference   type of meeting that brings together three or more people in two or more locations, using a combined audio and visual link through satellite or other type of network

Index